PORTRAITS
OF GUILT

PORTRAITS
OF GUILT

(On left: Drawing © Jeanne Boylan. Photo on far right: Photo © AP Photo)

THE WOMAN WHO PROFILES

THE FACES OF AMERICA'S

DEADLIEST CRIMINALS

JEANNE BOYLAN

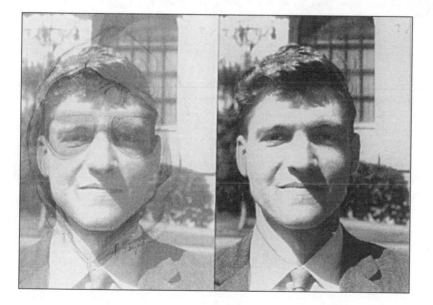

POCKET BOOKS

NEW YORK LONDON TORONTO SYDNEY SINGAPORE

All police sketches and police arrest photos are in the public domain.

POCKET BOOKS, a division of Simon & Schuster Inc.
1230 Avenue of the Americas, New York, NY 10020

ISBN: 0-671-03485-5

First Pocket Books hardcover printing June 2000

10   9   8   7   6   5   4   3   2   1

Designed by Jessica Shatan

Printed in the U.S.A.

For you, Polly . . .

CONTENTS

PROLOGUE

My "children" live only in a collection of photos I keep tucked inside my dresser drawer like some foster-family album. I hold their happy images safely in my hands and heart. I don't keep pictures of the brutal endings, yet their final moments are etched forever in my mind.

Polly Klaas, the beautiful, dimpled twelve-year-old aspiring actress, stolen from her slumber party, tied up in the darkness of a stranger's car for her final terrified ride through the night and into eternity.

Tiny brothers Michael and Alexander Smith, snapped into their coveralls and buckled into their car seats, drowned when their own mother shoved her car down a Union, South Carolina, lakeside ramp, her two children trapped in the backseat.

And the Oklahoma City babies—the nineteen little lifeless bodies carried from the bombed-out day-care center by emotionally weary rescue workers, their lives taken by a monster, their soft stuffed animals found still within their reach.

I want to remember them all in earlier days, long before I was called to come form the realistic faces of their killers.

According to the press clippings, I have an identified "knack" for interviewing "high-trauma victims and eyewitnesses." I unlock painful memories, ask questions, listen, and search for scattered fragments buried deeply inside emotions—eventually forming accurate descriptions of faces that sometimes even the eyewitnesses are without conscious knowledge of possessing.

The way I work defies tradition and rocks convention. My methods aren't detailed anywhere in police bureaus' tab-divided manuals, and that makes me an enigma in their pragmatic investigative world. Yet on the high-profile unsolved cases, they call anyway.

The ringing phone pierces my serenity. On the other end is an FBI agent, an exhausted detective, a desperate parent, or perhaps some small-town police chief asking, "How fast can you get here?"

I go because I have to. For years I've searched for the faces of two men who altered the course of my own life: age twenty-one, a rural road, one night, one attack, two strangers' faces forever seared into my soul.

No moment exists for me in which I don't search to find them again. My own case was never solved. But my understanding of what it's like to live without closure gives me the passion to provide for others what I may never know for myself: a simple ink stamp on a file folder marked "case closed."

Each time the call comes, I go. You see, I can't say no.

THE FACE OF A MADMAN

(Drawing ©
Jeanne Boylan)

"Miss Boylan?"

A tap on my shoulder snapped me out of my daydream.

"Yes?"

"FBI. We have a witness in the Unabom case. I need you to come with me."

My heart took a free fall inside my chest, pressing against my lungs, shortening my breath to a few jagged gulps. The Unabom case? But how had they tracked me down? I was merely trying to change planes on my way home after a long and exhausting case. I hadn't even noticed the clean-cut man in the dark blue suit. I must have passed right by him, searching for the gate number written in grease pencil on the face of my airline ticket.

Where would he take me? And why now? My mind raced for some legitimate form of resistance, some explanation.

"But, I can't go with you, I've got luggage!"

"We've got your luggage."

That change of planes in San Francisco in July 1994 represented a rare and needed break from my usual crazed rush through airports. The pressure from my latest case was finally behind me: my sketches were finished, and the presses were cranking out wanted posters for mass distribution. Finally I was headed home, just four hours and ten minutes to go.

As I dodged other harried passengers through the airport corridor, my mind drifted to my country home in Bend, Oregon. I imagined my yellow Labrador pup, Dillon, spilling out the front door of our log house, skidding sideways in the gravel driveway as he rounded the curve in his rush to greet me.

I could almost smell the welcomed aroma of the hot, dry air, a mixture of juniper and pine, tinged even in the high-desert summer with the faint scent of pine-fueled stoves. That pitchy smell always seeps into the airplane cabin the moment the flight attendant pops open the door, as if to provide confirmation that I'm really home. The locals around Bend say that if you inhale the rugged fragrance long enough, you start to take it for granted. I wouldn't know. My work steals me away too often.

I've spent most of my adult life probing the minds of crime victims and eyewitnesses to capture memories, exorcise fears, to draw out detailed recollections of the violators' faces so they can be apprehended before striking again.

I once read that some people study faces in a crowd in hope of finding their predestined lover. I used to flirt with such intentions too, but that was long before I started searching instead, for faces that steal dreams.

Faces haunt me: every nuance, every angle, every shadow, every line. I slip through the world sizing up their shapes and colors and textures. At a glance I notice if eyes are wet or iced, if they're squinty or withholding, if scars are new or smooth, if skin is oiled or abused.

On my way to an investigation, every minute matters. A suspect is at large and might soon leave his mark again. I'm brought in to bring to life the detailed face of the kidnapper or the bomber, the killer or the rapist.

My home town of Bend, Oregon, rests in the shadow of the Three Sisters Mountains, just east of the Cascades. If I hadn't been detoured by an FBI agent, I'd have arrived just in time to catch the last streams of evening sunlight sifting through the towering ponderosa pines and the tall blades of high-desert grass.

As I'd migrated through the San Francisco airport on my way to my connecting gate, the aroma of fresh-baked pizza had stirred my hunger—a lousy trick played on famished commuters like me, used to living on giant Snickers bars and lukewarm Snapple from pricey hotel minibars. To have something hot and edible seemed like a dream. But a lineup of newspaper front pages had diverted my attention from my empty stomach.

The word *murder* topped the local headline, and for a moment I nearly forgot which city I was in. The story drew me back to Albuquerque and Flagstaff, two Southwest cities on opposite ends of a stretch of old highway where a car-jacking had ended in the gruesome murder of sixteen-year-old Jonathan Francia. I'd just spent the past five days doing interviews and suspect drawings in an attempt to identify his killer. It was still too soon for any news on the case, yet I was hoping there might be an early breakthrough as I walked toward the concourse security checkpoint, but the sudden tap on my shoulder by the FBI agent interrupted my thoughts.

At first I thought I must have dropped something, maybe a receipt. The word *thanks* began to form on the edge of my lips. When I turned and looked into the eyes of the intruder, I immediately knew better. I recognized the look: the regulation haircut and the generic dark suit—all that was missing was the usual mustache, trimmed to the corners and above the lip line. He had to be a cop.

A leather badge case sprang open in front of me. "FBI," he announced, then apologetically added, "Max Nocl, ma'am." The airport crowd kept flowing around us, oblivious, as if he'd done nothing more than ask me for the time of day.

His presence meant only one thing: that once again I'd be turned away from my plans and back to the job that possessed me.

I feigned a "professional" smile and followed him back up the concourse, leaving my homebound flight on the other side of the terminal.

As we walked through SFO, past the glassed-in exhibits of antique toys, Agent Noel strained from the weight of the three-ring binders under his arm. They were stuffed with case reports and photocopies of evidence right down to canceled postage stamps recovered from the suspect's deadly packages. Wasting no time, he launched into a rapid-paced Unabom introductory course, with emphasis on the national security implications.

I listened, but my mind wandered between his words. Some of it I didn't want to hear. Instead, I kept thinking about the phone call I had to make. Agent Noel was talking about the biggest case in FBI history, and I was worrying more about what my husband would say. Would he see this as an unavoidable occupational hazard or just another shattered pledge? I shook the thought aside and forced myself to pay attention.

To keep the boundary strong between my two worlds, when I had time at home I worked hard to avoid the news, so when Agent Noel flipped open his badge case, I didn't know that the Unabomber was America's most wanted killer. I didn't know that he'd been on a killing spree for fifteen years. Or that he'd left a string of junkyard bombs that reached back to 1978, when he'd taken his first aim at a professor at the Technological Institute of Northwestern University near Chicago. The FBI agent filled me in on the case background as he walked me to a seat near our departure gate.

In 1979, the phantom bomber hit an American Airlines flight, where one of his creations malfunctioned and caught fire, forcing an emergency landing and injuring a dozen people. Had the bomb exploded at cruising altitude as planned, the casualties would have been beyond comprehension.

Next he targeted the president of United Airlines, then the computer-science departments at Vanderbilt University and the University of California at Berkeley. In 1985 he mailed a bomb to the fabrication department of the Boeing Company near Seattle, but fast-thinking security agents discovered it before it wreaked its intended havoc.

Other targets weren't so lucky. By 1994, the Unabomber's work had seriously injured twenty-two victims and killed a Sacramento man who was ripped apart by a bomb disguised as an ordinary package.

The FBI, the United States Postal Service, and the Bureau of

Alcohol, Tobacco and Firearms concluded that the tragedies were all the work of a single entity. The FBI organized a task force with two primary units based in the San Francisco and Chicago FBI offices. They named the case "Unabom"—*un* for *university* and *a* for *airlines,* the early targets of devastation; and *bom* as an abbreviation for *bomber.*

Agent Noel knew every detail by heart. For an FBI agent, this case was no easy assignment. They still had no suspect, there was no demand for money, and each detonation left no traceable evidence. The Unabomber crafted his own explosives and carefully covered his tracks, leaving no fingerprints, no strands of hair, no fabric fibers. But almost as a taunt, he "signed" his works by using unique homemade components where simple store-bought materials would have worked as well.

His bombs were meticulously constructed, the parts numbered prior to assembly and, based on analysis of the fragments, built and rebuilt repeatedly. He incorporated an indestructible piece into each one— etched with the initials *FC*—as if to say, "I was here. I have power." Then he'd enclose a clue or two, often some reference to wood—the material he used as a basis for his bombs and the topic for his cryptic comments—before sending them off to do their damage.

In the mid eighties, he changed his tactic, personally placing rather than mailing his bombs. He dropped out of the news until 1993, when he resurfaced, first with a letter bomb to the California home of a world-famous geneticist, and two days later with a bomb mailed to a computer-science professor at Yale University.

Then, as if to be sure everyone knew he was still around and kicking, he sent a letter to the assistant managing editor of the *New York Times,* claiming to be the representative of an anarchist group called FC. By that time, Janet Reno was attorney general, and in her no-nonsense manner, she lifted the lid off funding of the FBI investigation, fueling the intensified search that led to my 1994 interception in the San Francisco airport.

Agent Noel filled me in on the assignment: I would be interviewing the only person known to have actually seen the Unabomber. Her identity had been carefully protected; she and her family had relocated three times over the past seven years to escape detection by the media.

I took a close look at the seasoned agent in the dark suit, now in his

late fifties. In other circumstances, I would have found his kind face
and gentle manner endearing, maybe even charming. He'd done his
career stint and could have traded his badge in for a comfortable pen-
sion and a golf club membership, but he refused to abandon his decade-
long quest to capture the elusive murderer.

As we stood in line to board, I began to unload some of my own frus-
trations that went with being an in-the-wings resource in the investigative world. I was lamenting that by the time I got to an eyewitness, the
by-the-book investigative composite process had usually managed to all
but destroy the malleable impression of the suspect's face.

In a sentence, I was usually working against all odds to retrieve what
was once an intact image of the assailant, one that had inadvertently
been bungled by the very process of trying to create the face.

"It makes me crazy," I told Agent Noel. "The case I'm just returning
from, the Jonathan Francia car-jack murder, is six months old. Can you
believe that? The television program *Unsolved Mysteries* called to get my
help. They'd planned a feature around the case *six months after the fact*.
There were only contaminated eyewitness memories left to work with,
witnesses had been shown so many other faces they couldn't remember
what they'd actually seen, faulty police sketches had been broadcast for
months, leaving the police and the FBI no credibility at all in the public's eyes." I shook my head. The early swell of public interest, crucial to
the kind of break we needed, was all wasted on misinformation. The
trail was stone cold, and the family devastated. It was another mess—a
six-month-old mess.

It actually felt good to vent. An investigator of Agent Noel's caliber—
used to the highest-profile cases—would understand the frustration
when something so seemingly simple went so needlessly wrong.

He listened, then screwed his face into a knot, hoisted his shoulders
almost to his ears, and looked up through the thickness of his eyebrows
in a "don't kill me now" pose while he slowly squeezed out the words,
"Did, uh, I mention that, um, this Unabomber witness I'm taking you to
see . . . saw the guy seven and a half years ago?"

My jaw dropped. My feet refused to move forward. I couldn't make a
single word emerge from my mouth. He had to be kidding.

He pulled out the 1987 Unabom case composite of a pointy-chinned, ruddy-faced, redheaded, blue-eyed man with a mustache, wearing a hooded sweatshirt. "This is the image we want you to correct. It's the only thing we've had to go by, but from the day we first released it, we've had an unhappy witness. She's maintained that this is not the right face. We need you to reinterview her and find out what went wrong."

Noel could read the sentiment in my eyes. I looked away while he told me more. On February 20, 1987, a bomb had exploded in a parking lot in Salt Lake City. Three days later an initial attempt at a suspect sketch was prepared in haste by an FBI artist. But it was mechanical, flat, and according to the witness, "wrong." A second artist then entered the case, brought in through a social tie to a police lieutenant involved in the investigation of a potentially related 1985 event. That artist spent weeks toying with his version in a belabored effort to please the eyewitness but only took the image even further away from what she'd seen.

Left: The investigative sketch of the Unabomber, prepared by a freelance artist and released by Sacramento investigators on March 10, 1987. Right: This additional sketch, later privately released by the same artist, depicted what the Unabomber was supposed to look like without glasses, despite having never been seen without glasses by the eyewitness.

Out of desperation, though, his drawing was released on March 10, 1987, despite the witness's protest. To create more trouble, because of her complaints, the artist continued to tamper with it for yet another week. The artwork kept getting more refined, while the image grew even more unrelated to what the witness had actually seen. And worst of all, the sole witness's memory in the fifteen-year-old case was being contorted in the drawn-out process.

The misdirection of the case over the seven years had been costly, not just in departmental dollars and hours spent pursuing leads based on a wrong image, but in terms of public danger as the terrorist continued planning his rampage, unconcerned about being linked to the face then depicted on the wanted posters.

As much as I appreciated the Bureau's faith in my abilities, I was exasperated by the obstacles in my path. Every precaution should have been taken to protect the evidence. Yet even at the FBI level, investigators still seemed not to comprehend that a memory in an eyewitness's mind *is* evidence. And in this high-profile case, the primary evidence had been dragged through the mud—more than once.

The analogy is simple. If a fingerprint is found on a gun, a knife, or perhaps a glass at a murder scene, detectives guard that evidence with their lives, carefully picking it up with an implement and placing it into an evidence bag, untouched and protected. They'd never let it be smudged, knowing that once it was, those prints would likely be irretrievable. Yet, an "imprint" in an eyewitness's memory is *just* as fragile and in fact even *more* smudgeable than a fingerprint on a murder weapon, yet rarely is it treated with equal care.

Instead, the delicate eyewitness image obtained during the crime is routinely smeared, distorted, and contaminated by police agencies as they attempt to create a composite drawing of the suspect.

In standard police practice, witnesses are bombarded with mug shots and catalogs of facial photos so that they can point out a multitude of features that look something like what they've seen—like picking out your lost luggage by pointing to an airline baggage chart full of handles, fabrics, latches, and locks. If only the human psyche were so wonderfully simple—but it's not.

Shockingly, compositry is an aspect of investigations that has never been given academic thought. Few investigators question how a drawing is produced, just so long as they end up with one in hand.

Common belief is that if the artwork is good, then the information it conveys must be good as well. But that belief is dangerously wrong. There is no correlation between the impressiveness of the artwork and the accuracy of its information. The answers to uncovering memory reside not in artistic ability, but in understanding the powerful inner workings of the human mind—and more importantly, in the power of the human heart.

I started tallying up the odds against success as we taxied down the runway. Noel was describing the longest reign of terror in the country's history: multiple fatalities, overwhelming pressure from the media, and the highest imaginable scrutiny by the government. He was escorting me to interview the sole eyewitness from a seven-year-old sighting, and he was asking me to do—*what?*

"So tell me about this process of yours," Agent Noel said as he loosened his necktie. Then he posed the one question that really mattered: "And do you think we even have a chance at this?"

Despite all the bad news, I *did* believe we had at least a shot. With a two-hour flight still ahead, I'd try to use the time to explain why.

"Under ordinary circumstances, a seven-and-a-half-year time lapse might be an overwhelming obstacle to recovering a memory," I began, "but in this case, we're not dealing with ordinary circumstances. We have a couple of factors in our favor. The first is the high degree of emotional upheaval the eyewitness experienced. The mind holds great power to encode or record detail into its memory if an event evokes emotion, and especially if it threatens a person's own sense of security." I knew he'd understand the concept more clearly if I used examples that he'd lived through himself.

"Remember hearing the news about the assassination of President Kennedy, or perhaps about the explosion of the space shuttle? Both events took place years ago, yet most people recall them with precision and can even cite with detail the exact moment as they lived it, down to the temperature of the air, the song on the radio, the color of a teacher's dress when she walked into the classroom bearing the news. It's all still there. But asked to describe the day before, or the day after, the memory has long since released all nonpertinent detail." He nodded in understanding.

"The same thing occurs when the mind experiences the trauma of being witness to or a victim of crime. That's the good news, but there's a catch," I explained.

"Because the crime victim experiences the traumatic event personally, the mind, as a survival measure, acts with determination to protect the victim from reexperiencing the event by repressing the image that induced the trauma. Emotions arise and act to buffer the harsh reality from the conscious mind. The mind then strives to alter the memory in any way it can, to make that image more emotionally palatable.

"A crime victim will go through a series of 'if only's.' If only I had taken a different route, if only I'd followed my intuition, if only . . . It's part of the mind's effort to rework the event in order to master the emotion. The mind tries hard to achieve distance from the trauma to allow the victim to move forward, to move on to safety and to regain function. This sets the stage for disaster when interviewing high-trauma witnesses and victims, who are highly susceptible to influence and suggestion. You see, they are trying on a conscious level to recall the images of those who brought the experience of terror into their lives—while subconsciously their minds are trying to repress the same information. Their minds will willingly grasp at whatever information is presented, verbally or visually." Noel listened closely.

"The good news to investigators—and to this case—is that the subconscious mind often holds the true detail intact, though it's typically buried securely underneath what the conscious mind has allowed in as its new 'truth.' " Noel nodded in understanding and leaned in a little closer.

"Here's the irony. Without meaning to do so, investigators or police artists actually help to bury the image every time they present a victim with a photo of someone other than the actual suspect. Their hope is that the victim can simply point at something visual and say, 'The nose is just like that,' or 'The chin is like that,' based on the theory that recognition is easier than recall. The recognition method of 'identification' works sometimes, but more so in nontraumatic circumstances—for instance to describe someone who cashed a bad check. There's no trauma involved in that kind of an encounter, so the mind has no reason to protect itself from the memory. But to this day, that single approach is the one used by police when creating a drawing, no matter the scenario involved in the case." The flight attendant handed us our drinks as I continued.

"There are now decades of research proving that when emotion is introduced, every single dynamic of how memory functions changes. By showing eyewitnesses books of facial photos from which to choose look-alike images, the well-meaning police or police artists are literally handing to the eyewitness—at the very height of that person's vulnerability to suggestion and influence—the visual tools to effectively discard, distort or further entomb the actual image that created the trauma. They are, in effect, not producing but rather unknowingly aiding in *destroying* evidence. The academic world understands this, but the police system hasn't caught up. They still assume that this work is all about art."

His eyes lit up. "It makes so much sense! It's so simple, yet . . ."

I finished his thought for him while he began to realize the magnitude of the errors already made. "Think about this: What happens if you hold film still in a camera and repeatedly open the shutter? What happens to your original imprint on the film with each exposure? It is so simple, you're right; yet through lack of awareness, those who are trying whole-heartedly to help are potentially disabling the witness from ever having the ability to identify a suspect when one is apprehended.

"We might still have hope," I told him. "You see, if we can coach the conscious mind to move aside, sometimes we can still access the original untainted image—*if* there is reason enough for it to have been retained in memory. The higher the degree of personal trauma, the harder the mind works to discard or bury the image, but, also, the more likely it will have been encoded into memory in the first place, even if it's housed at a much deeper level of recall." Noel sighed as he listened.

"To put the concept into more tangible terms," I explained, "think of it like this: Searching for the encoded image in the eyewitness's mind is comparable to retrieving a fifty-cent piece that's been tossed into eight feet of water. The fifty-cent piece rests at the bottom of the pool, just as it originally existed, but the image of it is distorted through the eight feet of water—or, through the emotional aftermath that follows a traumatic event. Then to make it even more difficult to see, that same water gets muddied and rippled, as does the image of the suspect by the bombardment of visual contaminants offered by police artists and investigators.

"My job is to try to get through that muddied and rippled water and to bring that coin back to the surface of the pool—or, in real terms, to bring back into the eyewitness's conscious memory that original image, in its original condition.

"In the case of the Unabomber witness, the magnitude of the trauma she experienced was likely sufficient for her mind to encode the vision of the suspect into her short-term recall and—more important—to transfer it into her long-term memory. But the big question now is, Under how many feet of muddy water does that coin lie?

"The reason for optimism is, ironically, the eyewitness's aggravation over the last sketch. That frustration might have helped lock in her original memory at a subliminal level no matter how much contamination the image has since been exposed to."

Seat backs went up as we began our descent.

"We've blown it in this case without ever even realizing it, haven't we?" Agent Noel asked. "All those years, all those wrong leads . . ."

"Maybe not," I answered. "It will all depend on the emotional investment of your witness. We won't know until we try. But despite the odds, it's always worth trying."

The summer sun was just starting to sink over the Great Salt Lake as our flight landed. The Wasatch Mountains actually reminded me a little of the Oregon Cascades back home—except that they were on the wrong side of town.

I sighed, and the exhale made room for reality to invade. I was landing in the wrong state and still hadn't broken the news to my husband. For once I was grateful he'd never gotten into the romantic habit of seeing me off or picking me up at airports.

City traffic was sparse as we drove from Salt Lake City International to the downtown FBI office to pick up the witness's address from the local agents.

In February 1987, this crucial eyewitness was simply an unsuspecting secretary sitting at a desk shuffling papers for a small, independent Salt Lake City computer company when out of the corner of her eye she absentmindedly noticed a man walking outside the bank of windows that fronted her office. She registered the image as it passed from one windowpane to the next, but then realized that he'd not passed by the third. Thinking he might have fallen, she stood up and looked.

What she saw was a figure hunched down by the front driver's side of her own car, placing what appeared to be a wooden device beneath the wheel. As she yelled out to the business owner's mother to take a look, the stranger turned and stole a fleeting glance over his shoulder at her from just over twenty feet away. Sunglasses concealed his eyes. He looked immediately back toward the package, then stood up and casually walked off, leaving the device tucked underneath her front wheel.

By then, both women were at the window, though all they could see was his back, his face hidden entirely by the hood of the gray sweatshirt he wore on the sunny Salt Lake City winter day.

Odd, she thought. I'll just move whatever that is when I get off work. The two women laughed at the strangeness of his actions and commented on his "cute ass" as he walked away. A ringing phone drew away their attention and they returned to work.

"Whatever that is" was shoved into a canvas bag and appeared to be two two-by-four-inch pieces of wood held together by long nails that protruded through the top board and into the crisp Utah air.

Within an hour, the company's owner, Gary Wright, pulled in and parked in his assigned place several spaces away. As he passed by his employee's car, which he knew by her customized license plates, he noticed the package wedged near the tire. Concerned that she would run over it, he bent over to lift it out of the way. Instead, it exploded in his hands. Gary Wright's mother watched from just inside the office window as the blast tore through her son's body.

Injuries from his moment of unsolicited heroism were substantial to Wright's arms, legs, throat, face, and left hand. Years would follow before his body would heal, and the emotional injury would be far, far slower to mend. The mad bomber had blighted another life and left another victim without hope of reclaiming a carefree spirit. But the bomber himself had lost something, too: his anonymity. He'd shown his face—though only for a second—to his first and, as it would turn out, his only eyewitness.

The FBI, deep into its Unabomber investigation by then, identified many of the telltale fragments in the explosion remains. Their questions had less to do with who placed the bomb than they did with why it was placed under the car of this woman. Her custom license plates bearing her name indicated that his selection might not be random. If they could determine a rationale for how the Unabomber targeted his victims, they might be able to avert the next disaster.

To find their answer, the FBI seized the witness's privacy in the name of national security. For years, agents monitored her every movement, her contacts, friends, relatives, acquaintances, her mail, even her phone calls. Early on, they posted lookouts around her house, all in an attempt to answer the question "Why her?" Nothing about her life fit the bomber's apparent antitechnology agenda. Yet, the debris from the blast left unmistakable evidence that this was the work of the Unabomber.

By the time Agent Noel and I got to her home in July 1994, she simply opened the door and walked away, mumbling to the two of us, "Come on in, coffee's on," as we stood in the open doorway.

For the first order of business, I'd need to establish myself as a non-agent, almost the "anticop." Her irritation was with a system that hadn't listened to her. As amicable as her relationship was with the agency, and especially with Noel, I'd need to differentiate myself from "them" in her eyes, so she could feel assured that she wasn't just repeating her past experience.

"Heck, who am I? Just the witness," she asked and answered quietly in a single breath. "Never mind what *I* think I saw. They'll *tell* me what I saw, and when I tell them it's off base, they'll just tell me again. That drawing's never been right. I've tried to tell them." She smiled shyly after her words, but her frustration was justified, and her expectations understandably low.

Agent Noel knew exactly what she was talking about. He'd heard her loud and clear over the years, but he had lacked the budget and the nod of approval to start all over on a suspect depiction. That changed when Attorney General Janet Reno unleashed her resources to turn over every possible stone.

We started with two cups of coffee, while her three-year-old settled comfortably into Noel's lap on the sofa, oblivious to the weighty implications of the activity across the room.

I glanced around for references from her home which might lead me to topics that would elicit from her a positive emotional response: photographs on shelves, book titles—I wanted to immerse her in conversations around themes with which she was familiar and felt a sense of mastery and control. If she focused on subjects with which she felt safe, she might relax sufficiently for us to tap into the more sublime reservoirs of her memory. I needed to keep her attention diverted from the task we both knew loomed. The less she focused directly on the ominous task of re-creating the face, the more easily the real detail would surface.

Conversely, if I were to ask direct questions about the event or even about the suspect, it could revive her emotion regarding the bombing, and that upset could serve as an invitation for the cognitive or conscious part of her mind—where she now held what she thought she had seen—to take over. Cognitive recall is the portion of memory that's most susceptible to influence and change, so what she now *thought* she had seen was most likely to be incorrect. I had no interest in what she *thought* she saw. We needed to reach what she had *actually* seen. By this late stage, the two were inevitably a world apart.

At her kitchen table we discussed movies, the excitement of travel, the joys of work, and the rearing of a three-year-old, anything that would divert her from the weight of remembering. More than anything else, I wanted to avoid direct mention of the bombing. If we focused on the problem, we'd fail to find the solution and could conceivably end up only with her recall of the inaccurate sketch, which was by now securely and disastrously embedded over the original image in her mind.

The only reference to the task at hand was the infusion every fifteen or twenty minutes of a single, quick question—always phrased in *present* tense. "Would you create a shape that's longer than wide or the same length as width?" as a simple example. Keeping the conversation based in the present helped to anchor her emotionally in the safety of the current moment, and to distance her from the emotions connected to her memory of the event.

I'd insert questions only when she was in a state of relaxation. To assure that she maintained that relaxed state, I'd never refer to the suspect or to the crime. Instead, I'd only refer to shapes and textures in the context of an inanimate form, such as a pliable substance like clay, and how she might shape that clay into the form of a face.

Doing so took the image of the suspect, which aroused fear and terror in her, and transformed it into the form of a simple, harmless object—an object that existed in the present moment and over which she could have a feeling of control, something that the suspect, in real life, had taken away from her.

That inanimate form was lifeless, a simple imagined shape with no personality, no eyes, no arms, *no bomb,* and therefore, of no threat.

In every question, I monitored my voice tone so that no descriptor would carry more gravity than any other. Eye contact during a single question had to be completely maintained throughout or avoided altogether. Momentary eye contact, if construed as emotional support, could lead her toward the portion of the question during which the contact was offered. Every nuance mattered if we were to reach the original, untainted image of the elusive killer.

The 1987 bombing nearly caused the death of Gary Wright. He wasn't only her employer, he was her friend. His motive in moving the package was to help her. No matter how many years had since passed, this witness still wrestled with intense emotional issues. Honoring and understanding the weight of her psychological issues was the *most* crucial step in the interview and the missing element in the traditional police process.

Agent Noel listened from across the room. The questions were so minimal and indirect that they seemed like only momentary disruptions in an otherwise spirited chat between two old friends. But each time, she'd respond with answers that were crisp and precise. The distraction of our unrelated conversation didn't leave her time to dwell or second-guess. "Second-guessing" is, in fact, movement from the subliminal to the cognitive level of memory, or—figuratively—from the heart to the brain.

As in all of life, the heart is always right.

I showed her nothing—no standard police catalogs of facial features, no routine mug pictures, no suggestive visual aids. I asked no leading questions to prompt her answers. Instead I relied simply on the purity of her actual recall and the integrity of her wish to reach it. Slowly the deeply embedded image began to emerge, making its way past the newer image by then so ingrained in her conscious mind.

In contradiction to the existent suspect drawing, no ruddy complexion, no red hair, no blue eyes, existed or were ever seen on that day— although they'd been mysteriously depicted to the Bureau's bewilderment in an unsolicited drawing released by the first artist years after the bombing. There was also definitely no thin jawline and last but not least, there was no mustache.

She talked and I listened, quietly elated, as the answers gradually bubbled up throughout the conversation. I glanced over to Agent Noel to watch his reactions. He looked back with his brows raised, as if to say, "Let's get to the point. What is this, the friggin' *Oprah Winfrey* show?"

It probably did look like "girls' night out" to someone unfamiliar with this system of diversionary interview, but every question was carefully timed, toned, and phrased so as not to lead her in her answers. I wanted only the image encoded in her recall on that fateful day in February 1987.

We *were* getting to the point. We were just taking the back road.

The direct route, unfortunately, was covered with debris.

The eyewitness was at last content.

Agent Noel and I checked into our hotel rooms and reconvened in the lobby to go find dinner. To celebrate, we drove to Park City in search of a place fitting the occasion. The sun had already set and Utah's evening mountain air was sweet and sharp.

We ducked into a local brewery, pulled up two pine stools, and ordered. Max Noel was just the elixir I needed. He was one of those animated, instantly likable men I always wished could have been my uncle or brother or father-in-law. He talked for two hours about the devotion he felt for his wife and the plans he had to surprise her with a cabin he'd rented for the upcoming weekend. I watched his eyes dance when he described their long-term, solid partnership.

"So how did you ever find that, Max?" I asked.

"I don't know," he said, looking down. Then he let out a huff and smiled. "I was just real lucky I guess." Listening to his stories reminded me of the phone call I still had to make.

Before we said good-night, I slid the finished draft of the new drawing out of its carrier and handed it over for his inspection. We locked eyes in the sudden realization of what exactly we'd accomplished.

Against all odds, we held in our hands the first real look . . . at the face of a madman.

"Hi, sweetheart. How are you? . . . No, I'm not at the airport. . . . No, I'm not in Albuquerque either, that was yesterday. See, I got kind of, well, rerouted—by an FBI agent. I'm in Salt Lake. It couldn't be helped. It was an important case. I'll be home tomorrow though, not late, I promise."

Robert's exhale hurt my ear. "Damn it anyway, Jeanne. You know— they're *all* important cases, so what *else* is new?" I held the receiver away from my ear. His voice accelerated in speed and upped in volume. I knew that tone well. I could even picture his angry face. My elation over the day's success turned into a knot in the center of my stomach.

"Look," he said, "I had to fix my own dinner tonight. Yours is sitting here cold, and you know, Jeanne—damn it anyway—you're testing my limits! Tell me one thing, okay? Just tell me—why can't you just be . . . *normal?*"

2

OUT OF LINE

When I called my husband from Utah to break the news about being intercepted by the FBI, he was "downright pissed."

We both wanted to be home sitting at our own table, and sleeping in our own bed. Yet, the simple life proved elusive.

I knew that my work made for an insane way to live, jerked around by telephone calls, delayed flights, and task force meetings, carrying a suitcase that never got emptied, trying to hold a marriage together across fifty states and against the backdrop of the nation's biggest crimes. It was a real boon for Airtouch cellular, but something definitely had to change.

I had quit, many times, much like a smoker. In between, there were the placating pledges: "As soon as my contract expires." "I'll go just this once." "This will be the last case, I swear." Robert had perfected the art of eye rolling.

But my need to say yes always pulled at me harder than my wish to stay home. The drive was powerful, internal. It drove me. And it drove me nuts.

I met Robert Weldon in 1983 during an investigative-interviewing course in Portland, Oregon. Of course, he was a cop. Actually, I met his sergeant first, who had asked me to lunch but was too shy to take me out alone. So he invited six-foot-four-inch Robert to come along. Within minutes, the sergeant faded into the background and all I could see was the gorgeous man across the table, easy on the eyes, and with a gaze that bore straight into my heart.

But still there was this "complication." I had a cast-in-cement pact with myself to keep my social life completely away from my work. It was bad enough spending ten hours a day immersed in police drama. In off-hours, I needed a reprieve.

In a sentence, I didn't date cops and I wouldn't date Robert—even though I'd never felt that kind of reaction to a man, ever. Even though my heart fell through the floor when I looked into those huge green eyes. Even though he sounded like Sam Elliott, with that low, soft voice . . .

No, I didn't date cops, and I would not date Robert.

For months, I let his pink "while you were out" slips pile high in my in-box, until one day he had the audacity to show up at my Portland Detective Division office, refusing to give his name, and demanding that he see me.

I walked out from behind the security desk expecting to find another witness, but there he was, with those damned green eyes, the faint scent of Grey Flannel cologne, and stroking that signature mustache as if he knew his own power.

In person, I didn't stand a chance. He took me by the elbow, led me down a hallway, extended his massive arms around me, then pinned me against the wall and kissed me. I was in trouble—big, tall, sweet-smelling, green-eyed trouble.

I broke my own rule.

As the early-morning flight lifted over Salt Lake City's Temple Square on my way home, I thought of how Robert deserved an answer to his question. Why couldn't I just be normal? Maybe I needed to understand, too. I pushed the seat back, closed my eyes, and tried to come up with the answer.

I'd grown up the third of six kids in an Irish Catholic family with a rock-solid work ethic, raised by parents who defied conformity, and who made sure that we valued independence.

My father, a self-employed, highly principled Frank Sinatra look-alike, and my mother, the neighborhood's most beautiful mom, eloped at eighteen, fleeing from Brooklyn to a small Colorado mountain town with a population that matched the altitude and a setting as unlike New York as they could find.

Swimming lessons, 4-H, camping trips, horses, rabbits, and dogs: life was wholesome and good. One year rolled into the next, predictably, uneventfully, and peacefully. But through the eyes of a seventeen-year-old who'd never left town, it was not only perfect, it was perfectly boring.

The class president placed a rhinestone tiara on my head in October of my senior year: "Homecoming Queen, Montrose High School," as big an honor as a local girl could get. To the marching band's interpretation of "Lara's Theme," I reigned from the football field and, in what seemed like slow motion, waved to friends and family in the stands, thinking, Is this really as good as it gets? It can't be. I've *got* to get away from here and find out.

All my dreams followed the high roads over the Rockies. I wanted to see New York and Los Angeles, Rome, Moscow, to find glamour and excitement, have adventure, mystery, intrigue, become a news reporter or a foreign journalist. The specter of sitting in those bleachers, watching my own kids play ball twenty-five football seasons down the road, sent a chill from my crown down. My folks had found their dream in Colorado, but I still hadn't been more than sixty miles from their Rocky Mountain utopia.

The morning after the graduation party, the smell of wood smoke still in my hair, a total of $24 in my pocket, and the rest of my life in a green army bag borrowed from my brother, I boarded a seven-o'clock Greyhound and waved to my crying mother as the bus turned the corner at JC Penney's and vanished south down Highway 550. As breathtaking as the Colorado scenery was, and it was spectacular, I had to know what was on the south side of that San Juan Mountain Range.

I walked across the crusted snow on college campuses in different towns, watching classes in session from the outside in, but couldn't dig up tuition with desire alone. Road construction jobs in frigid mountain air kept me funded while I routinely stashed away every extra cent, determined to find my way inside a university.

In the meantime, there were other ways to get an "education"—like hitchhiking. The L.L. Bean catalog must have missed my mailbox, so with a knapsack, broom handles, and twine, I created a backpack. It wasn't pretty, but it was functional. I took back roads only, no rides over a hundred miles. The plan was to learn about the locals in every state, what they did, how they thought, how they lived, who they were. I filled up journals and wore out my Minolta SRT 101, like a budding "Jeanne Kuralt." If I couldn't be a photojournalist yet, I could at least live like one.

California, Canada, Chicago—I crisscrossed the country over two years. Highway junctions could get competitive. As soon as I'd tune in to the stories of a few dust-covered college boys bemoaning their languishing on the same highway crossroad for three days, the brakes would sound, the gravel would crackle under a set of tires, I'd shrug my shoulders and say, "Okay, well, see ya!"

It was the era of serial killers like Ted Bundy, out cruising the countryside looking for young prey like me. But it was also the era of Gloria Steinem and Helen Reddy. It was fashionable to be fearless.

Between towns and jobs I picked up an occasional college course whenever I could fit one into my budget. Early one fall day, I received a handwritten response from a small-college admissions office in Missouri. Instead of the usual "Dear Prospective Student," it was personally handwritten. I took it as a sign. They wanted me. I piled my things into my 1963 Ford pickup truck, tied the faded canvas down over the back, and drove nonstop.

Kansas City was "home" for a summer of hair-frizzing humidity followed by one long black-iced winter—both of which I'd never experienced before, nor I vowed, would I ever again. But my decision to leave within the year was prompted by more than just the weather. Disheartened but not defeated, I left with the faces of two assailants burned into my memory and drove west on I-84 until I reached the Oregon coast. I'd have kept going on to Tokyo if the road hadn't ended. If I drove far enough and fast enough, I reasoned, I could make believe that one night had never happened.

Nineteen seventy-seven brought with it the death of Elvis, the inauguration of a president named Jimmy, and the transfer of my college credits to a major Oregon university in Portland. It also brought the Proposition 13 tax revolt in California, which was threatening to spread into neighboring states. Anticipating that Oregon might follow suit, the local sheriff's office tested a pilot project to fill lost patrol positions with detectives, and to use civilians as criminal investigative assistants (CIAs) to pick up the slack, performing less critical tasks short of making arrests.

It was a finite twelve-month experiment, plus it paid well. As a bonus, the office was on the edge of town, so I could be fishing on the Sandy River by four-thirty on summer afternoons. I may have left the mountains, but I hadn't given up the lifestyle.

As one of five CIAs, my assignment was to conduct follow-up interviews with victims of Person's Crimes, the police term for the unit that handled rape, assault, robbery, and murders.

Daily, I listened to pained recountings by victims, piecing together facts missed by officers in their rush to get to the next call. But by taking the time to listen to the details of their assaults, I was discovering descriptions of attackers that were in conflict with the police composites created by the department.

The only consistency was the inconsistency between what I was hearing the victims telling me and what I'd later see in the sketches. Then I began seeing patterns emerge in interviews. Time lapses after a crime seemed to affect how people remembered things. Witnesses would have one account the night of the event, and another one five or ten days later.

But why?

Their memories could be swayed by something so simple as the way a question was formed or the tone of voice used. I could ask a question in two ways and get two different answers. If trauma was involved, recall became like putty.

If I supplied the words to use in descriptions, the witnesses seemed to grasp at the first thing I said before an alternative left my lips. If I showed them pictures to choose from, they'd change their descriptions from what they had already spoken to what they'd been shown. I could find nothing in police training about emotion or perception relating to suspect descriptions. Yet there had to be reasons.

The system, however, didn't seem to want explanations. It wanted hard data, obtained as efficiently as possible. Cops needed answers that were coded to fit into preformatted data-entry boxes, so the clerks could compile the statistics and police agencies could compare check marks. But the true answers just didn't fit into a multiple-choice format.

I collected a list of questions to take to the commanders, but never got to ask them. Instead, they were waiting to talk to me. I entered the conference room to find three supervisors with eyebrows lowered, all seated on one side of the table. On the other side, a single empty chair.

"Jeanne, have a seat," one ordered. "We've called this meeting to advise you that your position is in jeopardy. Your probing is outside your written job description and you're not adhering to the rules. If this behavior does not cease, we will terminate your employment. Are we understanding each other?"

"But there's a whole emotional end to this that isn't even being looked at and—"

They interrupted, repeating their warning. "Jeanne, either stay within the rules or be fired." I was, as they put it, "out of line."

Anyone who knew me could attest to the fact that staying within the lines had never been my strong suit. I looked at them all—with their matching haircuts, matching clothes, matching belts and shoes—and realized I'd be better served to just save my breath and nod.

"Yes, sir," I answered.

I had university tuition to pay, so I'd comply, at least during working hours. But they couldn't dictate what I did after hours, so I'd return to the victims and take the time they needed to talk.

The longer I listened, the more detailed their memories became. The information obtained during the first part of an interview was like a covering over the actual detail, like a bandage over a wound. Early thoughts were skewed by shock, emotion, and confusion. It took time to get to the real details, and investigators didn't have it. Plus, the regimented police system wouldn't allow it.

So much for evening fishing trips. Like an archaeologist stumbling over a stone and inadvertently uncovering a relic, I knew I was onto an area of investigations that was completely untapped.

Witnesses didn't describe in concrete terms like *large eyes* and *square chin*. They used an entirely different language that revolved around emotions and feelings, senses and perceptions. They used words like *confused, angry, terrified, mean, determined, distracted, nervous*.

But what did those words really *mean* to the witnesses? Checks in the same black box could denote something different to a fourteen-year-old boy than to a forty-nine-year-old woman, or to a black than to a Caucasian. It seemed not to be about what they *saw*. It was what they *felt* that formed their vocabulary.

Out of frustration, I began to doodle what the witnesses were trying to communicate, later saying to the investigators, "No, no, I think what they meant was more like this." The response was always the same: "What do you know—you weren't there."

No, I wasn't, but I knew what I'd heard, and the descriptions were not of the faces in the wanted sketches that were the primary focus of the investigations. As I'd drive home and see the drawings on light posts or on the evening news, I'd feel ill from the knowledge that the rapist or robber could be passing the same light posts—unnoticed and unsuspected—free to attack again, even given a sense of immunity due to the typical inaccuracy of the drawings.

But I had to be careful. I was stepping outside the box again, and I couldn't risk riling up the good ol' boys by "exceeding my written job description."

It didn't take brilliance to see that being young, unconventional, and civilian was not exactly the recipe for a warm reception in the tradition-steeped subculture of law enforcement. "Stay within the lines" was the prevailing rule on this playing field. Those who had ascended in the detective-sergeant-lieutenant-captain-chief hierarchy—in other words, the decision makers—were the same ones who had best followed the rules and were rewarded through promotion, making them, naturally, the least likely to bend.

When the CIA program ended in January of 1979, I sold my car, packed my green barracks bag, loaded up my Minolta and my journal, and bought a one-way ticket to Europe.

As the plane climbed, it banked east over Portland. A break in the low clouds formed a perfect frame for a departing view of the city. I looked down, picked out the pale beige sheriff's office building in the early-morning winter sun, and waved a final good-bye to the world of cops, uniforms and check marks with the appropriate gesture.

The Bavarian Alps of southern Germany revived my spirit. I spent spring and summer bicycling and writing. Even in fall it was perfect—*if* I ignored my savings account. I stood in the long lines for a work permit, but when it was my turn, the German official told me to try again—next time with a college degree. Unless it was under the table, I couldn't work. And thanks to a landlord who rationed hot-water heat to an hour a day, I also couldn't get warm. One early-winter Munich day I walked into a travel agency, pointed a frozen finger at the wall-sized world map behind the agent's desk, and said, "Just send me someplace warm." I left with a one-way ticket to Honolulu.

If Chaminade University in Hawaii had accepted all my credits toward a bachelor's degree, I'd have stayed in the sun forever. But the transfer would have cost a year of added time, so, reluctantly, I made my way back to finish college in Portland.

Something inexplicable still plagued me, something I couldn't forget: the faces of the victims I'd met in my year at the SO. Cautiously, I stepped back into the world of cops. This time, though, I approached the more upscale and downtown Portland Police Bureau rather than the rougher rural sheriff's office, and arrived with conditions: I asked for permission—free rein—to focus solely and unencumbered on the complex dynamics of eyewitness memory by reinterviewing high-trauma case victims. In a first for the department, I asked to create a new position.

I isolated myself from the beginning, setting up in an unused, unheated office, digging through a stack of dead-end files on which to test theories. I came and went quietly through the Detective Division's back door, hoping to draw no attention, working night school around daytime interviews.

In June 1981, in a rented cap and gown, I set up a tripod, hit the autotimer, and ran out in front of the lens. My bachelor's degree was supposed to signal a chapter change, but as each year rolled into the next, always at the last minute the Portland PD managed to scrape together funds to keep me on through yet another fiscal cycle.

Each year I was packed to leave and disappointed when the money came in. I was ready to move on to a sunny place and get back to creating a real life. But with each year's announcement of additional funding, I found I couldn't walk away.

The job title that fit the closest was "police artist," also known as a forensic artist, although both terms are incorrect.

Unlike a departmental police artist, I didn't use the "pick a nose" system of facial catalogs or spend time doing courtroom sketches, crime-scene drawings, or portraits of retiring police chiefs.

The next potential title was "forensic artist," but by definition, *forensics* means "the study and application of *science* to legal fact." There were forensic pathologists, toxicologists, odontologists, serologists. But "forensic artist"? No, that term was just another occupational euphemism. It didn't fit either.

I searched for training, but all I could find were the five-day, match-book-style sketchfest kinds of courses that popped up periodically around the country, offered by self-interested entrepreneurs promising anyone with a checkbook a "certificate" by Friday at five. Yet it held no more value than the paper it was printed on.

I contacted police agencies from New York to Los Angeles in hope of finding peers but also came up dry. Next I tried the universities. There, the answers began to emerge.

Dr. Elizabeth Loftus, University of Washington professor of psychology and author of *Witness for the Defense* and *Eyewitness Testimony,* led a field of scholars intensively studying eyewitness recall. By necessity, their work was based on classroom mock-drama studies, but I had a luxury they did not: I could take their statistical findings even further and test them in the field with real crime victims. Because no two cases were alike, my research could never be empirical, so I'd leave the stats to the academicians, but their hard work gave me the academic foundation on which to build.

Dr. Loftus was sought worldwide by defense teams needing an expert witness to discredit eyewitness testimony. The mention of her name sent prosecutors running for plea bargains. Her studies proved that memory is

not static, that ideas can be implanted, recall skewed, and images overridden if an eyewitness is exposed to suggestion in any form. She was
summoned to the courts in the country's high-profile cases. Her testimony helped overturn convictions and set imprisoned men free.

I didn't view her as "the enemy," even though many on the prosecution's side did. If she was working to keep the wrongly identified out of
prison, and I was working to get the correctly identified into prison,
weren't we in effect on the same "justice" team? I'd finally found my
mentor.

I took the scholars' findings and put them into practice on thousands
of cases over many years, continually refining interview methods, keeping what did work and discarding what did not.

But my low profile philosophy was slipping away. Local and regional
papers began to run stories on my work. National magazines picked up
on the interest. When television programs followed with occasional features, no one was more surprised by the interest than I.

Reporters seemed to pick up on my "nonconformity," personal and
professional, yet I could find nothing in the professional realm to con-
form *to*. Unintentionally, I was making waves again. The media began
raising the same question I'd been asking all along: "Why haven't these
issues been addressed before?"

In 1986, by invitation, I traveled throughout China to teach
investigative interviewing to a government trying to turn a difficult corner: they were trying to achieve an innocent-until-proven-guilty trial
process for the first time in their history.

Later I was invited to join the prestigious American Academy of
Forensic Sciences and was asked to speak at a national convention in
San Diego. An NBC crew arrived at the conference to tape a profile on
my work to air on the *Today* show the following month. A State
Department official followed the television cables into the room and,
after listening, asked if I'd consider making a series of trips to war-
ravaged El Salvador to teach investigative interviewing to a special task
force assigned to investigate political assassinations.

In January 1988, the Japanese government requested that I teach in

Tokyo. That trip was followed by lectures in Hawaii. By the time I flew back, I knew that things had gotten out of hand.

It was time to get back to my own life—a "normal" life. In June, I made the announcement. I quit.

I was sure that a move east over Oregon's Cascade Mountains to the small town of Bend would create a barrier that could break my ties with work. But the phone kept ringing. The PD wouldn't let me go. I agreed to commute to Portland for only two days a week; but the other five days were filled with calls from agencies even farther away. Though I'd left my job, my caseload only grew. I knew gate agents by name but I still hadn't met my own neighbors.

I had to choose. Robert waited for me in his world, defined in its entirety by county lines. His life was compact and blessedly uneventful. His idea of danger was thin ice on a frigid day of fishing. His idea of perfection was a lawn mowed to the correct height as he pulled in the driveway at the end of the day.

In the simple life we had planned, there would be no robberies, killings, or third-world wars. The biggest challenge in my day would be finding stemware to match the tablecloth and making sure the pot roast didn't burn.

On November 10, 1990, on a California beach at sunset, by a near-sighted preacher with Coke-bottle glasses who insisted on calling me Jennie, Robert and I were married.

Next we found the log home we'd held in our dreams. Depending on which deck we stood, we could overlook a show-horse ranch or face the snowcapped Cascades. Lodgepole pines brushed the crisp desert sky that was without even a hint of cloud. The occasional contrail from a DC-8 was the only flaw, visible only if I leaned back a little too far in the hot tub.

I hauled crates of furnishings out of storage. The Ralph Lauren cata-log had nothing on me. In my years on the road, I had acquired every Navajo blanket, old saddle, faded pair of chaps, and set of longhorns I'd come across. I hung my collection of Howard Terpening and James Bama paintings on the bark-chipped beams of our log home. Throw in a box-nosed, yellow Lab puppy named Dillon and our picture was complete, almost. The only missing element was a child. And time wasn't on our side.

Each time I got home my resolve to settle down got stronger. But before my carry-on could be emptied, another phone call would interrupt: "Jeanne, could you just help out on one more case?"

Detectives always apologized before telling me that their case was the biggest, the saddest, the worst, or the most important. Each time I'd pack and go, telling myself that I might be able to keep one foot evenly planted in each of my diametrically opposed worlds.

In November 1992, ABC television honored me as a "Woman of Distinction" during a nationally broadcast program filmed in Los Angeles. The producer also owned an outside production company, and within an hour of taping, I was cornered with a proposal to feature my life story in a television series. Robert wasn't pleased. I declined. I'd risen higher in this field than I'd ever expected to go. I decided to adjust my priorities and fast.

My husband had a birthday coming up and I had a plan. I'd use the occasion to soften him up on the idea of world travel. Travel for work was part of the job, but travel for pleasure was my passion. What I hoped for was a partner willing to go with me. I'd ease him in slowly.

I bought two round-trip tickets to Cabo San Lucas. I'd save Istanbul and Nepal for later. With a couple of margaritas on a warm beach, I was sure he'd be hooked. My world stretched far beyond the cast of his fly rod and I wanted him in it.

He went snorkeling, caught a marlin, and wanted to go home, all within three days, calling the place "perilous." I offered to drive him to the airport if he really wanted to leave, but the last thing I expected to hear was, "Really, sweetheart? You wouldn't mind? Great! You stay. It's your vacation, too. See you when you get home."

At the airport he hugged me good-bye, then called me "the greatest." I watched his large frame squeeze into the doorway of the aircraft as I waved good-bye and tried to coerce my jaw back into its original position.

The problem was clear: I couldn't stay home. He couldn't leave it.

Also, his values were rapidly shifting. He'd moved into a sales career and, for the first time, was making good money. He bought himself a

Rolex, although we still didn't have a washer and dryer. To entertain clients, he brought home bottles of wine worth more than my weekly grocery budget. He wore a diamond ring significantly larger than mine and traded his western boots for imported Italian Ferragamo shoes.

My Marlboro man was turning into Diamond Rob.

When I was home, I began to notice occasional muffled late-night phone calls. The office door would slowly swing shut if I passed down the hallway as he spoke. I didn't miss too many hints. It was time to get back to the ranch, this time, for good.

Coming home from Cabo, I scheduled one quick layover. It was a long shot. I'd worked a recent case with a strikingly pretty and unusual woman named Suzanne Jauchius, a world-renowned psychic who produced such accurate information that I'd been forced to rethink my own preconceptions.

Though she lived in West Linn, Oregon, a suburb of Portland, our paths hadn't crossed until we were brought together on a case in England. A woman was reaching outside British tradition to find the killer of her nineteen-year-old niece. Cradling a pair of the murdered girl's earrings, Suzanne envisioned the image of the attacker and a sense of the nature of the murder. She described the girl's body as being draped over railroad tracks, a detail she had no way of knowing.

Then, as if she were seeing through the victim's eyes, she described the killer as he struck his final blow. He loomed over the girl, his flesh sagging downward from gravity, strands of hair falling forward, partially obscuring his features. Together we formed the drawing of the killer's face.

The police later recovered the body draped over railroad tracks forty miles from London. The victim was last seen with a man having the precise face we had depicted.

It was enough to make me more than a little curious. I detoured on my return from Cabo long enough see Suzanne between flights. Maybe she could forecast my future. I'd resolved to quit the weekly commute and all other cases in just months when my two-day-a-week obligation to Portland officially expired, but when would I be starting my family? When exactly would my life become "normal"?

She sat facing me, holding my wedding ring in her hands, inhaled, and shut her eyes tightly.

"I see you taking a trip very soon," she said. "It's overseas, like Eastern Europe, or someplace very far, and it's a long trip, an important trip."

I wanted to laugh at the mention. Just what I needed—another trip overseas. I tried to imagine breaking *that* news to Robert when I walked in the door from Cabo. No, that was clearly wrong.

"I see a script or manuscript. Unfinished," she went on. "It's in the hands of a very tall man, someone with an accent whom you'll know instinctively you want to work with when you meet him. His name is Rod or perhaps Ron—I think it's Ron. Oh, wait." Her raised brows nearly pulled her eyes open. "And you'll do a lot of work for the FBI. I mean a *lot*."

I had worked for the FBI in the past, but not often. They prided themselves on being all-inclusive and seldom invited an outside expert into an investigation. When they did, it was only reluctantly and only if under pressure.

And what script? I wasn't writing any kind of manuscript. Some "psychic"—she didn't even know about my home, my waiting husband, my garden I was planning, my dog, and the softball team I was about to sign up for. She didn't even see my 120-day countdown out of this career for good.

She sat in long silences between her deep breaths, her eyes clinched shut in concentration, then suddenly said, "And you haven't found a mentor because there are none for you in this work."

I'd never mentioned my search for a "mentor." Yet she used that exact word? I guardedly tuned back in.

"Oh, and Jeanne—this is *big*. This work will grow to proportions you can't even imagine. Your work will be on major magazine covers, on the national news, there will be international news stories about your achievements—in Australia, Italy, England. . . .

"You'll be in demand by prosecution, and even by defense teams, also by media." Her voice accelerated. "A lot of media. And film, too. This is very clear to me. I see them wanting to make a film about you and what you do." She paused, sat up, and looked straight at me.

"But, be very careful. The higher you go, the more you'll be a target.

The press will embrace you because you are different; you're a noncon-formist, and quite simply, you make waves. They'll call you a ground-breaker, a pioneer, front-runner, but be careful not to trust too much. Your peers, especially, will resent you—viciously. They'll find you very threatening. You'll need to watch your back."

Some of this wasn't news—most of it was purely ludicrous—and none of it applied. After all, I was quitting completely in mere months. Press, magazine covers, a script, film, international news stories? No, *all* wrong. She was really losing me now. The room was seeming smaller than when I'd entered and the chair a lot less comfortable.

Suddenly she leaned forward, speaking loudly, almost shocking me with her intensity.

"My God, *this work owns you!* You have a job to do. You don't realize this, but you've been *chosen* to do this." Her eyes opened wide as she sat back and exhaled with certainty. Then she shook her head slowly in advance of her own words. "Jeanne—this work *will never let you go.*"

"That's it. I am so out of here," I mumbled, by then hardly caring if she heard. I grabbed my purse and jacket. I was leaving my job in June and I was leaving her home right this minute. I wrote a check, thanked her, and walked out her front door without looking back.

This work will never let me go? Oh, yes, it would. No job "owned me." I was quitting this stupid job, period. I had my log house, my mountain view, my yellow Lab, my handsome husband . . .

No overseas trips awaited. I'd tear up my passport first. No FBI agents would be calling. I'd change my phone number. No transcript or manuscript existed, nor did any writer named Ron. I didn't even like to watch cop dramas on TV. I sure had no plans to write about them.

I accelerated toward the airport to catch the day's last flight to Bend. I reached over and cranked up the radio dial, then rolled down the car window to let in the ice-cold air. Maybe B.B. King at high volume could help to erase her lingering words from my mind.

I was going home.

3

POLLY KLAAS: EVERYONE'S CHILD

"Welcome home." Robert smiled from the front porch. I looked at him leaning against the doorway. He had the same look he'd used ten years earlier, when he'd pinned me against the hallway wall outside my office in the Detective Division in Portland. I forgave a lot because of that look.

The big travel test was behind us and the results were in. I guess if I couldn't enlarge his universe, I'd just have to shrink to fit his.

I had only one last obligation to fulfill. An unexpected invitation came in to teach seven hundred Russian militia students. It would be my last teaching trip and a grand exit from my career. I returned from Moscow, and when the fiscal year ended on June 30, I clipped the final cord from the Police Bureau. I was done, ready to find a normal job, be a normal wife, maybe even to become an extraordinary mother.

Robert was again content. I'd closed my art case and thrown myself into yard work, promising to start a local job search once the snow fell. The area was loaded with resorts. I could move into public relations, marketing, sales, whatever. It didn't really matter as long as I could stay home.

On October 2, 1993, all the doors and windows were opened wide to take in the aroma of an Indian summer at three thousand feet. The morning news droned on, but my attention was turned to the aspen leaves, fluttering outside my windows like a million yellow canaries against the Cascade Mountains view.

A breaking news story in the background jostled my attention back inside. The reporter was live at the scene: "Last night twelve-year-old Polly Klaas was abducted from her Petaluma, California, home. Police say a stranger entered through a window shortly after ten P.M. and abducted the child from a slumber party she was holding in her bedroom with two school friends. Her mother and sister remained asleep in the next room."

I rushed inside to see the televised face of an agonized mother sitting forward, almost leaning through the screen, pleading for help. Her young daughter had been kidnapped while she slept nearby?

"No arrests have been made," the reporter went on. "However, police have released this composite of the suspect . . ."

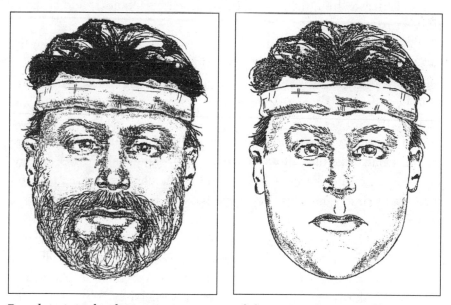

Based on initial police artist interviews of the two twelve-year-old eye-witnesses, the Petaluma Police Department released suspect drawings prepared only hours after the abduction of Polly Klass. The sketches launched the hunt for a bearded six-foot-three-inch-tall kidnapper wearing a bright yellow headband.

Oh, thank God, I thought, at least there were witnesses who'd seen the kidnapper's face. The drawing looked good—very good. I tried to turn away and force myself to begin folding the laundry, but the frightened faces of two little girls suddenly filled the monitor. One said, "He said, he told us, he said if we'd count to a hundred he'd bring Polly back." The strain wavered her young voice.

Our yellow Lab, Dillon, tugged on a sheet in my hand, and I pushed him down into a sitting position. "Hold still, sweetheart."

I shouldn't be watching this, I thought, yet, I still couldn't look away. The camera moved to a close-up on the face of the second girl.

Polly's mother watched as the two frightened twelve-year-olds tried to tell the nation their story. Her sunken eyes drooped into deep creases that ran to her earlobes, as if tear tracks had already marked her permanently. A chill crept past my shoulders. This woman's daughter was taken by a stranger, and for caring, I felt like a cheating wife.

I looked away from the screen, then turned back quickly and snapped the television set off.

"I can't watch this," I said to Dillon. I reached over and turned on the stereo. But the music couldn't erase the image of that mother's face. *Someone* out there has her child, I thought, and began refolding Robert's blue jeans, making sure that every crease was straight, exactly the way he liked them.

The story grew larger with each network's daily update. The frightening national wake-up call carried with it the implication that no one could assume safety, even at home. The whole country wanted to know *who* could have done this. Ten days passed, with no leads. Then the phone rang.

"Miss Boylan, my name is Mark Mershon. I am the ASAC of the Special Task Force on the Polly Klaas kidnapping in Petaluma, California. We understand that you have a special talent. We'd like to ask you to come to Petaluma to reinterview the two eyewitnesses who were with the child when she was abducted, to deduce if there might be additional, undiscovered details in the suspect description."

Dry, to the point, FBI all the way.

In the police lexicon, ASAC stands for assistant special agent in charge. The belated invitation was a surrender to the unrelenting nagging of a producer named Debbie Alpert from ABC television.

Alpert had arrived in Petaluma in response to a "cold fax"—the electronic version of the shot-in-the-dark call—received by the network from the grassroots Polly Klaas Center. Convinced that greater visibility would turn in some kind of lead, volunteers had faxed pleas blindly into newsrooms across the country, starting only hours after Polly's disappearance: "You don't know us, but we have a child missing. Will you please come cover this story?" The bold move was way outside the FBI's preference, which was to run a case tightly, in total control and by the book, but it had worked. Every news organization nationwide responded. ABC was among the first.

Once on-site, Debbie Alpert's maternal instincts bypassed her role as producer. She wanted every expert possible involved in the hunt for the missing child. We'd met briefly after an appearance I'd made a year earlier on ABC's *Home Show.*

"Yes, I know you say you have a drawing already," Alpert told the FBI agent repeatedly, "but have you seen this woman's work?" Agent Mershon finally acquiesced and agreed to look at a long list of my credentials, which Debbie had with her from the network's files.

The drawing the FBI had been using was not working. According to the eyewitnesses, it wasn't right. The Bureau put my résumé through their rigid background check, picked up the phone, and made the call. There was only one answer to their question. Robert's laundry would have to wait.

"Honey?" I said, looking across the kitchen counter to Robert. I watched him brace. Nothing on him moved. He already knew what the sound of the word meant.

I took a big breath. "The FBI called."

No response. No "Uh-oh," no "What's up?" no "Is everything okay?"

"They want me to come as soon as possible."

Robert had left his job as a police officer in Portland years earlier, not of his own choosing and under a great deal of stress. He resented my work, and especially my high-profile role in any case. I understood why. My notoriety seemed to shine light on what he perceived as his own failure. An unspoken rule in the house was that the subject of investigations was off-limits. In deference to his sensitivity I'd grown accustomed to keeping details to myself. But this case was big, an "important case." Those were combustible words. I had to ask.

His brow lowered. The anger-meter vein on his forehead throbbed. But he didn't actually *say* anything.

I walked to the upstairs phone to make the call.

"I need a seat on a flight to San Francisco as soon as possible please. No, I can't hold."

An ABC crew was waiting for me at SFO. Field producer Gordon Recht told me that the network had offered to pay my airfare in return for the first rights to air the drawing. The FBI accepted. On the sixty-minute ride north to Petaluma, Gordon filled me in on details.

We arrived at noon, though the day looked dusky from the weight of the rain clouds. Petaluma was quaint, yet weary, as if the last few weeks had aged it collectively. The houses seemed in want of paint and new porches. Even the trees were underdressed, their dry leaves already littering the small front yards. The town seemed the epitome of the word *safe*.

Downtown, though, was evidence to the contrary. The streets through the commercial area were lined with media trucks, their dish antennas reaching to geosynchronous satellites on the horizon. Reporters mingled with pedestrians, vying for stories, hoping to tape a cousin or a neighbor or anyone with a connection, fishing for another angle in the stalled case.

An unused storefront had hastily been converted into a kind of citizens command post, with search-team grids laid over wall maps, food donated by local restaurants, and work areas partitioned off for mailers, phone banks, media coordination, and family. Banners covered the walls, sent from children all over the country extending sympathy and wishing luck. Calls were pouring in from all points, offering assistance and providing tips on look-alikes to the kidnapper based on the existent sketch.

Then there was that face: "The Suspect." Poster-size blowups surrounded me. Rows of people sat at picnic tables rapidly folding flyers featuring the drawing alongside a photo of Polly, smiling shyly into the camera. Just a corner away, at a cost of thousands of dollars, the PIP printing shop was turning out more of the miniposters at full throttle.

Artistically, the sketch looked excellent. Yet, it also looked like *anyone*. It was without any trait that could single out an individual. A headband tied around the forehead was the only distinctive feature. The face was generic, but still I wasn't sure I could improve on it. All the written features were there: male, white, full beard, six feet three inches tall.

That height bothered me. In fact, it bothered me a lot. In the thousands of cases I'd worked, I'd seldom seen the words "six feet three inches" on a description. How did the investigators arrive at a precise height? What does six feet three inches mean to a twelve-year-old child seated on a bedroom floor looking up at a man with a weapon? To a frightened child, wouldn't he *have* to appear enormous? Did the six feet three inches come from the children's words—or from someone else's? It simply wasn't something a child would say.

I turned to Gordon. "You know what, I'll bet not. I'll bet he's a shorter man. I think we're going to need to open that up."

"How do you know?" he asked. I didn't know how I knew, I just did. Instinct told me that the height was the first mistake in the suspect's description.

I was led across the room to a slight woman sitting slump-shouldered on a folding chair. When her head lifted, I recognized her agonized face from the daily national broadcasts. It was Polly's mother, Eve Nichols.

Her presence at the volunteer center was rare. She was reluctant to leave home, certain that Polly would escape her kidnapper long enough to get to a telephone and call. The lines to her home had been tapped and traps set to trace the call.

She grabbed my arm and pulled me toward her. "Thank you for coming. I've got to know who has her, who took my baby. We have to see his face. The girls say the sketch is wrong. Did they tell you that?"

Her voice was hoarse from crying. Her pain was physically visible. I turned away just once, distracted by a bump from a cameraman. When I turned back, she was gone.

I had instructions from Agent Mershon to wait at the volunteer center for another FBI agent, who would escort me to a two o'clock meeting with the first of the eyewitnesses. Two P.M., three, three-thirty, came and went, and still no agent. Gordon paced and complained loudly over the hourly expense of his camera crew.

Then the room suddenly got quiet, as if the mute button had been punched on a remote control. The volunteers suddenly split into two groups, forming a passageway through which two blue-suited men swept with faces void of all expression.

"We need to have a meeting," Agent Mershon said quietly as he rushed past me, apparently my cue to follow. The second agent, a dark-haired man, came to a halt to prevent Gordon from following.

Nice to meet you, too, I thought as I withdrew my offered hand and followed down a back staircase into an empty basement. Agent Mershon spoke sternly but at a barely perceptible volume and in a single tone. "For reasons we are unable to disclose, you will not be interviewing the girls."

"Excuse me? Please say that again. Do you mean—?"

His volume edged up a notch as he interrupted my question. "For reasons we are *unable* to disclose, you will *not* be interviewing the girls. We apologize for the inconvenience. Thank you for coming."

With that, he turned and marched back up the dilapidated wooden steps.

Dazed and still filled with questions, I climbed the stairs behind him to break the puzzling news to Gordon.

Two local women overheard us talking and instantly insisted on taking matters into their own substantial hands. "You've got to stay! Never mind what the police say. The girls said the sketch is wrong and you've got to fix it."

I looked at Gordon. They were right, but after all, the FBI was the FBI. Before I could delve into an explanation of the intense political powers inside an investigation and how those lines are *never* to be crossed, one of the women linked her arm through mine and pulled me to the door and out to her curbside car, while the other ran interference. Gordon motioned to the cameramen to get this on tape, then followed us as we caravaned the short distance to Eve's home. They felt that if they couldn't convince me to stay, one more look into Eve's eyes ought to do it. I walked inside alone.

News reports called the house a "bungalow." It was old and small, but comfortable. Layers of thick enamel were built up on the woodwork. A three-panel bay window pushed out toward Fourth Street. The home was simple and unpretentious. Ransom wasn't a likely motive.

Eve sat with Polly's seven-year-old stepsister, Annie, cradled in her lap. A candle burned in the bay window, a symbol of faith that Polly would be coming back home again. When I explained the FBI's instructions, Eve fell back hard into the worn sofa and held her head in her hands. Tears pushed over the rims of her heavy brown eyes.

"No, you *have* to stay," she pleaded.

As she spoke, a white car lurched to a stop in front of the house. Four doors flew open. In a series of leaps, four suited men flew up the front steps and inside. One raced to the opened bay windows, three others ran to the various doors. No words, just movement and my apparent "cue" for departure. I looked back at Eve and rushed outside and down the steps. Everything slammed shut simultaneously, including the front door behind me.

Gordon and the two women snapped their heads toward each other, then at me, all of our eyes and mouths hung open to the brisk fall air. None of us knew what just happened. Still not dissuaded, the two women whisked me into their car again and drove me to the police station, then led me by the arm toward the chief's office, with Gordon right behind, barking orders to his crew to get every second on tape.

Police public spokesperson Mike Kerns walked out from behind a closed door as if rehearsed, looked just above my head, and announced coldly, "If you attempt to interview the girls, you will be arrested for obstruction of justice." He said nothing more, nothing less, then disappeared as instantly as he'd appeared.

"Excuse me?" I looked at the crew. Tape was still rolling. *"Excuse me? Was he talking to me?"*

Gordon was speechless—a first in the eight hours I'd known him. The two women frantically pleaded with the police receptionist to call someone else out to help, but there was nothing more we could do. We loaded the crew back into the van and drove back to San Francisco.

Two flights and five and a half hours later, I was home.

4

IF WE SPREAD ENOUGH LIGHT:

THE SEARCH FOR POLLY

Dillon was sleeping on the front porch but Robert was gone when I walked into the house. The light was blinking on the answering machine. I threw my purse on the counter and hit the play button.

"Miss Boylan, this is Agent Mark Mershon of the FBI. We would like you to interview the two eyewitnesses in the Polly Klaas—"

"Sure, right," I said aloud as I hit the stop button, "old message." Dillon's head cocked as it always did when I talked to myself. I pushed play again just to listen to the irony.

"Would you please get on the first available flight and return to Petaluma? Thank you. And, oh, by the way, we apologize for the inconvenience."

Return to Petaluma? It isn't the old message, but is he *kidding*? I asked Dillon as if he might answer. I was just threatened with arrest and now I'm to go back there?

Then I remembered Eve's desperate clutch on my arm at the volunteer center and saw her tears as she looked at me from her sofa.

I called Gordon, by now back in the ABC studios in L.A. "Are you ready to do this again?" I asked. I played him the confusing message, then used the downstairs phone to make a new reservation on the first flight the next morning. Rob never made it home that night. No message left behind.

Must have gone fishing with a friend, I figured.

Gordon met me once again at the SFO baggage claim. Different day, same drill. But not everything was the same. This time the FBI had turned my arrival into a news announcement. Media presence swelled, along with expectations. Cameras circled the ABC van as we pulled into the police parking lot, giving Gordon his first real footage of the chaos.

I wasn't a stranger to West Coast media, and on the heels of the announcement, I was quickly recognized when we pulled up. Our arrival and the second sketch were the day's new development. The camera crews crushed in around us as we stepped out of the van.

Inside the command center, the task force was waiting. I was accustomed to entering a case late, after an initial sketch had proven ineffective and the task force hierarchy was already in place.

The scene is always the same: the chief's office or a conference room—a bureaucratic setting—with doors securely locked, suits all the way around the room, tired faces, set jaws, and the scent of stale coffee in the air. Some investigators are anxious and filled with intelligent questions, while an inevitable few are slouched back with their arms crossed and lips pressed, plainly opposed to any intrusion by an "outsider." But in my case—a female, a civilian, *and,* my God, a blonde?—I had three strikes against me before I even walked in the door.

One thing I knew to prepare for. There was often an in-house wish for me to fail, in the minds of at least part of the team, inclined to feel that success on my part might be an indication of failure on theirs. Not valid, but the resistance was something I'd come to expect.

Mark Mershon made the opening comments. Most FBI agents are transferred often enough that they seldom adapt into looking "local," but Mershon was an exception. His good looks and California tan lent him the look of an L.A. news anchor, though his clothes and manner said "agent" all the way.

"Miss Boylan, we want to thank you for coming," he said, though the words *obstruction of justice* were still ringing in my ears.

"We apologize for your inconvenience in having to make two trips. You see, two nights ago a reporter scaled a wall to get to the home of one of the girls and managed an interview that ran yesterday under the headline 'Girls Think Kidnapping Is Hoax.' That, of course, is in contrast to what we want the kidnapper to think."

Mershon continued, "We've tried to keep reporters from the girls, but as you can see"—he tilted his head toward the windows and the forest of satellite antennas—"that's not been easy. We have concerns. Their stories are beginning to change. So we put a stop to *all* interviews while we regrouped to deal with this."

"And that's why the obstruction-of-justice threat?" I asked. "It wasn't aimed just at me?"

Mershon laughed for the first time. "Oh, no, did Kerns get to you, too?"

Now it all fit. Because of Gordon and the camera crew with me, police spokesperson Mike Kerns assumed I was a reporter, and on instruction he'd issued the blanket warning intended for the press—not for me. The "raid" of Eve's house that same afternoon was unrelated, a required FBI response to a cruel prank ransom call.

"It's a wonder you came back at all," he said, laughing.

Hmm, a crack in the armor? I wondered. Mershon might not be all bad.

"We have strong reason to question the girls' accounts," he continued. "We think that Polly may have an older boyfriend whom she's run off with. She might be pregnant."

Everything and everyone was suspect. The police artist who had interviewed the girls on the night of the kidnapping reported that their descriptions varied and agents said their recollections of the sequence of events differed. Those early reports had set a tone of doubt that had only worsened over the next two weeks. Tempers were by now hot between police and the families.

The public's perception of the kidnapping investigation was only half of the story. "Parallel investigations" were quietly under way behind the scenes, one looking into the possibility of involvement by family members, and the other pursuing the truthfulness of the girls' accounts.

"Do you have ways in your interviews to detect if these girls are lying?" Mershon asked.

"I do."

But to base such suspicions simply on different stories or different suspect descriptions made no sense. What would be *abnormal* would be for any two people to perceive an event identically. The discrepancies in their eyewitness reports should have served more as an indication of *truth* than of fabrication. The differences should actually have served to authenticate each girl's story, which would in turn have validated and more firmly implanted the images and details in their memories for later needs. Instead, they'd been doubted, a good first step toward damaging the memories and . . . destroying the evidence.

Mershon explained that the two girls had been interviewed *together* for the first drawing. Major problem. When multiple witnesses are interviewed together, one will always have the dominant personality, and that person's recollections can influence and even override the memory of the weaker witness. Meanwhile, the discrepancies between the witnesses' memories will cause self-doubt in the mind of the dominant person, therefore eroding the confidence of both witnesses, and leaving them both at an even higher susceptibility to suggestion.

Had the two eyewitnesses been separately interviewed, there would have been two chances to recoup an accurate description, but after the contamination of the tandem interview, I now faced *less* than one.

I scanned the room for someone who would slip me an understanding glance, but found only vacant eyes and tight jaws.

The dark-haired agent who had trailed Agent Mershon on his sweep through the volunteer center a day earlier sat at a corner table and was relentless in his glare. I was sure his thoughts were outside this discussion but had no time to try to read him. Yet his look was like a visual dare. Rick Smith was his name; his continuous stare distracted me.

Mershon continued, "We've not had an easy time with these kids."

"Frankly, we think they are hellions," another agent added.

"We think there may have been dissension in the household and that this disappearance may be part of a plot to somehow exhibit Polly's possible anger toward her mother. Will you watch for the signs in your interview? We'd like you to start right away."

The first witness would be twelve-year-old Kate, who'd arrived at Polly's sleepover after dark on October 1. By that time Polly and the second witness, Gillian, had already been "making statues" on the porch for a full hour, unaware of a man watching from the park across the street.

The three girls went inside to Polly's room to play a board game. Sometime after nine, Eve locked the front door for the night, flicked off the hall light, and took Annie with her to bed, leaving the girls in Polly's room just a few feet away.

Ten minutes later, the stranger was standing at Polly's bedroom door. "Don't scream or I'll cut your throats," he ordered.

The girls had never told the reporter they thought the kidnapping was a hoax, though that's what had been written in the earlier headline. What they said was that, at first, they didn't know to fear him. They were guests in the house and weren't sure he didn't belong until he entered the room and began to tie them up. He had pillowcases, which he placed over their heads, and then used pretorn fabric strips he'd brought with him, plus cords he cut from Polly's Nintendo machine, to bind their hands. He demanded money, but didn't take any. He took Polly instead, promising she'd be back after the girls counted slowly to one hundred.

As he carried Polly out, she selflessly pleaded with him for the safety of her family asking, "Please don't hurt my mom and my little sister."

Gillian was the first to wiggle out of her bindings, then she untied Kate. At ten-forty they woke Eve. She shook off sleep, looked at the girls' terrorized faces, and called 911. When police arrived, they found a dismantled bedroom, severed cords, a house filled with terror, and one child missing. No other room had been touched.

Kate's parents were waiting in a private room at the police station, protectively insisting on meeting me before allowing me to meet their daughter. Mershon stayed only for introductions. I closed the door tightly behind him after he left.

"Our daughter does not lie," the girl's father said, clutching his wife's hand as he spoke. Kate had been through not just one, but two polygraph examinations to test the truthfulness of her "story." She had since written a letter to the polygraph operator outlining her hatred for him, so traumatized was she by the experience.

They were wise to be defensive.

I moved my chair closer and explained that my approach is different from that of the police and from what they'd been through to produce the original sketch. "I'm not here to doubt her or bombard her with confusing photographs, in effect telling her what she saw. I'm not here to grill her or to judge her or compare her words to anyone else's. I just want to hear what she has to say."

"But they are saying Kate's lying," Kate's mother said. "Now she's trying to tell them that the image is wrong and they're casting doubt even on that. We are not going to put her through this again!" Kate's mother was insulted and justifiably angry. Still, she wanted to help.

I heard their concern and understood it. "Let me explain what's happened here. An image that is taken into memory under a traumatic circumstance is fragile. With exposure to as few as a dozen photographs, that image will start to distort and diffuse. Yet since Polly disappeared, your daughter has been exposed to nearly a thousand different suspect photographs just in the process of preparing the first drawing. It's no wonder there's a mix-up here. It's nothing she's done.

"Kate's confusion isn't about what she *saw*. The problems began in the way she was *asked* about it. I want to try to recover the image—the *actual* image she saw—this time by fully listening to her words. I promise you that I won't disregard or dismantle her memory by suggesting to her that I know more than she does."

I didn't go on to explain that after so much visual contamination, the chance of obtaining accurate recall was now slim. It would all depend on Kate's determination to be heard.

Should the case end up hinging on eyewitness memory, we were sunk. Now, without other tangible evidence, any defense attorney with the most basic knowledge on the topic of eyewitness contamination could blast these little girls' testimony right off the witness stand.

The local artist who prepared the first drawing was a kindly man, patient and well-meaning, but through no fault of his own he'd used an outdated system, just as he'd been taught in a five-day class, and one that provided the formula for catastrophe.

It was now time to pray for fingerprints, fibers, some other form of identification on which this case could be made. The damage, although inadvertent, had already been done.

By this time every news organization from NBC's *Dateline* to CBS's *Eye to Eye* to Fox's *America's Most Wanted,* to German and Australian and even Brazilian papers and television, was covering the story. All that valuable time and coverage was being spent circulating an image that the eyewitnesses were saying was "not the man." One and a half million flyers with an inaccurate suspect face were now in circulation. And a twelve-year-old was still missing in the largest child abduction case since the kidnapping of the Lindbergh baby.

The parents consented to the interview. I suggested that we work at their home, a place free of any of the emotion related to the kidnapping or the trauma created by the investigation itself. The police department as a location would never do. And no cops—I needed to be on her turf, in a place where she felt in control and where *I* was her guest.

Gordon drove me to Kate's home and parked the ABC van outside, still holding on to his promise from the FBI to get the first footage.

Kate's mother, Alice, led me to a back hallway in the house. "Look at this," she said, pointing to a wall on which Kate had been given free rein to draw ever since she could pick up a crayon. Symbols, faces, sayings—floor to ceiling—it was a vault of information, and it told me that Kate was highly visually inclined. It was, in fact, the primary way she expressed herself.

Every person perceives through his or her unique frame of reference. We encode things into our recall accordingly. We key in on sounds or symbols or feelings—or in more academic terms, we process information in audio, visual, or kinesthetic frames of reference.

Kate's "drawing wall" was a valuable clue to how she thought. It gave me a translation guide with which to structure my questions so that we'd be speaking in the same language. I'd be better able not just to speak with her but to *hear* her answers if I used the same frames of reference that she used to relate to her own world.

After two weeks of intense frustration, this child was as close to a "hostile" witness as there could be. She needed the freedom to emote, and any relative within earshot would inhibit that ability, no matter how strong their goodwill. I needed to have time with her alone.

Given the massive media coverage dedicated to the production of the new sketch, Kate's parents and grandparents had determined that the two of us together would be prime targets for the killer. To someone in the know, unlikely; to parents who'd almost lost a child, that thought was very real. They were terrified to leave us alone. It took convincing, but at last they complied.

The Donna Karan business suit I'd put on earlier was now in a bag in the ABC van, stripped off in a gas station bathroom while the news crew waited. I'd spent more money on that suit than I had on some cars I'd owned in my lifetime. It was indestructible, beige, double-breasted, and had enough fabric in it to make parasails for all my siblings. In it, I had no form, no breasts, no hips. It essentially turned me into a stunt double for a cardboard box and erased my body, leaving only my eyes to convey a message.

In the male-dominated environment of police work, I faced a choice: be seen—or heard. So, my formless dress-for-success suit was perfect for confronting a room brimming over with skeptical testosterone.

But to meet with a twelve-year-old? Never would I arrive suited in any way that conveyed authority. It was, after all, the "authorities" who had violated this child with their mistrust. I met Kate wearing blue jeans, a sweatshirt, and Nikes.

Kate sat at the dining room table, her huge brown eyes cast downward, her sturdy shoulders squeezed forward, her small hands pinned securely beneath her knees. In front of her was a sign she'd made from two index cards with a Popsicle stick stapled between as a handle. One side read I'M FINE, PLEASE DON'T ASK! Flipped over, it had the single word HUGS in a circle with a slash through it. Her message was clear: Leave me alone.

Luckily, engaging her in conversation was easy. She had a near–genius level IQ and conversing with her was like talking to a contemporary over a second glass of wine. World issues were well within her scope.

What was difficult was diverting her from my intent to get detail. When I'd casually inject a question, she'd revert right back to her early rigid posture. She'd turn sober, answering, "I don't know. I didn't see."

I'd give no sign of concern. I just carried on with the conversation and tried again in fifteen to twenty minutes.

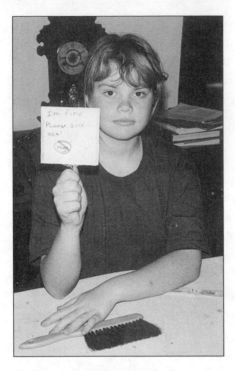

Twelve-year-old Kate McLean displays her frustration on a homemade picket sign reading on one side "I'm fine, Please don't ask" and on the other "No hugs." Her account of the Polly Klaas kidnapping suspect had been discounted by a sketch artist and by investigators because it differed from the description given by the second eyewitness. She subsequently endured two polygraph examinations to determine her truthfulness. (Photo: Collection of the author)

Again, a rigid "I don't know. I didn't see."

But I heard her clearly: She *did* know. She *did* see.

The drawing board normally lies low in my lap, away from the view of the eyewitness. If the witness watches the drawing progress, attention reverts back to the event and the task at hand, and the mind surfaces to the level of conscious recall, where only the contaminated images reside. By keeping the board low and unobtrusive, nearly out of sight, the sketching takes a distant second place to the unrelated conversation taking place. That's all assuming, of course, that things are going well.

With Kate, they weren't.

I understood her frustration—completely. In fact, I agreed with her. I'd heard what had been said about her in the task-force meeting. In her shoes, I knew I'd feel the same way. I felt strong admiration at her ability to protect herself from further injury through her closed-down stance. Kate was twelve—going on a well-developed thirty-five. I pulled the sketch board up from my lap, laid it open on the table, and pushed my chair back as if we were finished. An hour and a half had gone by and we had nothing on paper.

"Kate, you know what?" I hunched forward and looked her in the eye, then whispered, "If I were you, and I'd been through half the shit you've been through . . . ?" I spoke with sincerity. "And if I had that image in my mind . . . ?" She fidgeted with her miniature picket sign, eyes now diverted from me in confusion over what my tone was implying. I went on, "Make no mistake about it"—I leaned closer and lowered my voice even further—"I wouldn't tell *anyone.*"

Her dark eyes widened. She slammed her handmade sign down and yelled, *"Yeah!* Because every time I tell them something, they tell me I'm lying!"

At last, we'd found common ground. Validation was all she'd been seeking. Her experience was real. She'd just needed someone to believe in her, someone to listen to her words. As if we'd released the pressure from a valve about to blow, she began to immediately soften, and the detail emerged, piece by piece, until the face of the man who took Polly, the face inside her memory all along, was finally on paper.

Three hours later, I stepped down the front steps of her home carrying a drawing quite unlike the one already in circulation. Kate walked me to the van and hugged me good-bye.

"Son of a bitch!" Gordon complained loudly as we drove to the Petaluma Police Department that he hadn't gotten the hug from Kate on tape. "Why didn't you come tell me you were done?" he asked. The crew had been dozing and had missed the shot.

"Sorry, Gordon! It was a 'moment,' it wasn't preplanned." I laughed at his expectation. "I couldn't deliver you a script in advance. Give me a break, I mean, I'm not Kathie Lee."

They dropped me off at the PD back door. Inside the task-force command center, there was an odd calm.

Captain Pat Parks spoke first. "Any success?" Parks was a Ron Howard look-alike with freckles, invisible blond eyelashes, and a heart on his sleeve—a kind of antiauthority figure. I liked him immediately.

"I think so," I told him, "but I'm not prepared to show anything until I talk with the second girl and decide which sketch I'll go with."

This was part of the deal: I wouldn't homogenize descriptions, and I alone, based on my feel from the interviews, would decide which memory would most likely be intact—which sketch to bank on. I stipulated that each witness's recall must be regarded as a single entity. My credibility was built on my own set of rules.

"All right," he said. "Next, we need to get you out of here to the second interview somehow. We'll bring an unmarked car around back, slip you on the floorboard to get you through the media."

The interview with Gillian was scheduled to take place at an undisclosed location. With a big brother and an oversized dog named Arthur, the chaos of her home wouldn't provide the calm setting we needed. The media had been hounding the PPD all morning for our whereabouts, and all precautions were being taken to keep us hidden. As I waited in the hallway, a weary-looking female FBI agent came strutting down the corridor and introduced herself as the investigator who'd interviewed Kate and Gillian that first night.

"How'd it go with the kid?" she asked.

"You mean with Kate? Good. I think it was a productive morning."

She threw back her head and laughed, flashing a mouth full of fillings that matched her plain gray skirt.

"Well, good, because I really leaned on her and"—the next few words she said with a sliding jaw, her head bobbing back and forth—"I couldn't get shit. I wasted a whole day with that little bitch."

I felt my cheeks begin to burn. She'd *leaned on her? Little bitch?* A child who was feeling more guilt than a twelve-year-old should have to even fathom, a child who was having nightmares over what she might have been able to do differently, a child whose world had been turned upside down—and *this* was the attitude she'd encountered in her interview with the authorities?

It was no wonder Kate was withholding!

Police are taught to be skeptical, to look for the cracks in the story. That works fine with suspects. With witnesses, though, it's nothing short of disastrous. I was dealing with the aftershocks.

Captain Parks was ready to head out to the next interview. I hunkered down near the floorboard in the unmarked car as we made our way undetected through the police gate, past the cameras and reporters standing prepped for our expected departure through the front entrance.

Parks laughed out loud. "You can get up now," he said as we turned onto Petaluma Boulevard. Then he caught sight in the rearview mirror of a blue media van quickly closing in on us.

"Oh no, ever watch the *Streets of San Francisco?*" he asked. "Well, fasten your seat belt. We're being followed." And with that, he hit the pedal full bore.

We sped through traffic and around corners, circled on two wheels around a pizza joint, and tore off through a residential district. Parks had the home-field advantage, and we managed to lose them, but as we pulled up to a four-way stop, the blue van was now facing us across the intersection. Parks squealed like a kid and we sped off again, this time shaking them off before we reached the community center.

Agents met me at the door. Gillian and her mother, Diane, were already inside waiting.

Not a bad setting, I thought. Long blue table, slat blinds, and pale blue carpet. But Gillian was wound tight. She was goofy and giddy, the opposite in disposition from the introspective Kate.

"Look, Mom, my fish flop!" she'd yell, dropping to the floor and floundering like a fish out of water. Then she asked to be timed by the second hand on the wall clock while she crawled under the conference table from one end to the other.

Anxiety releases itself in all forms. I once worked with a woman who'd just seen her husband's head blown off in a residential robbery and who in our interview could not stop laughing hysterically, *hysterical* being the operative word. The line is thin between laughter and tears. The release of emotion, no matter the form it took, would help us reach the needed image.

A timid knock on the door diverted our attention. It cracked open. There stood Gordon, looking a bit forlorn.

"So why did you run?" he asked.

How was I to know that union rules had dictated a shift change for the camera crew? With the fresh crew came a blue van instead of the white one I'd been used to. Captain Parks and I had been the initiators of a high-speed chase through the back streets of Petaluma in an effort to ditch our own guys.

I turned my attention back to Gillian. The relationship between the young girl and her mother was so extraordinary that I decided it might be beneficial for the mother to stay with us—an unprecedented move on my part. Probing relatives can be disastrous. But nothing was typical about this mother-daughter relationship. They were clearly friends.

Every twenty to thirty minutes, I'd interject a question, making sure it was open-ended. If not, I could lead the witness with verbal suggestions. If I have to offer any descriptor, I have to counterbalance that suggestion with one of equal value from the opposite end of the spectrum.

Even voice inflection matters. If I use a higher tone at one point in the question, the witness might lean toward whatever word I stress, no matter at what point of a question the higher tone might fall. A simple, uplifted tone will be more "attractive" than one uttered in a base tone, and a crime victim, suffering from the depression that results from trauma, subconsciously seeks any form of relief.

But, boy, it was hard with Gillian. She was twelve years old all the way through. After two hours, I was still staring at a relatively blank sheet when her mother asked for a break. There's a momentum and a pace that is crucial in an interview, but in this case, I was the one who needed the reprieve.

This was, in effect, our last chance. Although Gillian's physical vantage point to the suspect had been stronger, I was getting virtually nothing from her.

What we produced would be released on national television in less than fourteen hours. The exhaustion and pressure were taking over. I laid my head down; my shoulders stung from the stress. It was time to call in the "*big* favor," which I don't often do—and never lightly. I could feel the sting of tears beginning to well.

"Dear God, I don't ask for much," I prayed quietly, "but Polly is still out there somewhere, and Gillian is our last hope for finding her alive. The face of that kidnapper went through her eyes, through those pupils. She was there. *Please,* I need you. Help me find the image. Take my arm, take my hand, just *use* me. If this little girl has ever had a serious thought, *please* help her to have one now. Help me reveal that face through the end of this pencil. I am asking you. No, I am begging you." I folded into a heap over the empty sketch board and used my shirtsleeves to blot my cheeks dry.

Thirty minutes went by before they returned. I'd sat back up to try again. This time Gillian sat still, focused clearly, and answered questions with fine detail. My pencil raced across the page as the elements I needed spilled forth:

The extra width in the center bridge of the nose.

Lines underneath the eyes.

Hooded eyelids.

The coarseness and waviness of the hair.

How the brows wrapped around the eye sockets.

Furrows in the forehead and between the eyes.

An indentation on one side of the cheek and not the other.

The lower lip fuller than the upper lip.

All the features that make a *single* face identifiable oozed up through her recall. There was nothing generic in this new face. This was the face of a singular man.

We had him. The image emerged from her recall like black-and-white film gently being rocked in a developing tray.

When it was all in place, it was time for Gillian's critique. The drawing has to be revealed in only one image and in life size, just as it was ingrained into the memory. When the suspect is seen by the witness, the mind accepts that image into recall as a holistic form, as one single entity, not in pieces. It doesn't compartmentalize the vision of a face in components—eyes in the eye bank, lips in the lip bank, nose in the nose bank.

Asking the human mind to recall information in components, as done by police using "facial ID catalogs," is asking it to perform a function that is completely foreign to the way it operates.

To avoid distortion, it's crucial to operate in conjunction with the way the mind actually works. That way we're sliding a *round* peg from a *round* hole, not bending it, not changing it, but retrieving the image *as it was seen,* which was as a whole. That's also how it must then be reviewed for the first time by the witness, so that the image she will see can be compared with the image as it exists in her recall.

By the time I show the sketch, the witness's memory is revived intact, cleanly refreshed, and not overlaid with new information. The "reveal" of the drawing lasts only a moment at a time, so that no matter how close it might be, the risk of the new images overriding the actual image in her mind is minimized. Every precaution *has* to be taken to protect the memory. There are no second chances to re-encode it—the suspect is not likely to come back.

The quick reveal acts to prompt additional fine detail, because it is already in alignment with the image in her mind. Any discrepancies between what she saw and what we've drawn are vividly evident. From her "critique," the final changes are made to fine-tune the sketch to align with her actual recollection.

Gillian quickly drew her conclusion.

"Yep, that's him exactly. Okay, Mom, can we go home?" She was casual and certain. But it felt much too fast. I cringed to hear those words. I didn't want to let her go. I needed every ounce of information she held, and with her departure would go any further chance. But she was pleased. I had to let it go, too. Within minutes, they were gone.

I collapsed into a lifeless form on the conference table and whispered, *"Thank you God."*

Before I could clear the relief from my face, Agent Mershon walked in and pulled up a chair. He shook his head as he stared at the drawing's fine details, so different from the original sketch. *"How*—do you do this?" he asked.

My exhaustion prevented any form of diplomatic answer. I turned my aching body slowly and shook my head back at him.

"Mark, you know, I thought you'd never ask."

The next morning, October 13, the ABC exclusive newsbreak was scheduled for seven A.M., followed by the national release an hour later. I met both Sarah Percell, ABC's "talent" who'd just arrived from Los Angeles, and the producer, Debbie Alpert, in the hotel lobby for a rushed cup of coffee before we shared a cab to the PD.

Barely daylight, reporters waited under the open-air awning, bracing themselves from the rain being blown in by a swift morning breeze. Television cameras ringed the room, news reporters filled the center, and a tabletop threatened collapse from the weight of the radio and network mikes up front.

Please, let this be right, I muffled my words under my breath. I waited just inside the door. At our early-morning briefing, Agent Mershon and the task force took the news of my belief in the girls' level of honesty with great relief. I had no doubts that they were telling the truth and that they had been from the beginning. Nothing in their eyes, their voices, or their descriptions made me believe one word from either child was untrue.

Public spokesperson O.J. Kerns, a nickname I'd given him since his first-day obstruction-of-justice threat, watched with me for the signal, and we stepped forward to join ASAC Mershon and the police chief behind the microphones.

After a few introductory words, Mershon turned the new drawing around. The air filled with the fireworks from photo flashes, mixed with shouts from reporters while the country viewed the enhanced image of Polly's abductor for the first time.

Assistant Special Agent in Charge Mark Mershon, San Francisco FBI, announces the release of a new drawing in the Polly Klaas case based on reinterviews of the eyewitnesses. The description was amended to include a reduced height of as low as five foot ten, the deletion of the headband, and different details of hair and facial characteristics. (Photo: Collection of the author)

Eve Nichols, the mother of Polly Klaas, anxiously gathers more information before the new suspect sketch is released to national media. (Photo: Collection of the author)

"Ms. Boylan, Ms. Boylan," their questions came in unison. "What about the headband?"

My chest constricted. Oh my God, I'd forgotten the headband! I reeled inside. The headband had been considered an extremely significant feature. A person either wears one consistently or not at all. It would be something that could trigger leads from neighbors or employers who would know of a man's habit of wearing one. It wasn't a minor issue and had been accentuated by the press in the early hunt for the kidnapper. A wave of heat screamed up through my body, but then stopped. There *was* no headband. A calm came over me as I realized the simplicity of the right answer.

"There *was* no headband," I answered. "I didn't go into this with the intent of replicating the first drawing. I went in to work off only what the girls actually had in their memories, and I can tell you that in neither description did any mention of a headband ever surface."

There also was no six-foot-three-inch kidnapper, of that I was equally convinced and had changed the description to a range—five feet ten *to* six feet three—to broaden the field of possibilities. Setting the height at six feet three inches was too specific. It didn't begin to take into account the emotion of the moment or the girls' physical vantage point when they looked up at the man who created the terror.

Yet I couldn't eliminate the extreme upper height used in the first composite or I risked adding material that a defense attorney could use to discredit both the case and the eyewitnesses, faulting them for too much conflicting information. It was sometimes a stretch to keep the original information within the new description's boundaries, but it was important to play the defense attorneys' games. Despite the odds, and despite that the height was a part of the description never initiated by the witnesses, the six feet three inches had to stay.

The tone of the investigation seemed to take an immediate turn after the release of the new sketch. The atmosphere became positive and revitalized. Suspicions about the girls' stories were withdrawn, tempers between family and police calmed, and the collective, cooperative effort to find Polly finally began. Eddie Freyer, an FBI agent from Santa Rosa, heard of the "little bitch" comment and, on his own time, drove to the homes of Gillian and Kate with stuffed animals and a dozen roses for each, apologizing to them for their early mistreatment.

The release of the second drawing also refueled the frenzy of media interest.

Because of the work of the volunteers, circulation of the drawing broke all previous records. It appeared in truck stops and on tollbooths and on airport sliding doors from the West to the East Coast and from the Canadian to the Mexican border. Over the Internet alone it was reported that an estimated two billion new images of the kidnapper were transmitted.

Eve summed up everyone's hopes: "If we spread enough light, we'll get her back." But as the days turned, all of us became afraid to add the word *alive* to Eve's statement.

Apologetic phone calls home to Robert became routine while I spent my days in the Polly Klaas Center, chasing leads and, on the FBI's instructions, fulfilling requests for media interviews to keep the drawing alive in the press.

We turned a back room into a heavily scheduled media center. The nation's major news reporters came, and international correspondents showed up. Senator Dianne Feinstein and Barbara Boxer dropped in with camera crews, and *America's Most Wanted* updated Polly's story weekly.

Actress Winona Ryder generously offered to up the ante with a $200,000 reward for Polly's safe return. Polly's hope was to become an actress, and like Winona, she'd practiced for her dream on the stage of the Petaluma Middle School they'd each attended.

A concert by Huey Lewis and the News also raised money for the search. There was little anyone wouldn't do to help bring Polly home.

The St. Louis FBI office called, asking me to leave Petaluma to come produce a suspect composite for use in the search for a serial killer who was suspected of murdering two twelve-year-old girls over the same

Marc Klaas lights candles at the search center in what would become a nightly ritual of prayer with the children of volunteer workers during the search for Polly. (Photo: Collection of the author)

period that Polly had been missing. I told Marc Klaas, Polly's father, that I'd be leaving for another child-abduction case, but this time, the children had been found—murdered.

"Why?" he screamed, slamming both fists into the office wall. "Jesus, Jeanne, why should twelve years old be such a goddamned dangerous age for little girls in this country?"

I couldn't answer him.

In St. Louis, a week prior to the FBI's call, an employee in a fast-food restaurant there delivered a numerically ordered, unusually large-sized sack of food to a customer, who, she noticed, had taken time to study a wanted flyer posted on the drive-through window. The flyer was about two young girls murdered within one month.

Near the crime scene where the first twelve-year-old's body was discovered, a crunched-up numerically traceable sack was found from the same fast-food restaurant. The contents in the victim's stomach proved she'd been held for a while by her killer, and a large volume of food would have been required to keep her alive all those days.

The restaurant employee had a week-old memory, gained only in passing, of a subject only possibly related to the killings.

There had been no trauma in the interaction between the witness and the subject, and trauma or excitement is what encodes the image into memory. The mind would be overwhelmed with data if required to remember every detail picked up in everyday activity. It stores in long-term memory only a percentage of all events witnessed and stores in vivid detail only that which it perceives to have the greatest significance.

Still, Special Agent in Charge James Nelson of the FBI wanted to pursue every possible lead, no matter how small. A freshman agent met me at the arrival gate, briefing me on case details over our long walk through the airport.

I listened, but his voice faded as my attention was pulled toward display after display of magazines in the airport newsstands and bookstores. At every turn, everywhere I looked, I was gazing again into the gentle brown eyes of Polly Hannah Klaas.

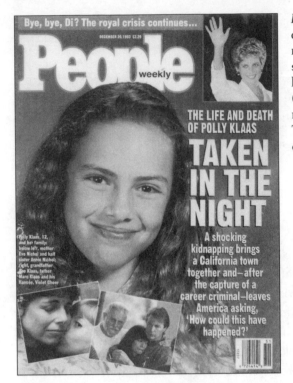

People Weekly, one of dozens of national magazines devoted to the story of the "shocking kidnapping" of Polly Klaas. ("People" Weekly is a registered trademark of Time Inc. Cover courtesy of People magazine)

The next morning, I awoke to the sounds on television of a press conference held to announce the release of the St. Louis case sketch. Still groggy from the all-night interview, I staggered to the hotel-room sink, rubbing my eyes as I took the cap off the crumpled tube of toothpaste.

The voice on the television droned on: "We called you here to announce the release of a drawing in the murders of . . ."

Under an overcast sky, the agent in charge spoke into the sea of media and microphones. I turned to my right to reach for my shampoo. It wasn't there. I reached for the cabinet; it wasn't there either. I rubbed my eyes again and shook myself awake.

I'd forgotten what city I was in, even what agent in charge was speaking. The weather, the voices, the crime, the hotels, the fatigue, the fear—most of all, the fear—were all the same. The name of the city had changed. Only the faces of the children were different.

5

TEARS IN HEAVEN:

GOOD-BYE TO AN ANGEL

"**J**eanne, they got him!" It was ABC's Debbie Alpert.

Almost two months after Polly Klaas was taken from her October sleepover, a parolee named Richard Allen Davis was arrested. The charge was on a drunk-driving parole violation, but his face was a giveaway. The Petaluma police and the FBI were convinced that he was Polly's abductor.

"He's a ringer, Jeanne. You nailed him. The press is all over this. Your drawing is amazing. You've got to see for yourself." She launched into producer mode. "ABC's arranged airfare to get you down here right away. We'll meet you at SFO and drive you to Petaluma. We want to film your reaction at the scene."

But Debbie wasn't able to answer the one thing I wanted to know most. Where was Polly? She wasn't with the disheveled Davis when they picked him up, and there was no sign of her in the FBI's raid of the rattletrap Ukiah home where he was staying for a few days with his sister.

In a void, hope takes over. If they'd found the man who took her and he didn't have Polly, the conclusion followed, then, that she must still be alive.

I stuffed my clothes into a bag and rushed to the Redmond airport.

The long search had been a real test of wills and camaraderie.

Marc Klaas, more than all others, never let up, offsetting bouts of depression with surges of action, his emotions raw, his efforts endless. His intention: to influence changes so that no other parent would have to live through the same ordeal. My friendship with Marc and his fiancée, Violet, deepened. I'd left my job in June to begin a family, but my "family" was taking on a shape I'd never expected.

Eve Nichols relied on her faith and quiet reserve to process the pain of Polly's disappearance. In so doing, she focused a world of believers on what might be, rather than what was most likely. The candle in her Fourth Street bay window burned as it had for fifty-eight days. With each passing hour after Davis's arrest, optimism grew that Polly would be home soon.

The arrest began to unravel the mysteries around what had happened on and since October 1. After Eve called 911, the Petaluma Police Department sent out a kidnapping bulletin to the California Highway Patrol and the Golden Gate Bridge District to avert an escape from Petaluma. Because it was labeled "not for press release," it didn't go to surrounding law enforcement agencies such as the Sonoma and Marin County sheriff's offices. A second alert, sent just after midnight, went out over only a limited number of radio frequencies.

Just over an hour after Polly's disappearance, the Sonoma County Sheriff's Department was called to Pythian Road—twenty-five miles from Petaluma—by Dana Jaffe, owner of a remote spread of land between Santa Rosa and Napa Valley. She wanted them to investigate why a beat-up Pinto was stuck in a trench on her private property.

The kidnapping bulletin hadn't reached the two deputies who responded to Jaffe's call, but despite that, when they encountered Richard Allen Davis, they didn't like what they saw. For over thirty minutes they held him in bright headlights while they ran "wants and warrants" on him, peered into his car, and ran his license plates to check if the car was stolen. Everything came back "clean."

As they stood on the remote private land—with Polly presumably alive, tied and gagged, and hidden in a heavily wooded area only forty feet away—they had no way of knowing that Davis was on parole from an eight-year state prison term for kidnapping and robbery. Their car radios lacked the technology that would have allowed them to run a detailed check on his mile-long criminal record. With no further excuse to detain him, the police hooked their car to his and pulled him free, escorted him to the property line, and let him go.

Upon return to their station later that night, they were advised of the kidnapping and shown the first composite drawing of the suspect. They'd just left Richard Allen Davis, but reasoned that the man they had stopped and looked at for over a half hour in good light was not relevant to the search for the kidnapper because of his height, the lack of the described headband, and his lack of resemblance to the newly released sketch. Dismissing any potential link between Richard Allen Davis and the kidnapping, they moved forward with the investigation.

By the morning of October 2, a full-scale search was under way, and the nation was fixated on one goal: find Polly's kidnapper.

It was a full two weeks before the new sketch I produced was released. By then the encounter with the man stuck in the ditch was long since gone from the deputies' thoughts.

"Look into his eyes," Marc Klaas said at the press conference. "That's what the girls did. You've got to look into his eyes." But the deputies' memories of the man they'd encountered weeks earlier had, by then, inevitably faded.

The national release of the new drawing in mid-October triggered a landslide of fresh leads. After a Portland police detective was quoted giving a complimentary review of my work to the *Los Angeles Times*, I called him to say thanks.

"You know, we're not seeing much on that case up here," he said.

"You're serious?" I asked. "It's getting coverage from South America to Europe, but it isn't making news in the bordering state? If the kidnapper were to flee northern California, where might he go? Back through a metropolitan area or north toward the remoteness of the Oregon and Washington woods? We've got to get Polly's face in the *Oregonian* and on the regional news. *Now.*" I packed photos of Polly that Eve supplied and drove to Portland to try to generate news coverage.

"Sorry, it's just not a local story," one editor said. Then he reconsidered and agreed to run it *if* they could key on my participation in the case to give it a local "hook."

I left behind the manila envelope filled with all of Polly's pictures and a page-sized, media-ready copy of the suspect sketch.

Two days later, the story ran statewide. The profile gathered from past news articles was four inches deep and two full pages wide, but with a minuscule one-by-one-inch blurred copy of the suspect drawing, not a single picture of Polly, and a four-by-five-inch, year-old file photo of me. I buried my head in my hands in frustration. The article had missed the point. The real story was about a missing twelve-year-old whose face we needed to get in front of every reader in the Northwest.

If the print media wouldn't help us, maybe the talk shows would. I called my television contacts in Portland and Seattle. Eve agreed to leave her telephone for the first time in three weeks, to fly up and join me on ABC sister-station talk shows in both cities. Each producer consented to our request that they air Polly's pictures continuously throughout the broadcasts, and that the shows would close out with a tape featuring video clips and slow dissolves of photos taken throughout Polly's life. The tape showed her in her parents' arms, clowning with her baby sister, performing on the Petaluma Middle School stage. Both airings lit up the station switchboards with people calling in to help.

In Portland, Eve and I sat on opposite ends of the studio lunch table in the darkened KATU newsroom-turned-greenroom waiting for the video to conclude and the show's closing credits to run.

A man was talking with Eve, but her gaze was beyond his shoulder, fixed on her daughter's face—smiling, laughing, playing—on the screen of the thirty-inch monitor. Oblivious to his presence, she folded her thin arms in a cross over her chest, and slowly rocked from front to back as if cradling an infant—her infant—in her empty arms. With her dark eyes filled with tears, she stared at the screen into Polly's face and slowly, silently mouthed the words, "There's my baby. There's my baby."

I'd heard of the powerful videotape, created by a volunteer to play during the Huey Lewis and the News benefit concert, but I hadn't seen it until that moment. The Linda Ronstadt song "Somewhere out There" lofted through the studio while I watched the images of Polly's young face.

Watching Eve sent a bolt of pain searing through my heart. The *only* thing that I could possibly do to help her was to show the authorities the face of the man who'd taken her little girl. And yet, when I entered the case, the odds were overwhelmingly stacked against any chance of doing that because of the simple blunders already and unknowingly made *within* the investigation. It was something like walking through a mud bog and being expected to emerge holding a bottle of Perrier.

I walked into the hallway out of Eve's sight and felt my suit catch on the texture of the brick wall as I leaned back, then slid slowly toward the floor in exasperation. Tears washed away the studio makeup. There *had* to be something more I could do.

I thought of Robert and his opposition to my work. I thought of my "peers" and how vehemently police artists shun the idea of delving into the discipline of psychology, out of an unwarranted fear that it might be something they wouldn't understand. I thought of the intense resistance of law enforcement to doing anything beyond the way things had always been done.

Then I thought of Marc and Violet, and of Eve's face. I thought of Kate and Gillian and of their pain, the frustration of the police, the determination of the FBI, the efforts of the volunteers, and all of their dependence on an image that I'd been forced to create out of the now sheer remnants of a once-intact memory.

How many times would this scenario be repeated? There had to be change, and this time, it *was* my problem. I couldn't just walk away. It was *everyone's* problem: every police agency, every parent, and every victim of a crime yet to happen. I knew something had to change, and I felt a power inside of me shift.

The two-month wait had finally produced a result: a man was in custody. I flew to San Francisco high with hope. Bringing Polly home was now just a matter of time.

Debbie Alpert and her crew met me at SFO. The route to Petaluma was by now a well-worn path. ABC perceived "ownership" over me as the result of their contributions, and while we maneuvered through the streets, they protectively hid me from any other news organization descending on the scene.

"Get down!" Debbie ordered as she surveyed her competition doing their side-by-side live remote broadcasts on the police station front lawn.

I peeked up over the back window just enough to see the commotion. Lighting from the media trucks cast a halo up into the low clouds, and generators hummed from every corner of the parking lot. The crews had all spent months covering this story, and in spite of the callousness acquired over years of hit-and-run accidents and political conventions, they'd fallen in love with Polly, too.

We slid into a tight parking space in front of the volunteer center.

"Stay in the car. We'll be back," Debbie ordered as she locked the door and disappeared with her crew through the front entrance.

"Locked doors and orders from a field producer to stay put? I don't think so," I uttered as I unlocked my door and walked into the neighboring tavern to use a pay phone. In my rush to get to the airport, I hadn't crossed paths with my husband. I wanted to reach him on his cell phone to share the news.

"Hey, honey! It's me. How are you? I'm down in—" Before I could explain where I was, the tavern door burst open. A breathless Debbie Alpert ran over and grabbed me by the back of the jacket.

"Jeanne, don't ever do that to me again!" She waved her arms in the air, frantic that she'd lost me to another news crew. In her hand, she held a color photocopy of Davis's mug shot she'd picked up next door at the center. It had been taken for an arrest made more than a decade earlier.

The cameraman reminded her that I hadn't seen it yet, but he was too late. My eyes were fixed on the image flailing in the air in front of me. I couldn't believe what I was seeing. The face I saw in the photograph looked *nothing* like the man I'd drawn. The press may have been raving about it, but why? I didn't understand it. I felt my heart sink to the floor.

"Sweetheart, can I call you back?" My words slowed. In three tries, I missed the telephone cradle. I pulled the photo out of Debbie's hands and stared. I'd never seen that face before. The soundman took the receiver from my hand and hung it up.

My God, what had I done? My spine weakened and I felt as if I'd be sick. I was looking at a flash of dark hair, thick and unkempt, a heavily bearded man much younger than what I'd portrayed. My drawing was way off.

Six weeks of a national manhunt based on a drawing that I'd done, and it had been all wrong? Horror racked my chest and body as I thought of the implications. We walked next door to hugs and praise and congratulations, none of which made sense to me. Thrilled that a suspect had been found, I still couldn't shake the sense of guilt and responsibility for such inaccurate work.

What if I had actually misled the investigation? Where was Polly while this wrong information was out?

What if the misdirection had cost her her life or she'd been alive and the leads had passed by her because my drawing was of the wrong face?

No matter the odds, that face and the decision to release it were still my responsibility. I went to the hotel and remained wide-eyed through the night, unable to sleep at the thought of having hampered the investigation or, worse, of having further endangered Polly's life.

By the next morning Davis had been processed at the Sonoma County jail, and his new mug shot, taken just twenty-four hours earlier, was released to the press. Copies fired through the volunteer center, but I couldn't bear to look again. An enlargement of the new photo made its way to the wall in front of me and was taped next to a blowup of my drawing.

Reluctantly I looked up, but shock began to replace the tension that had gripped me all night. I had to squint to believe my eyes. I stood slowly and braced myself along the tables, then walked over for a closer look. "Oh my God—that's him! *This* is the right face!"

The current mug photo contained the furrow to the forehead, the fuller eyebrows, the wave and coarseness of the salt-and-pepper hair, the fuller lower lip, the fullness of the cheeks, the nostrils, that glare, the lines around the eyes. Every feature on the face we'd drawn was there. He looked entirely different from the mug shot released the night before. Gillian and Kate had told the truth all along, and at last they had the proof.

My heart began to pound with fresh hope. The drawing could even be used to pressure the suspect to confess. Davis wouldn't be unable to argue when he looked into his own eyes on the wanted poster.

The new mug shot was Davis at his present age, with his hair cut drastically shorter than in the previous, decade-old mug shot. His beard

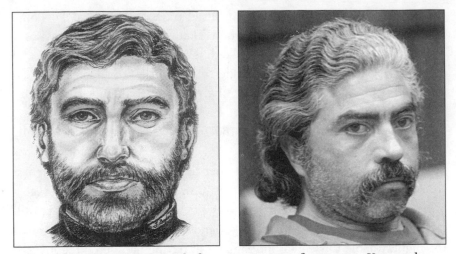

Left: Suspect drawing created after reinterviews of witnesses Kate and Gillian. Right: A photo of Richard Allen Davis awaiting arraignment in a Sonoma County courtroom, December 1993. (Drawing by Jeanne Boylan; photo © Associated Press/Ben Margot)

was now trimmed. He'd aged poorly and his prison years revealed themselves through the lines around his eyes and on his forehead. Every nuance, every crease, all there in the minds of the twelve-year-olds *all along,* but missed on the night of Polly's abduction.

The headband had, in fact, never been a headband. It had actually been the deep creases in Davis's forehead. The infamous headband had been produced on the first night when the two girls were shown a selection of headgear from a box of photos brought by the original artist. Showing any kind of visual aid strongly implies that the item exists.

Once the girls were shown a headband, it then existed in their eyes, overriding any chance of the actual detail being allowed to surface—a definitive example of the strength of the power of suggestion. Once the description had entered the early case reports, it had become part of the story.

The man the deputies encountered on October 1 was reasoned not to be the kidnapper because, "first of all," the sheriff defensively explained at a press conference, "he wore no headband. Secondly, he did not look like the first composite drawing available to them that following morning, and the third reason [was that] the description of the suspect was of

More than 1.5 million wanted posters portraying the incorrect suspect drawing were printed, bundled, and distributed in the crucial early weeks of the Klaas kidnapping investigation. The costs? Valuable time, man-hours, and $65,000 in material and mailing costs while the suspect remained unabated and leads grew cold. (Photo © Julie Colt/Polly 1993)

a man six feet three inches tall, and Richard Allen Davis stands precisely five feet ten inches tall."

The media immediately tracked down the one person who they felt should have most been able to link Richard Allen Davis to the crime—his parole officer. He knew Davis was out on probation, he knew he had a history of kidnapping, and he knew he had been given permission to commute between his residence and Ukiah, a route that goes right through Petaluma and only four blocks from Polly's house. Yet the parole officer never put it together, even though copies of the old and the new sketches hung on his office wall.

His response was telling: "Hell, we never pay attention to those composite drawings—they're never any good."

He was correct—far too often they're not. Typically, only 10 to 20 percent of traditional police drawings released are ultimately accurate, which leaves a best-case scenario of 80 percent inaccuracy. His words were, unfortunately, an accurate defense.

More details surrounding Davis's arrest poured in. Dana Jaffe, owner of the Pythian Road property where Davis was questioned on October 1, was walking her dog on November 27 when she noticed a piece of red fabric. She walked closer and saw that it was a pair of red tights, next to a big black sweatshirt with a piece of duct tape on it. Nearby she found strips of fabric. A condom heightened suspicions. But it was the Saturday following Thanksgiving, and when she called the Sonoma County sheriff, she didn't get through. The next day she tried again.

Jaffe reminded them of her October 1 trespassing report involving the same location. That linked the authorities to Davis's name. At headquarters, the task force ran Davis's staggering record and pulled up his probation photo. They laid it on the table next to the composite. As Santa Rosa's FBI agent Eddie Freyer explained, *"That* was when we knew we had our man."

They flew the evidence from Jaffe's property to the FBI lab in Washington, D.C. When the conclusive reports shot back, they made their late-November arrest.

By December 4, there was still no sign of Polly. It was time to get back to my husband. At the Polly Klaas Center, I tried to peck out a thank-you note to the FBI. It had been so long since I'd used a manual typewriter, I was wasting more paper than I was making progress. Instead, I decided to walk over and say my good-byes in person.

The police department lobby was oddly quiet. Investigators' cars were gone, no media were in sight, the lack of motion was ominous. Odd, I thought, while handwriting my note at the front counter. Just then Eddie Freyer walked out of the command center's side door.

"You leavin'?" he asked me quietly.

"Yeah, I think it's time. There's nothing I can do but hope, and I guess I can do that from home."

He looked up. "Jeanne, would you mind staying?" He bit his lip and put a fist up to his mouth.

"Oh my God, Eddie, no." He didn't need any words. I could see it in his eyes. They'd found her. Against every trained instinct, we'd all allowed ourselves to believe Polly would be coming home. But earlier on December 4, Richard Allen Davis had decided to put an end to all our hopes. He'd learned that his palm print unmistakably matched one found in Polly's bedroom and asked to make a phone call. He called Petaluma police sergeant and lead investigator Michael Meese.

Meese is a father, and like many of us—investigators, volunteers, news crews—he'd made Polly one of his own. A soft man in a hard field, his face is round, his shoulders are round, even his hands are round. Everything about him is gentle and good. And for his kindness, Davis chose him to confide in. When Davis called him to confess that he'd kidnapped Polly, Meese asked softly, "Can we go get her?" Davis gave him the answer he both expected and most dreaded: "No."

Polly Hannah Klaas, age twelve, was dead.

At the same moment that I was talking with Eddie, Davis was leading Meese and FBI agent Larry Taylor to Polly's body.

Davis said that on October 1, he'd come to Petaluma looking for his mother. He was on parole and in need of money, which he thought his mother might loan him. She'd long since moved on, but he hung around thinking he could learn her whereabouts. As the day wore on, he bought some beer and marijuana, which he claimed was laced with PCP.

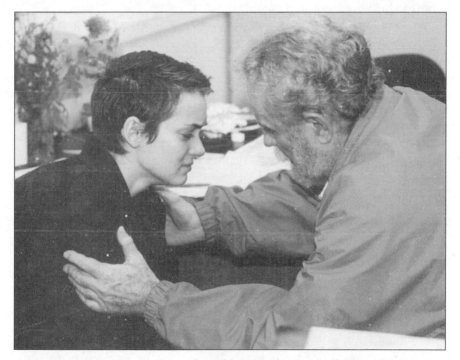

A grieving Winona Ryder is comforted by Joe Klaas, grandfather of Polly Klaas, after hearing the news of Polly's death. (Photo © *Petaluma Argus Courier*/Scott Manchester)

He blamed the PCP for a mental lapse, saying he had no idea how Polly got into his car. Facts differ: he had bindings and tape with him, indicating clear premeditation. His story was full of contradictions. Meese videotaped the interview.

Davis went from curt to coy, from coarse to remorseful. Finally, he said he killed Polly on the night of October 1, as the morning sun came up, only five hours after he'd been stopped by the two sheriff's deputies. Polly died by a quick snap of her neck.

The remains of her body told an even sadder story.

They found her on an abandoned mill site outside Cloverdale, north of Santa Rosa and forty feet off a major freeway, next to one of the rust-colored, cone-shaped, screen-topped sawdust burners that used to dot the logging country of the West.

It was dreary and dank when the first investigators reached her body. Yards away they found her dark, wavy hair, the work of animals over the months she'd been out in the cold, alone.

At the sight, they said Davis didn't say a word. Meese and Taylor couldn't.

Captain Pat Parks and FBI ASAC Mark Mershon asked Eve Nichols and Marc Klaas to come to the command center, to tell them first and together that Polly had been found.

"This has to be handled carefully," Eddie Freyer explained. Family at five, the girls at six, and then the volunteers; after that, the media and the rest of the world in a press conference at seven.

"Would you stay?" Eddie's voice broke. "Would you please be the one to tell the children? I think they should hear it from you."

I called the girls' counselor, Betty Resnick, and asked that she come with me. Gillian and Kate were at a friend's birthday party at a pizza parlor. They were asked to transfer the party to Gillian's, but not told why.

I thought I'd be all right as I started to drive away, but at each stoplight I felt more overwhelmed. My hands felt numb, my motions were automated, I couldn't remember starting the car though I was already blocks from the station. Polly's face was everywhere I looked, on streetlamps

and telephone poles, pasted to windows in cars next to me at intersec-
tions. I careened into the gas station where I'd changed clothes before
my interview with Kate, locked the bathroom door, leaned over the sink,
and wept uncontrollably.

An hour had passed and I had to pull myself together. It was near
dark and I'd need to be composed to go see the girls. Thinking that a
walk might help, I wandered around downtown Petaluma and found
myself looking through the plate-glass windows at the first volunteer
center, the old building where I'd first met Agent Mark Mershon and
which had been used during the early weeks of the search before the
space was outgrown and the center was moved to its new location.

Inside, the long room was empty but for a vacuum cleaner standing
near the back wall. One banner remained, partially coiled on the floor.
Only the words POLLY PLEASE COME H were visible, each end curled
from age.

Through the glass and into the empty, quiet room, I felt I was seeing
into the future. All the movement and all the energy that had filled that
room, day after day, were gone.

In the reflection, I could see people behind me, still walking briskly
past pictures of her face on posters, not yet knowing the outcome,
everyone filled with optimism, their hearts not yet broken, as mine had
just been.

I drove slowly to Gillian's house, the numbness having reclaimed me
just in time for the task ahead.

The lights of the Christmas tree were all that illuminated the front
room. On a couch antsy twelve-year-olds waited, unknowingly, for the
words.

"Polly won't be coming home—ever."

Their adolescent bodies filled the laps of their parents, who joined us,
and we rocked the children like infants while they cried. Later, I stepped
outside and watched through the living room window, the warmth of the
Christmas lights conflicting with the horror and sadness that filled the
house. The sobs carried hundreds of yards through the thick evening fog. I
tried with everything inside me to fathom the magnitude of the evil a single
selfish man could wreak onto these babies, so innocent and so sweet—and
the heartbreak he was callously about to inflict upon a nation.

Eve and her husband, Allan Nichols, went into seclusion at a donated beach house in Sea Ranch to escape the press and plan the funeral. Eve asked Winona Ryder and me to join them there.

I spent part of my time helping to distract Polly's stepsister, Annie, so Eve could attend to the details. We drew cartoons and played games. The few momentary respites of levity were courtesy of Annie her innocence. She'd dash through the house with pot holders, pretending to put out a fire on her chest, reenacting her favorite scene from the Robin Williams movie *Mrs. Doubtfire.* The laughs were our only relief from the tension and weight of planning her big sister's funeral.

The day before the service was dark and thick with fog. Winona and I left to give Eve the last day before the service alone with her immediate family. On my way into town, an idea occurred to me.

I stopped at a phone booth in the rain and called Susan Friedman, at that time the West Coast executive producer of the NBC *Today* show and a good friend ever since she'd produced a piece on my work for the show in 1987.

Candles flicker on a drizzly Petaluma night outside the Polly Klaas volunteer search center as the nation mourns the discovery of Polly's body. (Photo: Collection of the author)

"Susan, it's Jeanne. I have a favor to ask. Do you have any way to get in touch with Robin Williams?"

The plan was to ask Robin if he could meet with the girls, Annie, Kate, and Gillian, and maybe help lift their spirits, as he had already lifted Annie's and ours over the days of preparations.

Susan said she'd do what she could. Since she was a New Yorker all the way, "what she could" would likely be more than enough.

Petaluma's St. Vincent de Paul Church holds fifteen hundred people. Hundreds more stood outside for the December 9 service. Robert surprised me and drove through the snow from Oregon to attend the memorial.

Inside the church, the rich, soft light that filtered through the stained glass seemed to emanate from centuries ago, helping to soothe the pain of the moment with the hope of eternity.

Film producer George Lucas, who lives in nearby Marin County, wanted to help and sent his best lighting specialists to flood light through the rosette windows. The cathedral could be seen for miles. A single lamp shone on one unfilled chair in the children's choir loft—only Polly's seat was empty. Her friends sang her favorite song, Eric Clapton's "Tears in Heaven," which Polly had just learned to play on the piano.

Linda Ronstadt flew in to sing, as did Joan Baez. The California governor and Senator Feinstein both spoke, FBI agents wiped tears from their cheeks, crowds wept openly outside the church, and the Bay Area came to a standstill while all networks, in an unprecedented move, preempted their programming to cover the service simultaneously.

Polly Klaas had become everyone's child, and an emblem for missing children across the country. As a nation, we grieved for them all, perhaps acknowledging for the first time collectively the seriousness of their plight. Polly left a legacy that her father would carry on; Marc Klaas would make sure that no one would forget.

I felt the hand of Mark Mershon on my shoulder. He spoke my name as I turned, his eyes downturned in sorrow. I reached my hand out to shake his. Instead, he moved forward and gently wrapped his arms around me.

Robert bundled my coat around me tightly, then took my hand and squeezed it inside his. We said good-bye to Kate and Gillian and stepped through the cathedral doors, away from the lights and the press and the people and into the cold Petaluma night. I felt Robert by my side not just physically, but completely.

For the first time, I didn't have to explain to him the agony of watching a parent grieve, or the unfathomable frustration of having all you could do be just not quite enough. And I didn't have to worry about his being angry at me when I stepped off an airplane. This time, he'd been there with me. He'd seen it. He'd felt it. Not through his frustration over a missed dinner or a through a long-distance phone call, but in real life, and in real time. Robert had met this family up close, and for the first time, he had looked into their eyes.

Now he looked at me differently, too, and he clung to me tightly as if he finally understood what made it so hard to say no.

6

DRAWN FROM THE HEART

Robert and I strung red chili-pepper lights all through the house and draped swags of evergreen from the heavy, hand-hewn banisters that led upstairs, steeping our idyllic, protected world with the beauty of Christmas.

We were at last in emotional sync. In Petaluma, for the first time ever, we'd grieved together. Only a few winters earlier, I had mourned alone for the miscarriage of our only son. At the time, Robert had turned his back on me and the pain, later vowing to make up for his abandonment, yet never speaking of it again. Saying good-bye to Polly had finally caused him to face the reality of his not ever having been present for his own child.

His ice had melted. Usually I'd return from a case ready to pay a price for the first few days, working to "make up" for all the nights I hadn't cooked dinner, for the clients he'd had to entertain on his own. By necessity, I'd stuff all emotional needs from my most recent case out of his sight, so as not to violate the unspoken don't-bring-it-up rule.

But this time *I* wasn't the one reaching out—Robert was. He removed one kind of heat and replaced it with another. He was open and fully present for me, maybe for the first time, and we fell in love all over again. He'd rub my feet in front of the fireplace, or wrap me into his big arms for no reason.

This Christmas would be like a starting over, free from the burdens of my work and the intense emotional guilt he'd been bound by for so long. I'd forgiven him, and maybe, maybe, he'd finally forgiven himself.

"Jeanne, where are your ski poles?" His voice carried from the garage to the upstairs bedroom. The truck was almost packed for our Christmas ski vacation to Sun Valley, Idaho.

Okay, it was a working trip, too. But this time it was for *his* work, not mine. Robert's clients had invited us to their spectacular Sun Valley home. With clients, he was always "on," forever positioning himself for his next sale, but right now I was willing to overlook just about anything. It was the first time since Cabo San Lucas that we'd been on a "vacation" over twenty miles from home.

We'd had our tickets for two months to the renowned Sun Valley Lodge Christmas Eve event. I'd only heard stories of the 250 torchlight-carrying skiers who descend the mountain in formation, but couldn't imagine a more romantic setting.

"They're in the attic, Rob, I'll be right down." I had only to lock the balcony doors and we'd be on the road.

Robert was clamping down the skis in the back of the truck. I walked downstairs, double-checked the back-door locks, and turned down the heater just as the phone began to ring.

"Damn. Maybe I should just let the machine get it." I walked toward the front door ignoring the call, hoping he hadn't heard it.

"You getting that?" he yelled.

"Oh, I guess so," I relented. The roads were icing back up and we were already running behind.

"Jeanne, what are you doin'?" It was Agent Mark Mershon again. "We've got a situation here—a kidnapping—there's a hostage. We need you on a plane right away."

I felt the air rush from my lungs and looked out the open door. Robert was securing the bags behind the seat. My newly passionate husband was in the garage packing for our holiday, and I'd just endured the loss of a twelve-year-old with the man on the telephone asking for help. The energy drained from my body as I fell onto the deep cushions of the leather couch.

"Yeah, all right, Mark. Tell me what's up."

Less than forty-eight hours earlier, Ruth and Gene Mayer, a prominent Antioch, California, couple, had returned to their home from an evening out. After parking his car in the garage, Gene Mayer, a well-known jeweler in the San Francisco Bay area, heard the doorbell ring and walked around the house toward the front entrance.

When he asked, "May I help you?" one of two men spun around. Mayer looked at him for an instant, then looked down to the red point of light skittering over his chest. Prodded by the laser-sighted handgun, Mayer was pushed into his own home, then blindfolded, bound, gagged, and put facedown on his living room floor. His stately, dark-haired wife, Ruth, walked in from the kitchen.

"Honey, who was it?" she asked as she came down the hallway. When she rounded the corner, the invaders grabbed her, twirling and binding her before she could see a face.

They ripped through the house in search of valuables, rolled the safe out with them, then took Ruth Mayer as a hostage. One kidnapper drove away in the Mayers' Mercedes and the other in their Suburban.

Logic had it that at least one other person was involved since they likely arrived in their own vehicle, bringing the suspect total to at least three. Although the beam of the laser gun had distracted him, Gene Mayer had gotten a momentary glance at one of the men who'd kidnapped his wife.

After they left, he managed to free himself and immediately called the police. When the report hit the scanners, the news media heard it and—due largely to the prominence of the Mayer name—responded en masse, arriving at the family home at the same time the police did.

As the investigators entered and began to secure the crime scene, they found an open-faced note on top of the coffee table, unnoticed by Gene Mayer in his struggle to free himself and call for help. The note read, "If you call the police or FBI, we will kill your spouse."

Mayer panicked. The written message left him feeling that his call to the police was akin to pulling the trigger on his own wife. He wanted to take over, to fund the search, to do more than he felt the agencies could or would do on their own. He went on the airways frantically pleading for the kidnappers not to kill Ruth.

The Polly Klaas case, which involved many of the same agents—including Mark Mershon—had been a hard primer on what to and what not to do in an investigation. Mostly, they knew they had to move fast and without missteps.

The first thing Mershon did was to make sure that the image of that face, which only Mr. Mayer held in his recall, was guarded as fiercely as a fingerprint on a weapon.

My mind reeled.

I looked outside. Robert had already backed the truck out and was carefully placing our coffee cups in the holders on the dashboard. The snow was falling slowly, gently.

Ruth Mayer might still be alive. Every second mattered. What would I say? How would I explain this time?

"Who was on the phone?" Robert asked, his cheeks tinted red from the cold.

I swallowed hard. "It was Mark Mershon, sweetheart." I walked slowly down the front steps.

He stopped cold, knowing well from my tone just what would follow. His shoulders dropped.

"It's a kidnapping. There's a hostage—I've got to go."

He stood for a moment, then reached over and slammed the door of the truck hard, turning his face away. His body sank as he exhaled in resignation.

Ruth Mayer was in the hands of kidnappers, possibly in the hands of her own killers. A multimillion-dollar ransom request had been issued by her abductors, and her life was hanging in the balance. The publicity triggered by the police report heightened the danger. Gene Mayer was in a living hell, and his wife, if she was still alive . . .

No, I couldn't even let my mind go there. The pain from losing Polly was still too fresh. I couldn't think about whether this woman might be dead or alive. The chances that she had already been killed were staggeringly high.

The FBI had brilliantly guarded the image. There was reason to hope, but no time to waste.

Every step felt heavy and painful as I turned from the truck and walked back up the snow-covered walkway. I needed to make the flight arrangements as soon as possible.

"Wait," Robert yelled out to me. "Come 'ere." He came toward me, then reached out his arms, his eyes focused on the horizon. He held me tightly. "Can you meet me in Sun Valley? You know, when you get done?"

"Yeah, I'll be there," I whispered, though I wanted to say, "Wait, don't go. Never mind the case. I'm coming with you." He kissed my forehead and let go.

I walked inside and brushed the snowflakes from my hair, picked up the phone, and dialed the airline's number by rote. Through the frosted front windows of our log home, I watched the exhaust from Robert's tailpipe evaporate into the frigid mountain air like fine-spun cotton candy, while the on-hold music for Alaska Airlines droned on.

I had less than an hour to catch the first flight to SFO. I threw on my indestructible, wrinkle-free "uniform" and vowed to genuflect at the feet of Donna Karan if I ever saw her in person. Robert had taken my already packed suitcase with him, so I grabbed just a toothbrush, a purse, and art bag, locked the front door, and ran for my car.

Mark Mershon stood in the front entrance at the Antioch, California PD when I climbed out of my rental car. It had been only two weeks since I'd left him at Polly's funeral. He was back to all-business, though unlike our first meeting, this time he stepped forward and reached for my hand.

I entered the police briefing room in front of him. Coffee cups were strewn on long tables. Crammed along the walls were a few familiar faces among the new ones. No one took time for introductions.

Gene Mayer, the agents informed me, had deep financial pockets and was intent on hiring dogs, private investigators, helicopters, whatever it would take to find his wife. Privately, those in the task force inferred he was a "pain in the ass," no matter how noble, understandable, or justifiable his efforts. That every man in the room—given the same circumstances and the same resources—would act just the same if in Mayer's shoes was, at that moment, beside the point.

An agent's most dreaded words are *out of control.* Gene Mayer wanted to take control from the FBI and the police. The input of outsiders could complicate the lives of detectives, but even more important, it could introduce factors and issues that could muddy the chances for later prosecution. No matter his admirable intent, Mayer would have to defer to the experts.

"You'll be lucky to get him to sit still for ten minutes," Mark told me. The agents had even discussed seeking some form of sedation from his physician to help calm him down.

"**H**ello, Gene, I'm Jeanne," I introduced myself. The shaken man stood up in the sterile, empty meeting room. The setting wasn't ideal, but we'd make it work. As Agent Mershon left the room, he wished us luck, but the relief of having this man finally contained registered much more strongly in his voice.

Preconceptions rarely prove true. Gene Mayer sat calmly for hours. The key was to find a topic that not only soothed him, but that gave him a proactive role. He was a man deeply in love with his wife. "Tell me about her" was nearly all the prompting it had taken. He spoke for hours, telling me of their fortieth anniversary, about his plans for their future, his penchant for fishing, and his devotion to his family, all of it giving me the precise route needed to lift the image, gently and subtly, from his mind.

Around four-thirty, the door cracked open. "Excuse me, sorry to interrupt. We've got reporters all over the lobby. You done yet? They're hoping to make a five o'clock newscast." It was Rick Smith, the agent who had shadowed Mershon through the Polly Klaas Center on my first day in Petaluma. I was familiar with his perpetual stare, but this was the first time I'd heard him speak. Why now?

Achieving relaxation is a progressive process, which is why the more accurate details tend to surface in the latter parts of a several-hour-long interview. The early information is skewed by emotion and more likely cognitively based and distorted. The deeper the relaxation, the greater the level of precision we'd be able to reach. All my careful pacing of questions and structuring of moods could be thrown back to square one by the infusion of reality that came with this momentary interruption.

"No, but we'll let you know when we're done, thanks," I said, my bulging eyes meant to imply what my voice could not. Two months earlier, I might have felt pressured, but after what I'd seen in Petaluma, I wouldn't rush. Accuracy was more important than any network deadline.

By seven P.M. we emerged with the sketch of a clean-cut man with short hair, dimples, and a fresh face. It was nearly impossible to believe it to be that of a kidnapper—he looked more like a poster boy for Up With People. The simplicity of his features made him all the more difficult to draw, which made it all the more crucial that each scant detail be correct.

The press was waiting impatiently, the sound of their generators filling the cold and wet night air. The five o'clock evening news having passed, they'd now break into their regular programming to release the suspect sketch. Mark summoned them inside for the lobby press briefing.

The tripods and spotlights began springing up, illuminating the interior of city hall, while I ran into a darkened work area to make reproductions of the drawing for the networks. When I turned around, Agent Smith was looming over my shoulder. I'd endured his glares all through the months in Petaluma. At one point I swear he was even trying to read my lips as I talked on a telephone.

I braced for what he had to say, assuming it would be a reprimand or some criticism. "Can I help you?" I forced out the question, hoping he'd not answer as I bent away from him over the copy machine and held my breath.

"I'd just like to tell you how much I respect and admire your work," he said, his face inches from mine and without expression. "It's excellent."

I stopped what I was doing and stepped back, then squinted and looked at him closely, trying to figure out if he was kidding. His face concealed all expression, but his words gave his humanity away.

The press conference was beginning. I watched from the upstairs railing, thankful to be anywhere but in front of the cameras. This time, there was no need for me to provide a defense to the press. Nothing had been done wrong.

I watched Mershon speaking in front of the cameras, the enlarged sketch under the spotlights on an easel next to him, then skipped the good-byes and slipped out a side door to the rental car, driving off past the media vans, their doors wide open to release the heat from their equipment into the cold night air. I dialed the airline from my cellular phone to try to book a flight out. No luck. The first flight to Salt Lake was six A.M., and from there I'd have to grab a commuter flight to Ketchum, a fifteen-minute drive from Sun Valley.

After a quick call to Robert's voice mail, I settled into an airport hotel room just in time to tune in to the eleven o'clock broadcasts. Thankfully, the release of the drawing would likely head each network's news so I could get some sleep before my four A.M. wake-up call.

I clicked through the dial and caught the story on every Bay Area channel, then hit the off button and climbed into the freezing-cold king-size bed.

This wanted poster, with a suspect drawing based on an untainted description by Gene Mayer, was released by the FBI in the Ruth Mayer kidnapping case, Antioch, California, December 24, 1993. (Drawing by Jeanne Boylan)

I'd barely gotten warm when the wake-up call came. No pajamas, no travel bag, my back hurt from tension, and my hair was like twine after its run-in with the cheap hotel shampoo. My miracle suit was the only thing that looked flawless as I rushed to catch the early flight to Salt Lake.

Working the case meant that Robert had made the drive to Sun Valley alone, but I'd really missed only one day with him. It was December 24, the day we'd planned for two months, and I would still make it in time for the big Christmas Eve celebration.

Inside the terminal, stacks of the *San Francisco Chronicle* waited in front of the locked doors of each bookstore and newsstand. Thin plastic straps bound the piles. Under them I could see the Mayer story across the top half of the page, with the hand-drawn scrubbed face of the kidnapper ready to stare into the eyes of every Bay Area morning subscriber.

I stopped at a phone booth to call Robert and let him know it wouldn't be long now, I was on the way.

After boarding at my assigned gate, I had to look again at my ticket before settling into seat 8-A. I was in the front cabin and I knew the ticket I'd bought was for coach. I guessed that due to the holiday, they'd bumped me up to first class. The flight attendants all were wearing Hawaiian leis. Hmm, I thought, . . . festive.

I put my art case in the spacious closet and buckled in. A 747 going to Salt Lake? Go figure. I'd arrive in Utah, catch my commuter to Ketchum, and be in Sun Valley by two P.M. I was so excited I was talking to everyone seated around me while the attendants began to secure the massive cabin doors.

"Good morning, ma'am. Would you care for some orange juice or champagne?" the flight attendant asked.

"Sure, I'll have some champagne." A one-day turnaround on a case was unheard of, and I'd actually done it. I'd toast to that. I raised my glass in the air and took a sip. Just taking the case put me on thin ice with Robert, but reuniting with him so soon would land me back on solid ground.

The attendant returned up the aisle with her empty tray and leaned on the seat back ahead of me.

"So, tell me, are you going to Honolulu on business or pleasure?"

"*Excuse me?*"

She took a quick look at my ticket and screamed, "Grab your bags!" then yanked my arm to help me move even faster toward the exit. She threw her arm out to block the closing door and frantically ran me across the concourse to the right plane. There had been a last-minute gate-change announcement that I'd missed while on the pay phone calling Robert with the news of my early arrival. The gate agent had also missed the error when I boarded. As we tore across the concourse, my Salt Lake flight was just closing its door.

"Federal regulations, ma'am," the flight attendant said. "Once the door is sealed, we can't reopen it." I could have reached out and touched the nose of my plane.

I was, to put it mildly, inconsolable. Five and a half hours until the next flight. I stood, arms dangling, and my purse dropped with a thud to the floor as I watched through the terminal windows while *my* pilots put on their sunglasses inside the cockpit of *my* airplane. I wasn't on it. My shoulders began to shake and the floodworks began.

The gate agents on each side of me offered cocktail coupons and free prime-rib lunch tickets, but I stood motionless, my eyes still locked on my flight. I wasn't listening, I was sobbing. Soon, customer service representatives came along, picked up my purse, turned me by the shoulders, and escorted the weeping woman in the Donna Karan suit down the concourse into the Red Carpet room, and out of the public eye for the duration.

I t was after seven at night before the commuter flight from Salt Lake finally descended toward the Ketchum airport. The swelling of my eyelids had gone down nicely. I put my hands up when Robert came rushing toward me in the quaint ski area terminal. "Don't even say it." I shook my head.

"We might still make it if we rush," he said. In the cab of the truck, I pulled on the jeans, knee-high Sorel boots, and thick, white ski coat that were in my still-unpacked vacation suitcase as we slid around icy street corners and raced for the Sun Valley Lodge.

The crusted snow gave way underneath our boots when we cut

through the lawns to the lodge, then wound our way into the center of the decks where our friends held a spot open for us in the crowd. Rock tiers lined with planters stepped down to the ice rink, where Olympic skaters Brian Boitano and Nancy Kerrigan were performing under black lights. The white streamers attached to their costumes trailed gracefully behind them. I stood atop a planter for a better view and braced myself with Robert's shoulder, still in shock at having arrived in time.

In front of us, the famous slopes of Mt. Baldy glittered with criss-crossing chains of torchlight-carrying skiers weaving past midmountain on their way to the base. We'd made it with less than two minutes to spare. Symphonic strands of "Ave Maria" through loudspeakers filled the air, and stars were sprinkled across the clear night sky. The scent of expensive perfume surrounded us. Finally standing at my husband's side, amid all this beauty, I was nearly lost in the sheer magnificence of the moment.

"Hey, I almost forgot to tell you," Robert brought me back with a touch on my elbow. "The FBI called and said to tell you thank you."

"Thank you? For what? The FBI doesn't make calls to say thank you . . ."

"They said when the drawing came out, the kidnappers freaked. It was all over the news. Apparently they'd already dug that woman's grave and intended to kill her, but instead, realizing their capture was imminent, they cut their losses, drove her into a neighborhood, and rolled her out of the car. She's alive."

The elation of the news flooded through me at the precise moment that the skiers arrived at the base of the slope. Suddenly fireworks shot high into the pitch-black night air, filling the sky with light. I leapt off the planter into the crowd, grabbing hold of fur coats on the people around me and shaking them by the shoulders shouting, "She's alive! She's alive!" I was out of my mind with undiluted joy.

Even "Ave Maria" on loudspeakers couldn't drown out my shrieks of elation. Robert stood way back as if to say, "I don't really know this woman." I jumped, I laughed, I hopped, I cried, I shook and hugged total strangers, and finally, in sheer relief, I fell into a seat on the planter, put my head in my hands, and, silently and profoundly, thanked God.

All during the interview with Gene Mayer, I'd tried to think of how he'd live without his wife—*if* he could live without her, he loved her so much. But after Polly's case, hopes were at rock bottom. This time we'd gone into the case assuming she was already dead. None of us could have endured another heartbreak like Polly. Now, three days after the kidnapping, they'd let this woman go.

Nothing could bring back Polly Hannah Klaas, but it was Christmas Eve, and Ruth Mayer of Antioch, California, was alive, safe, and at home with her family.

We went to our hosts' home and sat in front of a golden fire framed by huge handpicked river rocks. I climbed inside the security of my husband's arms. Bayberry candles burned and snow fell softly outside the windows.

On Christmas morning, before anything else, I needed to make one important call. The FBI was monitoring all calls to the Mayers. Ruth was home, but the kidnappers were still at large. Gene Mayer had told the FBI to let me through if I called.

"Hey, Gene, it's Jeanne!" We'd joked about our matching names over our hours together. "Hey, I hear you're having a pretty good Christmas."

December 28, 1993, four days after the release of the wanted poster, Brian Tomasello was arrested for the kidnapping of Ruth Mayer in Antioch, California. (Photo courtesy of Antioch Police Dept.)

His voice was calm and tranquil. "Yeah, we are ... thanks to you, sweetheart."

The investigation involved the hard work of many people, in many capacities. I knew that, but his simple words to me were the greatest Christmas gift I could have received. In that moment, everything in my world seemed eerily perfect.

The media spread the news of Ruth Mayer's release on Christmas Day. The headline in the *San Jose Mercury News* read:

KIDNAP HAS HAPPY ENDING

I watched my husband out near the fireplace modeling his gifts in front of the mirror and thought of Gene and Ruth Mayer and the importance of family. I thought of how lucky I was to be soon beginning mine. This new year would be all ours, with nothing in the way to stop us. Robert held up my hot chocolate, a signal that it was getting cold.

Christmas Day, 1993. Ruth Mayer celebrates her survival with investigators at a revisit to the location where she was held hostage by armed gunmen after being abducted during a home invasion robbery. (Photo © *San Francisco Chronicle*/Michael Macor)

I walked over to the morning fire and put my arms around my husband. But my serenity was haunted by the echo of the psychic's words: "This work will *never* let you go."

Robert and I grasped each other's hands all through the Christmas Mass. We'd survived the interruption of the Antioch case intact.

Finally, like two halves of a split prism lens, we were in perfect alignment. We'd been in Sun Valley for nearly a week before obligation weighed in and I checked my Oregon voice mail early New Year's Eve day.

"Ms. Boylan, this is Randy Leaf with the Manhattan Beach Police Department. We have a crisis here. One of our police officers was executed and we need your assistance. Could you please get back to me immediately?" The phone felt leaden in my hand. Slowly, I dialed the number in Southern California.

"Sergeant Leaf, yes, this is Jeanne Boylan returning your call."

I listened to the report, then got up to go join the others. I sat down at the breakfast table to break the news.

Officer Martin Ganz was an only son from a large family of girls. He had one nephew, thirteen years old, who was visiting from Florida for Christmas. The boy also wanted to be a police officer, and Uncle Martin—his only uncle and his hero—had let him ride along on a post-Christmas patrol.

Under the strands of shopping-mall lights, and through the rear window of the idling patrol car, Ganz's nephew watched as his uncle was shot in a cold-blooded execution before he could get his own pistol out of its holster.

"Of course, Jeanne, if you've gotta go, you've gotta go," my husband said. I knew Robert was "on" again and I was grateful for the audience. "I'll drive you to the airport." It was agreed that he would leave with me and then drive on home to Bend.

It was bone cold on the road to Ketchum. The snow danced in lacy patterns above the highway, too dry even to stick to the frozen pavement. The heater didn't begin to take the chill out of the truck. I wished for my ski clothes rather than my beige suit. I wished for many things.

I'd be gone just a few days, but when I put my arms around Robert to say good-bye, something had noticeably changed.

Through the porthole of the ascending morning plane, I looked out over the empty New Year's Eve highway. Only Robert's truck rolled down the quiet road, the snow, like dry-ice trails, swirling all around it. I was flying away in one direction, he was driving away in another.

I wiped the moisture away from the window in circles with my sleeve, but by the time I could see out again, he was already gone.

Martin Ganz wasn't even thirty years old when he became the first officer to be gunned down in the quiet seaside community of Manhattan Beach, south of Los Angeles.

He and his thirteen-year-old nephew were in his patrol car waiting to pull onto Sepulveda Boulevard when a car stopped practically under the stoplight at the intersection in front of them. The officer turned on his loudspeaker asking, "Please back up to the line." But the driver didn't comply.

When the light changed, the man turned left into the parking lot of a shopping center, and the police car followed. Both cars stopped near a branch of Bank of America. Ganz got out of his car, leaving the door

Manhattan Beach Police Department officer Martin Ganz. (Photo courtesy of Manhattan Beach Police Dept.)

open as he walked the thirty feet without his ticket book, intending to issue only a verbal warning. But instead of producing a driver's license, the stranger pulled out a handgun.

Ganz tried to run behind his own car for cover. He fumbled with but was unable to free the safety snap on his holster. The driver bailed out of his car, chased after Ganz, and fired. More than once.

Ganz's nephew was curled up, terrified, on the floorboard of the front seat of the police vehicle, the driver's door still open. As the killer walked casually back, he noticed the boy's movement inside the patrol car. The thirteen-year-old peered up over the dashboard.

The murderer then turned toward the patrol car and slowly assumed a full-combat stance, both hands wrapped around the grip of his gun, the barrel pointed directly at the face of the young boy. Miraculously, he didn't fire. Instead, he turned away, continued walking slowly back to his car, got in, and drove off, braking fully at the stop sign, then signaling for a right-hand turn before disappearing down the street.

Detective Mark Lillefield filled me in on the case as we drove from the airport to the Sepulveda Boulevard hotel he'd booked for my stay.

"We'll pick you up first thing in the morning, and, hey, whatever you do, stay away from the windows," he warned. "By the way, Happy New Year."

"Yeah, thanks, Lillefield." I could read the sarcasm in his voice. My New Year's Eve would be about as festive as his would. We were both working.

Being a Caucasian in DKNY was not exactly an attribute inside this infamous airport hotel. I didn't even live in L.A. and I knew this segment of Sepulveda Boulevard's reputation for hookers and drugs. I wound through the New Year's Eve crowd to my room and bolted my door. Then I pushed a dresser up next to it. Then a chair.

As midnight neared, I learned why I was advised to stay away from the windows. Gunfire erupted in the streets. It was a local tradition in the *spirit* of the holiday, but deadly if you found yourself in the wrong spot. Lillefield would owe me for this night.

The next morning I met him in the hotel lobby with my bag in hand. The look in my eyes told him how my evening had been.

"What, you didn't like it here?" He laughed knowingly. "I'm really sorry, Jeanne. Really I am. Everything was booked." By noon that day, Detective Mark Lillefield had personally arranged for the remainder of my stay in a suite on the top floor of the Manhattan Beach Marriott, overlooking the golf course.

Officer Ganz's nephew Don was a beautiful boy with soulful, dark eyes, thick brown eyebrows, and a labored tone tied to a heavy heart.

By the time I interviewed him, a suspect sketch was already in circulation. It had all the ingredients, but not the needed details to make the face identifiable. Putting ego aside and the interest of the Martin Ganz case up front, the agency's original artist graciously called to offer me his support and to ask what he might do to help. He'd interviewed the boy just after Ganz's death.

Consistent with the original drawing, we developed an Asian man's face, but the similarities stopped there. The new sketch showed his full checks, the angle of his eyes, his full brows. It portrayed the sternness of his gaze and the posture through his neck and shoulders. Ganz's

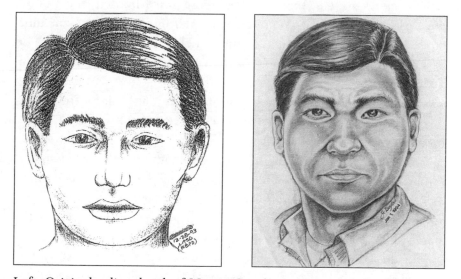

Left: Original police sketch of Martin Ganz's executioner. Right: New sketch released after reinterviewing the eyewitness for greater detail. (Right-hand drawing by Jeanne Boylan)

nephew was smart and determined. At least on paper, we captured his two-second vision of his uncle's executioner.

The case was high on the minds of not just those in Manhattan Beach but those throughout the greater L.A. basin. But the news stories had surged the day after Martin's death, and the police needed a new twist to get the story, along with the new more-detailed sketch, back on the front page. The police commander asked if he could utilize my name as a means of giving the Ganz story a fresh angle and a revitalized round of media attention.

I complied. If it would help get the drawing in front of the public, I said I'd stay, but first I'd have to call Rob at home and explain the delay.

The PD put out a press release announcing my involvement, and within hours my hotel voice mail was jammed.

First up was L.A.'s preeminent anchor, Linda Alvarez, who stayed for two hours asking questions that far exceeded the content of her report. Then reporters from several coastal newspapers arrived. If the suspect was from L.A., the southern California press would be saturated with the new drawing.

Next came the *Los Angeles Times*, represented by Bettijane Levine, the Walter Cronkite of L.A. print media. Her interest in the Ganz murder extended into an idea for a feature article that included my work on past cases, to be run as a cover story in the paper's widely read Life & Style section.

I agreed to do the interview, though I didn't want to sit for the obligatory photo. But the *Times* photographer, Al Seib, said he wasn't asking for a snapshot.

"You know, it's not really about what you draw, but rather what you *see* through these," he said, grabbing a handful of sharpened pencils from my hotel desktop and spreading them out like a Chinese fan.

Having never been formally trained in art, my favorite pencil was the standard No. 2, just like the ones used in grade school.

"Put these in front of your face," he suggested. "I want to shoot you looking through only the tips of those pencils."

His photo moved me into the background, my face buffered from the camera by the sharp graphite pencil points. He saw what so many others didn't. He wanted to symbolize that this work is not about the artist or the artist's ego, it is about carefully extracting and capturing on paper delicate information from a painful memory in order to give investigators the best possible tool to help solve a case.

I raised the pencils and peered through the tips, ecstatic for his insight behind the photograph.

The film captured the simple truth. It didn't matter that I was exhausted, that my eyes were tired, or that I needed to get home. The story wasn't about me. It was about the reality of a killer at large. From the heart of a victim and through the tips of those pencils, the truth could be found. Everything else was secondary.

7

AN UNCONVENTIONAL FAMILY

At home, my culinary skills were on a steep upswing. In a good week I could master five new recipes, each entrée looking precisely like the photos in the *Good Housekeeping* cookbook. Apple cobbler was the house specialty—more for the way it made the log house smell than for its actual consumption. After each attempt, the kitchen looked as if a powder-filled bomb had exploded, but I'd have it all back to Robert's standards before he walked in the door at night. Dillon and I were just grateful he didn't come home at lunchtime.

My new role of hausfrau seemed to be working out—until the morning of January 12, 1994. By the paper's count, on that day more than one million copies of the *Los Angeles Times* were circulated, though the reverberations I felt in Bend, Oregon, made me think they underestimated their numbers, or at least their impact.

Bettijane Levine's article on my work hit the L.A. streets at dawn. Even before the sun began to soften the fresh layer of overnight snow, I was aware that her story on my work practically filled a section cover and one interior page of the newspaper. The headline read "Drawing Attention." Apparently, it did.

The feature included a rundown of how I work and why I'm called

At home in Bend, Oregon, with yellow Labrador Dillon and one of
the many reporters to delve into past criminal case mishaps. (Photo:
Collection of the author)

unorthodox by investigators, plus laudatory comments from agencies
around the country that I'd worked for in the past. It ended on a quote
from Dr. Elizabeth Loftus, my academic mentor.

I yelled out to Robert as an L.A. friend read to me over the phone.
"Boylan has a real talent," the article quoted Loftus. "She's done incredible things. She can create images amazingly close to those of the real
perpetrator. She did it in the Polly Klaas case, even though the witnesses' memories were highly contaminated before she arrived on the
scene. That she was able to pierce that contamination and get back to
the witnesses' original images is remarkable. You ought to either bottle
her and sell her, or else analyze her to death in hopes that her skills can
be taught to others."

With one large and prominently placed feature, Bettijane Levine used a blowtorch to light a flame of interest in my field.

The four days following her story's break were wild with calls. Progressive thinking artists called wanting to be tutored. Agencies called wanting training for investigators. In between, offers from more than two dozen production companies poured in, wanting to secure rights for movies of the week, television series, and feature films.

I started answering on the upstairs extension. I was still on thin ice and afraid of how the attention might rattle my husband. I sat on the edge of the huge log bed scribbling details of the offers and information on a yellow legal pad.

Maybe this was the answer to the looming question of what project would come next. If there was an antithesis to the police world, it had to be the film industry. *This* could be fun!

"Honey?" The corner of the morning paper quickly flipped down, exposing only one eye across the table.

"No!"

"But—"

"The answer is no."

But I hadn't asked the question yet. I'd been afraid to bring it up. It was mid-January and I had to begin returning calls. Plus, two of the companies had already FedEx'd plane tickets to Los Angeles and invitations to the first of the face-to-face meetings.

On the night before the first scheduled flight I built a fire, made Robert's favorite meal, put on his favorite music, and broke the news over dinner. The meetings at Paramount were set for the next day. The offers hovered over six figures. Robert offered to drive me to the airport.

The following morning, the phone woke me yet again.

"Jeanne, turn on the news," a neighbor called to clue me in. "I don't think you're going to L.A. today." The Northridge earthquake had struck Los Angeles with tremors that reached a magnitude of 6.8. Gas jets shot fiery columns a hundred feet into the early-morning sky. Swimming pools exploded into torrential downpours. Whole sections of the Santa

Monica Freeway were knocked out. Nearly two thousand square miles were rearranged by the earth's violence. In all, fifty people died.

As only tragedies do, the terrible news put everything else in perspective. I put the plans for Hollywood aside in favor of prayers for the earthquake victims, and unpacked while glued to CNN as L.A. began its recovery.

But true to Los Angeles style, the setback was temporary. Within just two weeks, businesses were wobbly, but up and running again. Meetings were reset and the tickets reissued. Plans were back on.

If I'd wanted a change in routine, I'd gotten what I'd wished for: Warner Brothers, Paramount, 20th Century Fox, dinner at Spago, contract talks, lunch in Beverly Hills, film sets, movie lots, writers, producers, entertainment attorneys—nothing even resembled the milieu of an investigation. A month flew by and the streets of West L.A. were becoming as familiar as the road to the Redmond airport.

Hollywood was tantalizing. But at the same time, I couldn't seem to make myself take any of it seriously. No one's life was hanging in the balance, no children were missing, no murderers were at large. Everything in it was make-believe.

With each flight home, I'd sink into my seat and go over all the places I'd been, the celebrities I'd met, and the sets I'd walked on. But I never quite had the feeling that the producers fully understood the real message in the story. I continued to turn down their offers.

Television had something called "formula." It was only safe, their conventional wisdom dictated, to create what had worked before. A lone female protagonist as the lead was risky, they believed. So they wanted to give the story a pretested hook and make my character into another Cagney or Lacey. But I didn't smoke cigarettes, live in New York, swear like a thug, or even pack a .38. If it couldn't be done authentically, my preference was that it not be done at all. Yet the offers kept on coming.

Eventually I did sign—with a company run entirely by women. Under the Hollywood Boulevard umbrella of Stephen J. Cannell Productions, I'd encountered two insightful and compassionate executives named Ann Gross and Marcy Westin. Their offer wasn't the most lucrative one on the table, but they assured me that the topic of a single female working on high-profile crimes could be portrayed with meaning, depth, integrity, and heart. If I could lend my name to a project with a purpose, I'd sign.

One evening, I dialed Eve Nichols from my Beverly Hills hotel room. Her husband, Allan, answered the phone.

"Everyone's in bed early tonight. The kids had a heck of a day. Eve's asleep." He sounded different, almost upbeat. "You would not believe what happened today. We got a call to get the kids—Annie, Kate, and Gillian—and Eve and I were to take them to a pizza parlor. They had a back room set up for us, so we ordered, and you won't believe who walked through the back door and joined us."

"No idea. Who?"

"Robin Williams! He walked in with his wife, their arms filled with gifts for the girls. Gillian and Kate sat speechless, their mouths just hanging, but Annie jumped right up on his lap as if she'd known him all her life. Jeanne, he was great. He was incredible. I haven't seen those kids that happy or excited in—well—let's just say, in a very long time."

"Let Eve sleep, okay? Please just tell her I called."

The Oregon snow was melting, my marriage was on solid ground, and as if my prayers had been answered, the cases had quieted down. I'd lost count of the trips to Hollywood, but March 3 took me to California for a more important reason.

On a stage in the Petaluma Community Center, in front of Bay Area news cameras and as many Petalumans as could pack in the hall, the Klaas case investigative agencies hosted a "Celebration of Courage" to pay tribute to Gillian and Kate for their roles in the Polly Klaas case. Agent Mark Mershon walked to the podium.

"We are here tonight to honor both Gillian Pelham and Kate McLean, two courageous young people who, despite intense pressure, held strong to what they knew to be true. We've been through a lot together and we salute you, your courage and your truth. This night is for you."

The Petaluma police and the FBI broke all tradition by allowing their vulnerability to be seen that night. Pat Parks, Mark Mershon, Eddie Freyer, Mike Meese, Rick Smith, and Chief DeWitt all attended on their own time, at their own expense, letting everyone see into their

Top: FBI Assistant Special Agent in Charge Mark Mershon, who headed the Polly Klaas kidnap/murder case, shakes hands with Kate McLean at the "Celebration of Courage," during which the two young eyewitnesses were honored by police and FBI for never veering from the truth throughout the case. March 3, 1994. Bottom: Santa Rosa FBI Special Agent Eddie Freyer, left, presents a Special Letter of Commendation for Outstanding Work from FBI Director Louis Freeh, while Assistant Special Agent in Charge Mark Mershon, right, looks on. March 3, 1994, Petaluma, California. (Photos: Collection of the author)

hearts as they bowed to two little girls who, despite the pressures of the most intimidating law enforcement agency in the country, had never veered from their truth.

Before the crowd could clear, Mark Mershon and Eddie Freyer called me over to the side of the stage. Eddie pulled a page from a large, thick envelope—a "Special Commendation for Outstanding Work"—signed by FBI director Louis Freeh.

Portaits of courage: Kate
McLean (top) and Gillian
Pelham, eyewitnesses in the
Polly Klaas kidnap/murder
case, are photographed as
they begin to pick up the
pieces of their lives after
Polly's death. March 1994.
(Photo © *Petaluma Argus
Courier*/Janet Orsi)

Letters from the director are rare, but commendations to civilians are
nearly unheard of.

"So, what did you think it was, an arrest warrant for obstruction of justice?" Mark laughed. Then he added, "Your singular belief in those two
kids turned this whole case around."

The evening wasn't over. Gillian's mother presented me with a two-
page document, written in lofty legalese, titled "Certificate of Adoption."
I read it aloud:

> The party of the first part, does hereby undertake to receive,
> retain, and accept as its own that which was not so originally, and
> to otherwise adopt the person, property, and personal effects of
> Ms. Jeanne Boylan, hereafter referred to as the party of the second
> part, for the purpose of integrating said second party into a subset
> of the familial assemblage.
>
> All parties named are happy, delighted, and otherwise ecsta-

tic to receive into our family the party of the second part hereafter to be known as "Aunt Jeanne."

Signed heretofore this day by the power vested in me, one family under God, indivisible, E Pluribus Unum, etc., etc., ad infinitum, ad nauseam, with cookies and milk for all. God Bless America. Welcome to the family, Aunt Jeanne.

I took pen in free hand and signed my name, right above the silver seal reading—in Latin and in English—"To Know Us Is to Love Us."

Every sense seemed heightened when I walked back in the door of our log house. I wanted to bring with me all the sincerity that I'd felt in Petaluma and never to allow that level of authenticity to fade from my life.

With my husband's approval, the movie contract in L.A. was secured and under way, and a business plan he'd undertaken was moving along, though oddly he was keeping all details to himself.

Three weeks later, the phone rang, but it wasn't the movie industry calling again. This time it was a mother, pushing words out between heaving sobs, asking me to come help her find the murderer of her only son.

"I'm sorry to bother you at home. Marc Klaas gave me your number. My son's been murdered, and the police are saying that there are no witnesses. I need your help. Can you come right away? Please?"

Tragedies have a way of putting everything in perspective.

8

WHAT THE BLIND MAN SAW

Even through the haze of her deepest grief, Lisa Dahl could see that the police had thrown a wall between her son's death and the search for his killer. How a murder could take place during early-evening hours in a heavy tourist area without a single credible witness made not a shred of sense to her.

Twenty-three-year-old Justin Jones was her world. His broad smile sat as a permanent fixture above a square jaw. His *Beverly Hills 90210* face was topped with a tousled mass of curly, dark hair. Lisa's union with his father had been brief, yet it left a joy that was hers forever—or so she thought, until March 27, 1994, when a solitary moment extinguished the brightest light in her life.

Justin had hopped on his bicycle to ride from their Marin County home across the bridge and into San Francisco's Haight-Ashbury district in search of a rare-record store. The route was long, and the warmth of the new spring day was perfect for rationalizing the exercise. But in his path, he saw a blind man waving his white cane into the air, frantically calling out for help.

Justin Wesley Jones in 1994. (Photo courtesy of Lisa Dahl, Justin's mother)

What happened next would alter Lisa Dahl's life forever.

Justin never made it back across the Golden Gate Bridge. The police maintained that there wasn't a single witness who could attest to what took place in the last moments of his life.

A week passed with no suspects, no leads, no witnesses. Lisa's hopes were shattered and her patience on empty when she decided she had to look beyond the system for answers, beginning with a call to Marc Klaas.

She'd watched the sad ordeal of Polly's murder from her luxurious Marin County condominium, never imagining that within months she'd be sharing the same anguish. Marc understood her pain. He comforted her and offered her my telephone number, which she turned over to the San Francisco Homicide Department on April 4. But SFPD presented her again with the same worn-out words: "We have *no* credible witnesses."

Any search is virtually futile unless you know whom you're looking for. The investigation needed a face. Someone saw something. Somehow, she had to find out who and what.

Lisa waited for the police to take further action. Her son's killer had been free to wander, unrestrained, for two full weeks. With each additional day that the case languished, the trail was getting colder. When questioned, one inspector tried to reassure her by touting his thirty years of investigative experience, saying, "Look, I know how to solve homicides." Lisa cared about only one homicide, however, and no one seemed to be solving it. On Sunday, April 10, she picked up the phone and dialed my number.

"My son's been murdered," she said, gasping for breath between words. "He reacted from his heart because someone called for help. That's how he was. The person who killed him is still out there, and no one is doing anything. I owe more than this to my boy. Marc Klaas gave me your number. Can you help me, please?" Her voice quivered through the phone line.

"Possibly," I said gently. "Just tell me what happened."

For an hour, she cried and talked, and I listened.

On the last Sunday of his life, as the sun was just starting to set, Justin Wesley Jones arrived in the busiest part of Haight-Ashbury. The famous 1960s center of "flower power" had transformed over the 1980s into a commercial center surrounded by a seedy underworld of drugs and prostitution.

Justin was slowing to a stop when he saw a man emerge from between two parked cars, yelling for help while flailing his white cane in the direction of a young man running down the busy street carrying what appeared to be the blind man's backpack.

Justin pushed his pedals back into high gear and raced after the thief, jumping the curb with his bicycle to block the path of escape. The robber slid to a stop and, with a single sweep, punched Justin in the chest. But concealed inside his hand was a sharpened wood-chisel that plunged deep into Justin's body, boring straight through the center of his heart.

Reeling from the blow, Justin collapsed over the legs of a disabled veteran seated curbside in a wheelchair. The Vietnam vet pushed back, spitting an explosion of curses, furious at Justin for dying at his feet.

Media immediately dubbed the tragedy the Good Samaritan Murder. Recognizing Justin as a hero was the only easy part of the aftermath.

To Lisa Dahl, a more fitting tribute to her only son would be to find his killer. In that effort she ran into roadblocks on every front. The lack of information or assistance from the police made her question the workings of an investigative system in which she had formerly placed an unconditional trust.

Were they even trying? How were they able to say there were no witnesses when Justin died during active hours on such a busy street? The
disabled veteran was there. Who else saw? Someone had to have witnessed enough to provide a description of her son's murderer.

I hung up the phone and called the San Francisco Police Investigative
Division to obtain permission to step into their case. When I identified
myself, the officer recalled my name from my involvement in Petaluma,
though with him, the link didn't begin to break the ice.

"Yeah, well, what do you want?" His tone made clear his disinterest in
an answer.

"Sir, the mother of your March twenty-seventh, Haight-district homicide victim, Justin Jones, has asked me to come assist in the investigation. I called first to advise you of her request, and secondly for your
permission to enter the case."

"It's Sunday," he snarled back in annoyance. "I'm not calling the two
case inspectors at home on their day off. Do whatever you want." He
hung up without a good-bye.

Politics are complicated and egos are touchy between agencies, but as
an outsider, treading on an investigator's territory can be a tough road. I
didn't want to do anything that could hamper Lisa's relationship with
the agency. But "no witnesses" usually indicates only that the right questions have yet to be asked.

We needed to find people who were on that street that night, to
obtain information that we could turn over to the inspectors on the
case. What we might uncover could be of great value to them, but they
would have to decide that they wanted to view it that way.

I pushed RECORD on the phone's answering device and called back for
round two. If I couldn't get a definite answer from the SFPD, I needed to
at least have my effort noted. If the officer later claimed to have forgotten, I'd have the conversation on tape. Orthodox? No. Necessary? Yes.

"Listen, lady," the same weekend commander answered, "I said do
whatever you want. We are so used to people sticking their noses in our
business that we don't care what you do."

"Are you sure? Then I'm informing you that I will be arriving to
assist."

"Like I said, do whatever you want." He hung up.

Those were the magic words. As a professional courtesy I'd followed protocol and apprised the agency of Lisa Dahl's request. I popped the tape out of the recorder, grabbed it in midair, and tossed it into my purse.

All that was left was telling Robert. He'd left his job months earlier, and his weekdays were filled with hushed meetings regarding his new business idea. Evenings he spent with friends, and almost every weekend he'd leave to go skiing or fishing. I'd finally quit asking to tag along. The plans, he always said, included "just the guys."

Despite all his talk of wanting me there by his side, since I'd quit my job to stay in town, I seemed to be spending more time alone than ever. My Rolodex was filled with names of news anchors, correspondents, talk show producers, and FBI agents from coast to coast. Yet, f I wanted to go have a cup of coffee, there was no one local to call.

In mid-March, *People* magazine had sent a photographer out to do a shoot for an upcoming article. When he was done, I wanted to shackle the poor man to the front porch, just for his friendly conversation. So, when Robert and I were invited to a first-day-of-spring party, I grabbed at the opportunity to finally begin making some local women friends.

"Jeanne, I'd like you to meet Harriet and Leslie and Sharon." I was thrilled as the host began introducing a circle of professional women, well dressed, pretty, most just a little older than I.

I held up my hand. "Oh, just a moment please, I'd love for you to meet my husband, too." I turned toward the kitchen to call him into the room, but their responses came in unison, like some off-key chorus by the Lennon Sisters, "Oh, we know Robert, we go skiing with him all the time."

My heart hit bottom like an anchor in a wading pool. "Oh, you do?" I choked on the words. "Okay then." I kept smiling while swallowing all pride.

So, these are "the guys." Nice to finally meet ya—*fellas.*

I didn't let much time pass between Lisa's request and dialing Alaska Air. A few hours later in the SFO terminal, I looked right past Lisa Dahl when I scanned the baggage-claim crowd. The forty-one-year-old woman with the outstretched arms looked more like a *Vogue* model than a mom, with her slender Audrey Hepburn neck, pale porcelain skin, and black hair slicked back to frame her symmetrical features. Her designer clothes were immaculately pressed and color-coordinated. Only her eyes revealed her sadness.

She struggled with tears as we walked from the gate to her car, which she'd left at the curb in the care of Andrea, the Italian man with whom Lisa shared her life.

Andrea stepped out of the car and gave me a hearty European hug. We skipped introductions and jumped right into strategy. Tragedy tends to strip superficialities away.

"Have you got police reports? Are any witnesses at all listed?" I asked. Lisa lapsed between strength and devastation as she answered.

"There's only one man, John Mitchell," Lisa said. "He's the one who was being robbed, the man who Justin tried to help. The police say they don't know where he is now. But they don't see any need to interview him again. They say he's an addict. And, they say, he would not be a credible person on a witness stand so they don't plan to go back to him at all."

"Do you mean the blind man? The blind man is our only witness? Is there anyone else?" I dug in my bag for writing paper, largely as an excuse to turn away from Lisa's line of sight. I didn't want her to see the incredulous look on my face.

Here I was involved in a case that was less than vintage and my primary eyewitness was . . . was a blind man?

"No," Lisa answered. "They say there's no one else."

Since the murder had occurred on a busy street, Lisa and Andrea doubted that as much as I did. Andrea had created flyers featuring Justin's photo and Lisa's home phone number and plastered them on district storefronts and phone poles, begging anyone with information about Justin's death to please call. But so far, nothing.

Lisa's brother Jay flew in from Philadelphia and immediately upon arrival wandered into the San Francisco underworld to find someone who could help them produce information on Justin's murder. They needed someone good at locating people. In his innocence he asked, "Who better than a bounty hunter?"

The city's bounty-hunter offices were concentrated right behind San Francisco's City Hall, on a short street that catered to those down on their luck. The bay-windowed, old-world storefronts could have been on a street in any Bavarian village, but for the heavy metal grates over each pane of leaded glass and the multiple dead bolts on every door. At random, Jay stopped at a plain brown sign reading MACKENZIE GREEN. BAIL BONDS. He walked down the steps and into a dark, one-room office. The sign outside proved as ordinary as its occupant was not.

MacKenzie Green had been a flight attendant back when they were still called stews, but even in those pre-ERA days she was probably pushing the pilots around. There wasn't much she hadn't seen, and probably nothing she hadn't done, and she could tell you about it all in the low whiskey voice that she used to call the world as she saw it. She didn't say *stomach* if *guts* worked better, and she didn't say *please* if an expletive got faster results.

MacKenzie stood five feet tall, but never stood still. Criminals didn't scare her. Complacency only made her mad. She was Angela Lansbury with steel-toe boots and a don't-fuck-with-me attitude. When asked to help by Justin's family, she said yes to the job.

Both Jay and MacKenzie were waiting for us when Lisa drove up to the grand Nob Hill Fairmont Hotel. While I was en route, MacKenzie had secured an executive suite with four phone lines to serve as my hotel room and our central headquarters during our hunt for the killer. A quick check-in and we could get to work.

I left Lisa, Andrea, Jay, and MacKenzie in the hotel's ornate lobby and hurried to find the second-floor corner room, to toss my overnight bag in the massive mahogany armoire and run a brush through my hair. Cable cars clanged past the windows, and Grace Cathedral towered across the street.

I raced back to the lobby, but when the elevator door opened, the sight in front of me left me frozen in place.

Marc Klaas had operated the Hertz rental-car franchise in the Fairmont Hotel lobby prior to his daughter's death. The man now making frequent trips to the Oval Office in a push for legislation to protect

the safety of children had been cast into his new role from an anony-
mous position behind a five-foot-long car-rental counter. Now his sister
managed the franchise, and she'd lined the office shelves with a memorial to her slain niece.

Staring into the soft eyes of Polly Klaas, I felt as if I could hear her
message: "Hurry, don't let him get away." I kissed my fingertips and
touched her cheek as I walked by.

MacKenzie and I headed out, rattling down streets in her beat-up burgundy Honda. While her intentions and her bail shop may have been in
perfect order, her car was a disaster on wheels. All the better, I thought,
for moving unobtrusively through the Haight's weary underbelly.

Justin had wandered into a world in which he didn't belong. The
Haight's quaint shops and trendy restaurants were just a thin skin over a
highly organized and political drug culture. No matter who was on the
street the night of Justin's death, it wouldn't be easy finding anyone who
would talk. The tourists were gone and the locals were mute. This culture was one in which you saw, you heard, and you said nothing.

We found our first exception. A Portuguese-speaking Brazilian man,
Justin's age, was working in a take-out pizza store. He'd stepped onto the
street at the precise time of the murder, and Justin had fallen within
twenty feet of him. He'd rushed back inside the store and had an
English-speaking friend help him call the authorities. The police took
his number. He delayed his scheduled return to Brazil while waiting to
be questioned, but they never called him back.

It didn't make sense. He'd made it clear that he had witnessed the
murder. San Francisco is a cultural amalgam—surely the police had
every kind of translator they might need. Language could not and
should not have been the reason.

With his English-speaking friend at his side, we brought him to the
Fairmont and got to work. Within hours we had our first roughed-out
vision of Justin's killer. The Brazilian described him as a light-skinned
Latino with a bald head—young, agile, ethnic, and deadly. His description was enough for our first completed sketch.

Lisa was too frail to go on. She returned to her condo in Marin to be
near the phone in case calls came in response to the posters still lining
the streets.

Justin's best friend, Michael, joined us in the hunt for more witnesses. He knew the streets of the Haight almost as well as MacKenzie, and on his motorcycle he could move between leads with greater speed, keeping in touch by cell phone.

The name "Chicago" kept coming up. It was the street alias for John Mitchell, the man with the white cane. But the information was tenuous. And no one would fill in details, in spite of MacKenzie's relentless pushing.

"MacKenzie, you look like a damned cop. Did anyone ever tell you that?" I said.

"Well, fuck you. You look like a fucking prima donna." She threw the transmission into gear and sped between cars.

It hadn't taken long to understand her challenges. If you were to enter into MacKenzie's world, you did so on her terms. I had only to change my looks, my demeanor and my vocabulary and we'd get along just fine.

"MacKenzie, there is no lane here, what are you doing?"

She laughed. For the first forty-eight hours, every move was just another can-you-keep-up-with-this test. I liked this woman. There were stories behind that steel-cased facade that I had no time to excavate, but I suspected her toughness was well earned.

We both needed to change our look if we were to mingle with drug dealers and pimps on the evening streets of the Haight. Word passed like wildfire in the tightly controlled underside of the district that we'd been snooping around asking questions about a drug dealer.

Drug dealers and pimps had problems, but they also had eyes. Before they'd open up, though, they'd need to trust us. They needed to know that we weren't cops and that we had no interest in prying into their lives beyond finding out what they had seen on the night of March 27.

SFPD hadn't returned our calls. We were ready to turn over the drawing we'd done from the Brazilian's description, but neither of the two inspectors assigned to Justin's murder responded.

Something was wrong. This was a high-profile case. Why weren't the leads getting through? We decided to run our own test, so we began calling in strong-sounding tips and asking for return calls ASAP, leaving numbers for the hotel room, a pager, and MacKenzie's shop.

We got no calls in return.

Further upping the ante, to be sure the results were consistent and not dependent on the time of day or operator errors, we made more calls, one even so brazen as to offer a confession to the murder to test the limits of their reluctance to help.

No calls came back.

Each side of each block of the Haight district was split into two territories, which were worked by dealers in shifts that changed every eight hours.

The more established the dealer, the more prominent the spot on the sidewalk. Territories were not to be crossed, and shifts not to be violated—or else. The street system protected the hierarchy, keeping the sidewalks off-limits to all dealers but those who'd fought their way up to earn a designated time and place to conduct business.

The man named Chicago worked from four P.M. to midnight. Since MacKenzie tired easily, she'd quit by dinnertime, but I'd return after dark with Jay as my cover.

It took time. Word began to circulate that we were working for Justin's mother and not the SFPD, and slowly tips turned to leads.

"I think Jim was down here that night. He works a gig with a band in the Tenderloin. Plays guitar. His girlfriend lives above a deli on San Francisco Street. Go talk to her."

"No, no one here by that name. But there used to be a girl living here named Lynn something. I think she used to work at a restaurant."

"Yeah, she worked here, but she went into rehab last month—you know, the one by the bus station."

At rehab they sent us away, but on our way out we heard a whisper from a drunk on a couch: "She's here, but she comes in only at night."

Lots of leads. Lots of phone calls. Lots of disappointments. But still no Chicago. He was gone from his post.

Word had it that the drugs he sold were fake—that the robbery was a payback from one of his customers.

"Jay, what do you think, maybe we should—" I turned around and Jay was gone.

Justin's uncle Jay was a paradox. Easygoing, funny, and kindhearted, he saw the world through his wire-rim glasses that perched about five feet five inches from the ground. He had the appearance of a suburban accountant and father of three. But Jay was single and, as a career, sold custom-made costumes for strippers in nightclubs. Under his arm he proudly and constantly carried a three-ring binder with full-color glossies of half-naked models and was always ready to make the unforeseen sale.

I took a seat at a bus stop under a flashing neon GIRLS, GIRLS, GIRLS sign and waited for Jay's return. Each time we neared another club, I'd find another seat.

Being alone had a payoff. Nearly every time I'd sit to bide time, someone would come by and slip me information. If we'd been pegged on the street, we'd been pegged as good guys. The drug dealers had their own code of ethics, and murder was not among them. Everyone in the Haight, no matter his station, understood that Justin had died a hero. They all wanted to help, and in quiet bits and pieces, they did.

We verified that Justin had been killed at the favorite begging spot of a disabled vet named Dan. But beyond his first name and the fact that he never looked up from the ground in front of him, no one knew much about him.

We found a Chinese witness who lived on the third floor of a building directly across from the scene. He described the suspect as Asian. He'd seen the murder from his bay window facing the street, in dim light, looking over and down. Good information but not enough for a drawing. We could try again the next day.

So far, the only common denominator in the descriptions revolved around the suspect's clothing. By all accounts, he wore a hooded sweatshirt and oversized denim shorts, high-top sports shoes and long socks. With that information, we cruised the streets with eyes wide open.

MacKenzie, or "Mac," was at her best in the morning. Her temper would swing with the heat of the day, and by dusk she'd be downright nasty.

I'd just found a spot for my feet among the Burger King bags on the floor when my shoulder slammed against the car door as she swerved around a truck and jerked to a halt, leaving the Civic double-parked in the street. Before I could unbuckle, she was out of the car and had a man at least a foot taller than she was slammed flat up against a wall.

"Let's see some ID, buddy, I mean now!" she yelled while holding his arm in a twisted clinch behind his back.

"MacKenzie! What the hell are you doing?" I screamed at her as I leapt from the car.

"Jesus, Jeanne, look at the clothes! ID. Now, you asshole!" she yelled as the six-foot kid frantically unloaded his pockets onto the sidewalk.

He was wearing the hooded sweatshirt, baggy jeans, and high-top shoes all right. As were at least three eighteen- to twenty-two-year-olds on every block. We needed to get with the program. Styles on the street had changed. Using urban grunge as a distinguishing feature was hardly a primary clue.

"MacKenzie, I'm buying you Prozac—a whole damn case of it," I said as her assault victim sauntered off in a daze.

We were a good-cop/bad-cop combo, however unintentional, and in some situations it worked. I may have had a six-foot-four-inch husband back home, but I felt safer with five-foot Mac by my side.

Justin's friend Michael uncovered a lead on Dan, the disabled vet. Michael's sleuthing led to a street address in a low-income-housing area, from where the witness to Justin's murder would wheel himself up and down the steep hills of the city. According to sources, ever since March 27, he'd shown up on the streets only after dark. Jay and I were determined to find him.

So far, we'd talked with twenty-six people who'd been on the street the night of Justin's death. By piecing together their reports, we knew that Chicago had been walking down the sidewalk when the suspect grabbed his backpack and ran. But there was also a woman on Chicago's left side as they'd walked. Just minutes before the robbery, the woman had talked face-to-face with the suspect. Our informants said that following the killing, Chicago had walked the woman by the arm and handed her over to the police. She told the officers that night that she'd talked with the suspect and was willing to help.

That made four direct witnesses: the Brazilian, the Chinese man, the disabled vet, and the woman. We had to find her, and only Chicago knew who she was.

Word leaked to the media that I was involved, and reporters put two and two together. If I was involved, they deduced, someone had to have seen something. SFPD had its own resources including an on-staff artist. Why was an outsider necessary? Why hadn't the police come up with sketches on their own? After reporters began to speculate, I put in a call to the SFPD artist as a courtesy to let him know how I'd become involved.

I thought the territorial wars between drug dealers were rough, but I'd never before encountered a barrage of obscenities quite so volatile or delivered in such an artistic fashion. The artist made it clear that I was on his turf and—though significantly paraphrased—in essence, he wished first for an upswing in my sex life and then most sincerely for my untimely demise.

I hung up, remembering the psychic's warning: "Your peers especially will resent you, viciously."

Rita Williams, a prominent reporter from Fox Television, had become a friend through our mutual ordeal in Petaluma. She phoned to ask for a story, but I declined. We needed to keep out of the press. If SFPD had said there were no credible witnesses, we had to be discreet. Lisa still needed the SFPD's help. Our sole goal was to hand them the face, not to humiliate or upstage them. To protect their egos, we had to keep a low profile.

But the media doesn't know the term *low profile,* and Rita and her crew caught up with us on the street. Despite my telephone pleas, she approached with a camera rolling and settled for a few words as MacKenzie and I walked through the alleys of downtown San Francisco.

Rita's report aired on the evening news. It detailed how a mother of a murder victim had been forced to initiate her own investigation. The clip showed Mac and me working with no cover, in rough areas, out looking for leads. Within an hour, Lisa received a call from an unrivaled powerhouse in the city, a woman named Angela Alioto, head of the Board of Supervisors. Politically, she had power over the SFPD, and she was *livid.*

Angela wanted the names of the Good Samaritan case inspectors and vowed to take this matter up with the chief of police. Within hours, we received a call at the Fairmont from one of the two inspectors.

"Miss Boylan, I am Inspector Zahler of the San Francisco Police Homicide Division. We are investigating the homicide of Justin Jones.

We understand that you are, too, and we would like to offer you our sincere assistance in anything at all you may need from us."

Thank you Rita Williams, thank you Fox News, and thank you Angela Alioto! I could barely believe my ears. Heads must have landed on a SFPD platter, topped off with just a touch of marinara sauce.

Not only were we offered their full cooperation and support, but to close on their offer, I invited them to our hotel for tea. Under the circumstances, however short-lived it might be, they had no choice but to attend.

"I'm not wearing a damned dress." MacKenzie was steaming when I told her the plan. But our power was only temporary and we needed to cement the deal.

"Come on, Mac, just do this for me. We need more than a patronizing phone call from these guys, we need some eye-to-eye contact to let them know we've been working hard and that we're not going to let up until this case is solved. Right now they think we are just an annoyance, just a couple of broads—minding *their* business. I want to give them what we've found and find out what else they have. One dress, one afternoon. It won't kill you."

Lisa was getting stronger and had driven over from Marin. Mac looked pretty good in her navy blue skirt. She had legs. Little stubby ones, but legs. I picked up a dark dress in a shop in the Haight, and Jay showed up as, well, as Jay—less his infamous three-ring binders after I took them from him and hid them in the armoire.

"So, why the stupid outfits?" Mac could make a little whine last all day.

We'd talked to dozens of people who were on the street the night Justin was killed, and even more who knew something about it. We'd be unveiling information that the inspectors had missed. They'd stated publicly that they had found no credible witnesses. No matter how pleasant our "tea," they were meeting with us against their wishes, probably following a hearty reprimand by the chief of police. They'd walk in the door gritting their teeth at having to meet with us at all. We needed to make ourselves as blatantly subservient as possible so as to give them the illusion that they held all the power. This was not a war of egos, at least not on our side.

"Come on, work with me here, Mac. Tea and crumpets, anyone?" I arranged the doilies on the sitting-room table just as they knocked on the door.

"Good afternoon, ladies." The two weathered detectives walked in while I reached behind me and signaled MacKenzie to knock it off. She ended her curtsy just as they rounded the corner into the room.

If MacKenzie and I were Mutt and Jeff, they were Schwarzenegger and DeVito. The two could not have been more opposite in appearance—or in demeanor. One white, one Chinese, one round, one thin; one all smiles, the other refusing even to make eye contact—not even when Mac placed the pastries under his nose.

"Are you sure, gentlemen? The crumpets are simply delightful," she said. Mac had gotten perhaps too thoroughly into the game. I shot her an evil eye. Lisa sat in her demure and elegant manner, her eyes still revealing her excruciating pain, yet her mouth curling into an occasional smile at MacKenzie's antics.

We handed them a list of names, phone numbers, and a schematic of locations of the various witnesses we'd discovered.

"We'd like to know more about the original robbery victim, the man called Chicago," I said.

The friendly one spoke, while the other rhythmically tapped the heels of his wingtip shoes on the floor. "Yes, we are aware of him. He's a drug dealer. He is afflicted with a number of problems and is not, shall we say, credible. He's of no use. We cannot have him on a witness stand."

"Well, that's fine, but we just need to find him to get another name. He was with a woman that night. Do you know the name of the woman he was with? She gave her number to the street officers on the scene." Lisa and I tried to peer over and read the reports on the inspector's lap. He didn't answer.

"We hear from two sources that the suspect is from San Jose," I offered.

The investigator responded with a loud laugh. "Now listen, if you were going to buy some drugs and, say, maybe stab a kid to death, would you tell anyone where you were from?" I watched Lisa suddenly wilt as she recoiled from his uncensored words.

"You'd say San Jose to throw someone off, not because it's where you actually lived." His laughter spiraled into a scoff while he continued shaking his head.

At my request, the jovial one followed me into the hallway to look at the drawing we'd produced from the description by the Brazilian man. I wanted him to view it out of Lisa's sight.

"Please take it. It's valid information, the witness was good." I handed him the sketch wrapped in paper to carry it, but he thanked me and laid it back on the hall table.

"You ladies call us anytime," he said, making no note of Jay in the room. "If there's ever anything more we can do—*girls*—you have our numbers." They nodded good-bye as they walked out the door.

"Yeah, right," Mac grunted. "And I dug out my pearls for this? They never even touched the crumpets." She kicked her shoes off as she plopped into a chair.

"Yes, but there is an accountability now," I said. "They met us and listened to us. Now we have a right to call them. And we have faces to go with their names. It wasn't a waste, Mac. They had to look us in the eye."

I looked over at Lisa standing at the window, her back to the room. The afternoon sun created a halo around her jet-black, perfectly styled hair. She stood staring out at the cathedral, her shoulders shaking gently as she silently cried.

Jay and I waited until late at night. We went to the low-income building where the Vietnam vet was reported to live and waited for him in the darkness. Through the shadows on the steep San Francisco street, we watched Dan laboriously powering his wheelchair with his massive arms, his head down as he entered the orange glow in the cinder-block entrance.

"Dan?" I asked, speaking softly and moving slowly, walking far out to his side to give him a chance to see me first from a distance and to allow him to feel that he could access his entrance safely. I stopped and held my hands out with palms up, moving into the light so he could see my face.

"Who are you?" he asked as Jay walked up near me.

"My name is Jeanne." I walked forward and squatted beside him. "I need your help. May I talk to you?" His glance was brief and he kept his head low while I explained that I meant him no harm. When he learned that our efforts were for Lisa, not for the police, he led us up to his tiny apartment on the second floor.

The only light inside came from a meticulously maintained fish tank that sat at his eye level. The rest of the room was in shambles. The living-room pane of glass was missing, and the water-stained drapes wavered with the inflow of cold, damp night air.

Dan was in Vietnam at the same time as my older brother, Tommy, 1966 through 1968, and also like my brother, he'd been the lone survivor when his entire platoon had been killed before his eyes. Dan had been left paralyzed. He began drinking first to ease the emotional pain and later to dismiss the memories of the death he'd witnessed all around him, which he'd almost accomplished until the night of March 27, when a twenty-three-year-old hero collapsed at his feet. The sight of Justin dying in front of him cast him back into his own private pain.

We talked for over two hours. It was clear that he wanted to help, but the truth was, he had never looked up—not on March 27—not ever. To watch people look at him would force him to see what he was, and that was a mirror he couldn't face, so he'd grown accustomed to keeping his head tilted down and to hiding inside his disgrace.

I looked over at Jay. It was time to move on. I reached over and put my palm over Dan's strong, dusty hand and clutched it tightly. "Can I tell you something?"

He didn't answer. The entire time I'd spent talking with him, I was struck by the strength of his features. Under the street dirt and beneath the matted hair and disheveled clothes, he had a beautiful, masculine face.

"I just want to tell you that I think you are a strikingly handsome man."

At first he held still and I was afraid I'd been out of place. He turned his face upward and toward me.

"Really? Do you think so?" I was sure he'd heard it many times—before Vietnam. "Thank you." He paused. "Very much." He smiled, his neck and shoulders held upright for the first time.

As Jay walked ahead of me through the dark apartment, a path of light suddenly flooded into the room through a brusquely opened bedroom door. Behind it stood a man, thin, haggard, a junkie, and stark naked.

"Are you gettin' the fuck in here, or what?" he yelled at Dan. I looked back. Dan's shoulders suddenly slumped again, and his head fell downward as we walked out and closed the front door.

The next day brought welcomed news: MacKenzie had a solid lead on Chicago's whereabouts. He was living in a halfway house in the Tenderloin district. Given the area's abundance of strip clubs, Jay would be of no use to me at all and I'd need cover. I opted for the company of a five-foot-tall, fifty-year-old woman instead.

"I told you, Mac, you need to be softer. You look like you're here to make an arrest." I talked with my lips pressed together as we crossed the sparsely decorated lobby and approached the bulletproof glass of the reception desk. "You could get us in big trouble."

"That's only because of you," she mumbled. "Jesus, I'm walking around with Miss Goddamned Georgia. You're the one that's gonna get us killed. Did you bring your baton? You can fucking twirl us out of it."

I stepped on her toes so she'd keep her mouth shut while I talked through the slot in the glass. Mac was not especially skilled at endearing herself to strangers, and we needed all the help we could get.

The graffiti on the outside walls may have been a forewarning about the interior, but it didn't do the place justice. Rooms ran $100 a month with a maximum stay of thirty days. If Chicago had slept here on March 27, those rules would have moved him out by now. The trail was not de-icing.

Used to dead ends, we braced for disappointment, but the clerk looked at us suspiciously, then haltingly handed us the room number and discreetly nodded toward the elevator.

When the steel cage bounced to a stop, I cranked the wire grate open and stepped out ahead of Mac. The stench of urine in the narrow hallways made it tough to inhale.

"Mac, this is it!" I whispered—Room 412. The door was cracked open. She tucked in under my arm to peek in, and our hearts surely pounded as one. We'd *finally* found Chicago.

"What are you doin'?" a loud, quick voice barked out from behind us.

We jumped back, stumbling over each other and bumping into the wall. A man in a ripped Deadhead T-shirt walked down the dank hall behind us, but kept on going past. Even Mac had been scared. The noise had been enough to stir Chicago from his slumber, and he groaned as he began to wake up.

Mac pushed the door open and in her most delicate style screamed, "Hey, Chicago!"

I threw my arm across the front of her shoulders and shoved her back out into the hall.

"Jesus, MacKenzie, don't give the man a heart attack!"

"Excuse me, Mr. Mitchell?" I asked softly. Chicago was a vet and I'd learned enough from my brother to understand that waking him suddenly could startle him into an instant defense.

He was asleep on a single mattress just inside the door of the tiny room, the plain white sheet pulled up to his waist. Chicago's back was a mosaic of open lesions. On the sheet under him was an imprint of blood, exposed when he'd turned toward the wall. Flung partially over his legs was a tattered Mexican blanket. Used syringes poked through the old woven fabric. MacKenzie turned in disgust and walked back outside the door.

"Mr. Mitchell?" I took a step closer.

His head rose up. He peered through swollen eyelids and seemed to scan the room around him. Suddenly he threw off his top sheet and jumped to his feet.

"My television! Where's my fuckin' television? Who the fuck took my goddamned television?" He flew right past me and out into the hall, then came back in and began slamming the old drawers of his dresser as if he might find it inside them.

"Damn it to hell!" He sat down among the bare needles and lit up a cigarette. "And who the hell are you?" He began to slide into the jeans that were lying crumpled on the floor.

"Oh my God!" I gasped, still braced against the wall in disbelief. He's not blind? Chicago's not blind? My mind reeled between questions and possibilities. We'd just struck gold—and in more ways than one.

On his bedroom wall was one of the posters that Andrea had tacked

on lampposts the day after Justin was killed. It had been refolded so
often that the folds were worn thin, and it had been taped and retaped
to his wall. The spots from the multiple tapings gave evidence of his
routine. Why would he do that?

Above the poster were words in red crayon, two inches high, written
so neatly as to seem almost stenciled: "Number one thing to accomplish
in my life," apparently referring to the search for Justin's killer. An arrow
angled toward the photo of Justin's face.

"Get your ass the fuck out of the hallway, lady," he slurred to Mac.
"Jesus, you look like a goddamned cop. You'll get fuckin' shot out there."
MacKenzie reluctantly walked inside and pushed the door partially
closed. I rolled my jacket around my bare arms and sat down on the
edge of the bed to speak to him at his eye level.

Justin died trying to help him, and now this man was desperate for a
way to repay him. He'd seen Lisa Dahl on his television pleading for
anyone to come forward with information about her son's death.
Chicago had waited for the police to contact him again after the first
night, but they never did. He told us about the woman who'd been with
him, then gave us a first name and a cross street where she lived.

"Shit, I walked over and handed her to the goddamned cops that night,"
he ranted. "She was talking to the guy, you know. She saw him like I did,
right there. Man, she was standing there fuckin' talking to the guy."

"Talk to me now, Chicago." I watched him glance suspiciously at
MacKenzie. "It's all right. Really, she's cool. She's working for Justin's
mom, too. We gotta find this guy. We can't do it without you, Chicago."

Would he be able to help us? Was he lucid when he saw the killer's
face? Finding out would take more than one day. Chicago was coherent
for only twenty-minute spans after waking, after which he'd get fidgety
the way a smoker gets when he can't find a place to light up—but
Chicago needed heroin, not nicotine, and once the urge hit, we'd lose
him. He'd have to go work his "shift," and we'd be out of touch until the
following day.

We conformed to his schedule, hoping he might have the will to stick
with us as we searched for the details we needed from him, and hoping
that in response to our respect, he would entrust us with his story.

John Mitchell got into drugs right after the war and blamed them for destroying his marriage, ruining his relationship with his two children, and leading to the loss of his job. His tenure on skid row was long, not unlike his record with the police. He was so ashamed of his life that he had made sure his children believed he was dead. He didn't want them seeking him out; he didn't want them to learn what he'd become.

He spent most of his waking hours in a prime spot in the busiest section of the Haight. Over time, he had managed to get the four-to-midnight "swing shift" hours—the most lucrative time slot in the area's drug trade.

From his post, he sold repackaged portions of herbs that he purchased in local Asian food stores, which he carried around in the backpack Justin Jones lost his life trying to save.

His white cane signaled safety to passersby, and as a result they'd come closer to the "blind man" than to others on the strip. This let him safely size up their potential before making his offer. After each cash transaction, he'd turn over the "drugs" with confidence that their consumption would occur far enough away to protect him from retaliation.

Chicago held a belief—a sincere belief—that by selling fake contraband, he was sparing others from taking real drugs and therefore sparing them a life like his had become.

In his own skewed reality, Chicago had a doctrine. He paid his rent and for his food, and with any extra money, every month, he bought toys for the children of the prostitutes on the block where he lived, an effort to make amends for the gifts he was unable to provide for his own children. In his own way, Chicago was a good and noble man.

For three consecutive days, McKenzie and I returned to the urine-stained hallways that led to the dismal room, trying to piece together through the series of twenty-minute installments a recollection of what he'd seen. In between visits, we tracked other leads. We found the girl who'd been with Chicago on March 27, but she demanded money for her cooperation, and I lost trust in her input. Her motives were tainted by her greed, and I was concerned that what she'd provide couldn't be deemed reliable. Chicago was invested only in the outcome. His devotion to the task was as high as his habit allowed.

Memory lies at the bottom of emotion. I didn't really need to hear about his children and his brother and his regrets about his life, but he needed to tell the story, and most of all, he needed someone to listen. When he had emotionally unloaded and our trust was built, we were gradually able to reach the image of the killer's face.

The blind man became our primary eyewitness.

No thanks to Mac. I needed her as cover, but in every other way she was a distraction. She refused to sit down, insisting that she remain on her feet, standing in the doorway that she couldn't bear to have closed behind her. Every time I'd glance in her direction, she'd grab her hair in two fists as if to pull it out, or else she'd crank her hands wildly and point at her watch, my cue to "speed it up." She was the dearest thing I ever wanted to slap.

In all, we found forty-two people who had been in the Haight the night of March 27. Seven had seen the suspect well enough to provide a description.

The police report was wrong: There had been witnesses after all. And all of them, especially Chicago, were "credible."

A ngela Alioto was the only angel we encountered in the system. Head of the San Francisco Board of Supervisors and daughter of the city's famous longtime mayor, she was also planning to toss her hat into the upcoming mayoral election, so she packed plenty of punch when she spoke.

We knew from our effort to give the police our first drawing that the likelihood was high that they'd just file this new image away—if they even accepted it at all. That left us no choice but to call our own news conference. Over dinner together in Marin, Angela agreed to help.

I called in my media contacts. Angela faxed her own media list to my hotel room, and she helped us out further by letting us use a pressroom at City Hall. We faxed a special invitation to the SFPD inspectors, hoping, though not expecting, they would attend.

We knew we had only a single chance: we'd make the top of the news, but only once. When the image went out to the public, we needed to know that incoming tips would be logged in and acted on. Yet we'd received no follow-up on any of our test tips to the PD, either before or after our meeting with the police. So, we hired our own answering service and briefed the operators on our purpose. Most were mothers themselves, and they jumped at the chance to help, assuring us that every call would be answered and every caller listened to.

My two days' of clothing had long since worn thin. I called Nordstrom's personal shoppers and asked for a suit—black, button-up, conservative, size eight—to be delivered to the Fairmont by nine A.M. That taken care of, Jay, Andrea, Michael, and I drove to an all-night Kinko's print shop in Marin County. By morning, we had managed to get the image onto a thousand media-ready flyers.

I packaged the stacks of paper and drove back to San Francisco for the early-morning preparations. There was still time for one hour's sleep, but when I lay down, my eyes refused to close.

Monday, April 18, in San Francisco's City Hall, the media gathered for the release of the sketch. The *San Francisco Chronicle,* the *Examiner,* Fox, CBS, NBC, ABC's *Prime Time Live,* the *San Jose Mercury News*—all major news agencies turned out.

Lisa and I stood nervously in the back room, waiting for MacKenzie's late arrival. We decided that Andrea and Jay would sit in the gallery. Lisa, Mac, and I would sit behind the long wooden councillors' dais, from where we'd field reporters' questions. Angela would make introductions.

The last person through the door was Mac—in a dress. Walking in behind her was a sight we'd not expected—the reluctant inspector nodded hello to Angela as he made his way to the end of the panel.

At ten o'clock sharp, Angela spoke briefly, then turned to have me present the image of the suspect to the media. I stepped forward and talked into the mass of microphones.

"The San Francisco police have been wonderful in providing us with all of the information we've needed," I began. Lisa kicked me under the table, knowing I was having to lie. But we wanted to help them by giving them the face we'd found, not to call attention to their failings. Diplomacy was on the top of our list.

"I'd like to introduce the drawing," I continued while cameras rolled. "As you can see, the suspect is in his early twenties, with—"

"Excuse me, excuse me, Ms. Boylan!" It was the KCBS reporter

During twenty-minute interviews between heroin-induced sleeps, the main witness provided the description for the sketch that focused the search for the murderer of Justin Jones. (Drawing by Jeanne Boylan)

who'd been at every Petaluma press conference. I remembered the sparse strands of blond hair artfully arranged over his balding head.

I knew what he was up to: he wanted to publicly question the lack of police involvement. I wondered how strongly I could beg him to be quiet with a simple look in my eye, but it was no use.

"How many witnesses did you actually interview, Ms. Boylan?" he asked deliberately.

I couldn't have a face-off with the SFPD—not here.

"Several," I answered quickly, "and as you can see by the drawing—" I turned my body away from him and toward the sketch, hoping that he'd take the cue.

"Excuse me, excuse me, Inspector." The reporter redirected his attention toward the white-haired inspector, whose chair was separated from ours by the most distance the space would allow, his arms crossed and his body leaning toward the exit.

"How many of these witnesses did *you* interview?"

"None of them," the inspector said. Then he sat up and spoke with force. "These witnesses were only available weekends—and we don't work weekends."

An audible gasp suddenly filled the room and bodies shifted uncomfortably. Eyes darted around, sizing up the reactions of others, making sure they'd all heard the man right.

Angela bolted from her chair, grabbed the drawing out of my hands, and shouted in a piercing tone into the otherwise stone-silent chamber, "I don't care who did what! We're not here to discuss the past. We're here to discuss who murdered this woman's son." She flailed her arms in the air and pointed at Lisa, who was sliding even farther down in her seat, tears streaming down her pale cheeks from the finality of the words.

As the press conference concluded, the television cameras locked onto the drawing displayed on the pressroom wall, while newspaper reporters took copies from the pile.

Still numb from the outburst and the inspector's shocking words, we stood and walked out single file. Mac hurried off to change out of her dress.

Angela led Lisa and me to her ornate back office, connected by a back hallway to the meeting room. Exhausted, we collapsed into two desk chairs, surrounded by the gilded features and heavy red velvet draperies that hung from iron rods near the high ceiling of her chambers. Without saying a word to us, Angela picked up a black and gold antique phone receiver and dialed the chief of police.

"Hey, this is Angela. Who is this goddamned son of a bitch you sent over here?" Her voice filled every inch of the room, if not the hallway. "He was an embarrassment to me, an embarrassment to this city, and what in the f—" She stopped when she looked at Lisa, now almost under the chair in pain. "I'll call you back." She slammed the museum piece back into its cradle.

"Just . . . just stay here," she ordered, waving her arms in the air as she stormed out of the room.

I reached over and took Lisa's hand. We were emotionally wrung dry. Five minutes of silence would seem like a tonic.

Within moments, a uniformed police commander came in and took a seat, apparently on orders from Angela. He was small and fit and exuded all the warmth that the reluctant Schwarzenegger did not.

"I'll tell you what's going on here," he whispered, leaning forward from Angela's chair. He glanced at each of the connecting doors.

He took a deep breath while I squeezed Lisa's hand, then he further lowered his voice to carefully avoid being overheard. "The investigators who were assigned to this case have been the top producers of overtime in this city for a lot of years."

In a calm, soothing voice he continued, "Over the past few months, they've had their overtime cut. That's why they're not going out of their way on your case—because they're using it as a political forum to protest having had their overtime cut. The publicity you've brought them, unbeknownst to you, has only aided in their cause."

I fell back into my chair, stunned. We had gone through all this for their political agenda? Despite risking our necks, despite the danger, the time, the frustration, and the expense, they didn't want to solve our case because they wanted to win some kind of labor dispute? And a killer was being allowed to run loose so they could make a point?

My temples pulsed with anger. I looked over at Lisa, now crying unabashedly with her head buried in her pale hands. It would take time for the magnitude of what we'd just heard to settle in—if it ever would.

I'd checked out of the corner room at the Fairmont before the press conference and left my bags at the front desk to pick up later. But the hotel generously offered us a temporary suite high on the twelfth floor so Lisa, Jay, Andrea, and I could at least watch together and in privacy the news coverage at the top of the five o'clock broadcasts.

Lead story, every channel. The drawing looked good. We'd done it. The face was at least being seen. We flicked the television off and sat still for a moment in silence. The good-byes weren't going to be easy. We stood up and huddled in a mass in the quiet room, our arms around each other. Now all we could do was hope—and pray.

Justin Wesley Jones died a hero. His mother was also a hero—to me and everyone who witnessed her reach through her pain to make a difference in his memory. I watched the others walk to the end of the long hallway and disappear around the corner, then went back inside the room and closed the door.

I waited alone for the front-desk clerk to notify me that my airport taxi had arrived. The sun was setting over Grace Cathedral and the city was bathed in a warm peach glow that masked the harsh realities of the underworld we'd encountered, the world in which Justin Jones had lost his life.

I pulled back the sheer white drapery to watch the changing light. Far below, I saw my three comrades crossing California Street and heading west. The long shadows of the sunset stretched across the pavement behind them. Jay and Andrea wrapped their arms around Lisa's shoulders, supporting the weight of her exhausted, frail body while her feet only brushed the surface of the ground.

Cars sped by them, radios played, people walked briskly past on their way home from just another ordinary day's work—life in the city went on.

I looked at the trio and knew that, no matter the outcome of the case, they could finally go home now and rest, knowing that for Justin, they'd done everything that could have been done.

Robert was out of town on a trip to see old clients all the while I'd been gone. I picked Dillon up at the kennel and opened up the house, stepping back into my other life.

Lisa called daily with updates. Our 800 operators were deluged, handling calls and compiling lists of names and numbers, which we filtered through Angela to be certain of follow-up.

Weeks passed, hopes rose and fell, but at last, on a Tuesday, we had a solid tip: the suspect, the informant said, was from San Jose.

Angela helped us make sure this tip didn't slip through the cracks. We forwarded the information to the San Jose Police Department, which then promptly pulled the suspect's mug shot from their files. The answer was clear. By Friday, San Jose PD had notified SFPD, which then joined them in pursuit. By Friday afternoon, an arrest was made. With the sketch as evidence, twenty-one-year-old Jose Avina confessed to the March 27 murder of Justin Wesley Jones.

San Francisco police called a press conference to announce the arrest in the Good Samaritan Murder. Every station covered the story.

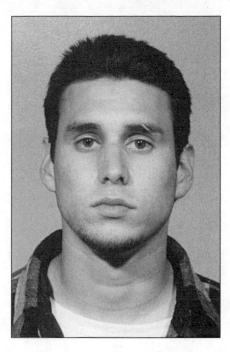

Twenty-one-year-old Jose Avina is arrested for the stabbing death of Justin Wesley Jones in the Good Samaritan Murder, San Francisco, May 1994. (Photo courtesy of State of California Corrections Division)

"Excuse me, excuse me." The same relentless KCBS reporter was punching his arm up through the crowd. The same inspector took his question.

"So, Inspector," the reporter said slowly, knowing the story behind the story, the one that city politics would assure would never make front-page news, "how much did the resolution of this case have to do with the involvement of Lisa Dahl and Jeanne Boylan?"

The inspector looked past the reporter and into the camera as if talking not to the reporter, but directly to the two of us. "It had nothing at all to do with it," he said slowly. "It was good old-fashioned police work. We just knew which rock to look under."

9

A MATTER OF PERSPECTIVE

In every investigation, the end always takes its time. Lisa Dahl last saw her son on Easter Sunday, 1994. Five weeks later, the confession of twenty-one-year-old Jose Avina to Justin Jones's murder cranked into motion a long trial process that, if all went well, would someday lead to justice. The news came first from Angela Alioto, then from Lisa. I flew back to San Francisco for the arraignment.

That SFPD jumped to take credit for the capture was worth little more than a shake of the head. They were now beside the point: Justin's murderer was behind bars.

Lisa, Andrea, Jay, Michael, Mac, and I hung on to each other waiting to look him in the eye, but we weren't allowed the luxury. Instead, Justin's shackled killer walked past us in the courtroom and never looked up.

In the thousands of faces I've formed on paper, the only universal feature has been my signature buried somewhere in the graphite lines. There is no other common thread. Eyes are not always an eye's width apart, and the corner of the iris does not always align with the outside corner of the mouth. There simply is no art school "formula" for human anatomy. Faces are as varied as are rocks in a quarry, even within the same race.

So what does the face of a killer look like? This one was only Justin's age, wide-eyed and youthful, and with an almost mocking look of innocence. He was one of many siblings, each with a long history of crime.

On the night he murdered Justin, Avina's weapon of choice had been a sharpened wood chisel—for good reason. Avina had a record that included weapons possession and robbery, but he also had big brothers who'd taught him how to dodge the system. He knew that a released prisoner would have his parole revoked if caught with a weapon. But a wood chisel was defined as a tool, and a tool was legal to carry, even though, when sharpened, it could be as deadly as any knife. It was a legal and lethal catch-22 that could spare a killer from the harshest sentence.

Jose Avina knew the street rules and was thinking ahead—his graduation to murder had been only a matter of time. His mother sat alone across the room and quietly cried.

I leaned forward to study his face more closely. A dark-skinned Brazilian boy had described him as "light," but light in relation to what? A Caucasian had described him as dark-skinned, but dark in relation to what? An Asian described him as Asian, relating most strongly his own sense of self.

Every witness had, in fact, been correct in his or her own perception. Their different words reflected only their different points of view.

By steering free of any bias as to how one's ethnicity "should" look, we created each of their drawings as a compilation of only the forms, textures, shapes, and tones that each witness actually saw.

When releasing any drawing to the press, I intentionally omit an ethnic assignment. To have called this suspect Latino or Mexican or Asian would have required that I accept only one perspective or stand behind the eyes of only one witness. By avoiding any ethnic designation, every person who then views a drawing can perceive the suspect's face through his or her own set of filters and experiences, without any assigned labels to suggest what they *should* be seeing.

It's through the shapes, not the labels, that the real answers surface. Each time a police description designates the suspect's ethnicity, the first question to be asked must always be "But, according to whom?"

Jose Avina's trial was set for the fall. Chicago would be called to testify. But would he come through for us again? The blind man had led us to the killer, not with his eyes but with his heart. Something told me he'd be there.

When the snow melted in Bend in late April, the grass underneath was a winterized mess. When we purchased the log house, Robert penned a contract stipulating that I'd do every bit of the yard work. I actually signed it, assuming he was only kidding. I was wrong. Yet the yard ended up becoming a refuge for my soul. I loved every fingernail-wrecking moment of the time I spent outside. I'd just gotten the spring plants put in the gardens when a summons came to go back to court. It was time to face another killer.

Five months after the December 4, 1993, confession of Richard Allen Davis to the murder of Polly Klaas, the preliminary hearing was set to take place. Petaluma district attorney Greg Jacobs would be the prosecutor. Kate and Gillian were his star witnesses. Jacobs agreed to let them each be accompanied on the witness stand by one adult of their own choice. The phone rang twice that day with not one request but two.

I drove to California on May 10, checked into a Santa Rosa hotel for the night, then met Kate and Gillian at the Sonoma County courthouse the next morning. Captain Parks secretly ushered us past the onslaught of reporters, through the back door, and down hallways toward the back room where we'd wait.

Polly's mother testified first. She returned silent, weakened, and pale, then moved mechanically toward a chair, using her thin arms to brace herself as she slowly collapsed into her seat. No one dared ask her feelings. She wore them on her weary face.

The prosecutor called the kids next. Kate was first up. We stopped within feet of Davis. She raised her right hand and swore to tell the truth while I kept an arm around her shoulder, using my body as her shield from his gaze. When we took our seats, she gripped my hand below the beveled wooden ledge.

"Can you look around the courtroom and point to the man who took Polly from her bedroom?" Jacobs asked her softly.

Violet and Polly's grandparents sat clutching each other in the dark seats of the courtroom.

"Yes, he's here. He's that man right there," Kate answered firmly. Unknowingly, she tightened her grip.

The first written description of him as a six-foot-three-inch "monster" had impregnated even my own preconception, but Davis was surprisingly small. The tattoos on his thick arms crawled out like snakes from under the short sleeves of an untucked yellow shirt, and the cuffs of his gray slacks landed high on his short, hairy legs. He hid behind oversized glasses with heavy black frames. I watched his hands writhe in rings around one another as Kate spoke, the same thick hands that he'd used to steal the life from a twelve-year-old child.

Next it was Gillian's turn. All her giddiness was erased, as if she had evolved into an adult overnight. Her voice was strong and decisive. When asked to point out Polly's killer, she didn't flinch.

I couldn't take my eyes off Davis. I knew every angle of his face. I expected to feel hatred, maybe even needed to. But instead, I found myself feeling only pity. My lack of antipathy shocked me and I tried hard to will it away. But it was as out of my nature to hate as it was within his nature to kill.

T he work to capture Davis and Avina had yielded results, and both murderers were now behind bars. I kept glancing in the rearview mirror as I drove home, watching a once prevailing part of me fade. Every mile seemed like a hundred, each one distancing me further from the past.

By the time I got back, the ski crowd would finally have stowed their gear for the season, at least so I hoped.

Our time had finally arrived. Robert and I could focus completely on our life, our home, our family, and our future. This time, no one would take this away.

I turned my wheels in from the country road and slowed the car on the gravel driveway. Robert was standing on the porch holding Dillon back by the collar. I snapped off the stereo. Something was wrong. I could see it in the slump of his shoulders and in his narrowed eyes. I left the car door swinging open and rushed up the walkway toward the house.

I reached out to hug him, but he tensed, then turned his back.

"The business deal fell through," he said, leaning back against the massive logs of the front porch.

I reached toward him again, but again he pulled away. Over the past five years he'd been surrounded by those with money, a lot of it, and he craved the same wealth for himself. The business he'd planned to buy was his way of buying the social status that his sales position had never allowed him. He didn't want to cater to businesspeople, he wanted to be one. The deal was officially dead, and the loose ends suddenly seemed to be knotting around his neck.

For me, the order was reversed. My career had never been about making money. I'd get by, but I'd sometimes nearly forget to send a bill when I got home. Where someone was hurt, missing, or murdered, I'd go. If the call came from an investigative task force, I'd charge my full fee, but if a family called, I'd charge next to nothing. If there was no money for expenses, we'd find a way. Together, we'd search for discount airline tickets, organize garage sales, appeal for help from victims' groups and foundations—whatever it took to break even.

The media, however, was relentless in its determination to delve into the financial end of things. The inevitable question at every news conference was always "So, Ms. Boylan, how much were you paid?" I always avoided the question, never withholding because the amount was so much, but more often because it was so little.

In light of the clash between Robert's high taste and his new lack of income, our picture had to change. I now had to make money a priority or watch him self-destruct from the pressure.

In a twist of fate that I could never have imagined, I began to hope for the phone to ring.

In late June, the television program *Unsolved Mysteries* called, wanting to feature a profile on my career. After waiting for the right case, they'd found a five-month-old unresolved murder they wanted me to work as the foundation for the piece. Once they settled on the details, the producer called again, asking me to fly immediately to meet their crew in New Mexico.

The honor came with a needed paycheck, but I'd be in front of the cameras again, and not just speaking at another press conference. This time, I'd be the center of the story, resulting in more visibility for me and for the career I thought I'd finally managed to leave behind.

It was the wrong time to step back into a spotlight when Robert now had none, but I had to take it. His worries had begun to manifest in his behavior and he was scaring me. Even Dillon would cower under the table when he raised his voice. His temper was escalating. The pressure he was under would either kill him or it would kill me.

I boarded a flight to Albuquerque and checked into a spacious room at the famous old La Posada Hotel.

I f I thought my heart couldn't break again, I was wrong. Sixteen-year-old Jonathan Francia was a great kid. Six months earlier, in January 1994, he'd driven a friend to an Albuquerque Denny's to pick up a paycheck while he waited with his engine idling in the parking lot.

At the same time, two renegades on a bus trip to Flagstaff were booted off midhighway by a driver who'd run out of patience. Not about to let an eviction interrupt their trip, they jumped down the freeway embankment in search of a car to steal. Jonathan's engine was already running. Instead of just taking his car, they drove away with the boy still inside.

That night, before reaching "Flag," they needed to rid themselves of their passenger. They pulled over, stabbed Jonathan, threw his body into the trunk, then drove on to the city, where they stopped at a girlfriend's house to shower the caked blood off their hands.

Later that night, the three took the car out again, but heard a thud as they drove down the road. Jonathan was still alive. They pulled his wounded body back out, and this time, with the girlfriend's help, they cut him open from neck to groin, filled his body cavity with gasoline, and returned him to the trunk. While searching for a place to dump the

car, they became stuck in a ditch. Two Indian men working on a construction site nearby towed the car out with a pickup truck for a $5 pay-
ment. The suspects drove away, then later set the car on fire in the
remote mountains outside the city. Jonathan's body was incinerated
inside the trunk of his own car.

One of the killers was quickly captured after using stolen credit
cards, and subsequently hung himself in jail. The girlfriend was awaiting
trial and not speaking to the authorities, but the second man was still
running free. The FBI needed the face of the missing killer on paper to
spearhead the regional manhunt.

While taping in the Francia home, I sat on the floor in the hallway
with Jonathan's father as the *Unsolved* producer interviewed Jonathan's
mother in the living room. I dialed Marc Klaas's number, got him on the
phone and asked him to help console Jonathan's dad. Marc understood
his loss all too well and was always there to comfort a parent who'd lost
a child in so brutal a way. I also called because I knew his counsel was
another way for him to heal.

While waiting, I watched Mrs. Francia sitting in front of the television camera, pleading for someone out there watching to come forward
and help. She choked on deep, pained breaths between her labored sentences.

Her sixteen-year-old son would never come home again, and the
chances of finding the man who'd killed him were slim at best. The only
identified witness had a highly contaminated memory. Again, baseless
early sketches had been haphazardly prepared, and the most valuable
time in the investigation had long since passed. There were dwindling
leads and fading public interest, and the odds for success were at rock
bottom.

Same scenario, same old mistakes—different family. Would law
enforcement ever wake up to what it was they so routinely did to the
fragile and crucial eyewitness memory of a suspect's face? And would
they ever understand the emotional complexity of the mind, of why and
how memory works, or would they simply stay entrenched in their insistence on doing things the way they'd always been done?

If so, this same scene would play out again and again, just a different
town, a different year, a different mother pleading for help without ever

knowing how much more could have been done had the early investigation gone just a little differently.

After the meeting with Jonathan's parents, I asked *Unsolved Mysteries* and Albuquerque FBI agent John Shum to set up two more last-resort meetings for me in Flagstaff. The two Indian men who had helped pull the suspects out of a ditch on the day of the murder had early on been discounted as potential eyewitnesses by the police. According to the detectives, the men were "uneducated" and reportedly neither of them spoke English.

But that oversight was potentially the very break we needed. If they'd been overlooked as eyewitnesses, that meant their memories hadn't been tampered with. If they didn't speak English, we'd simply find an interpreter. And "uneducated" has nothing to do with an ability to observe. A four-year-old is capable of observation.

If anything, the discrepancy in the language between the witnesses and the suspects likely served to keep the two men even more on guard. In the absence of trauma in their sighting, it might just be the single factor that would allow them to remember details from so long ago. What was construed by police as a detriment could be our lucky break.

Agent Shum agreed and called a detective at the Flagstaff PD to locate the two.

"We can't pay you for this, but we'll pick up your expenses. Just hang on to your receipts. Oh, and Jeanne—good luck." The *Unsolved Mysteries* producer and crew left me in the airport lobby and flew back to L.A. with the footage they needed for their segment, letting me pursue this lead on my own.

When I sat down to interview the men in Flagstaff, they initially spoke in their native tongue, then stunned me when they broke into English—perfect English. They laughed as they explained that one held a master's degree from the University of Arizona. They'd only spoken their native language in front of an investigator six months earlier because they'd overheard him discussing his assumptions about their lifestyle and their level of education. They'd never let on that their English was flawless. By the end of our day, finally, we had a full, clear, and untainted drawing of the wanted man's face. Next would come the hunt for his identity.

I called the *Unsolved* producer with the news, and the next morning, after overnighting the new drawing to the studio in Los Angeles, I took a commuter flight to Phoenix with one last change of planes in San Francisco, so I could hurry back home to Bend.

I was worried about Robert, seriously worried to be away from him. His depression over the collapsed business deal had him on edge. Afraid of what he might do, I wondered if he might turn his anger inward.

But during the change of planes in San Francisco, I felt an unexpected tap on my shoulder, the tap that redirected me overnight to Salt Lake City in the hunt for the face of a bomber who held the whole country in terror.

This time the face the authorities were seeking already had a name: the Unabomber.

"**W**hy can't you just be *normal?*" The drone of the airplane engines didn't phase out the memory of Robert's angry voice. His words still echoed through my mind from the previous night's call in my Salt Lake City hotel room. Throughout my flight home, I'd searched for an answer. But maybe the problem rested in the question instead.

What exactly was "normal"? Better yet, what was "*ab*normal"? Was it really so out of line to care about creating change in an antiquated police system, or to help a grieving family, or to try to find a missing child?

It really all came down to definitions, to perspectives and points of view. I suddenly realized that I'd let Robert's single perception take root, to embed in my own thoughts and even skew my own beliefs. I'd been fighting for years to get away from this work, to be something else, some definition of "normal" that he wanted me to be. Yet, each time I reluctantly left on a case—thinking it was to help someone else—in fact, the reality was that the victims I met ended up helping *me*.

Adversity creates depth, stirs movement, and ignites passions—not just in the crime victims and their families, but in everyone touched by their traumas. These events can jar us from the anesthesia of daily living and the inertia that we construe as contentment.

Sometimes what arrives in the form of a tragedy becomes the very event that spawns growth and rekindles souls. No one I'd met who was connected to these cases ever remained unmoved—*no one*. We were all made better, stronger, wiser, more appreciative, more loving, more real.

I didn't need a Rolex or diamonds as proof of my prosperity. My wealth came in a much different form. By brushing close to death, I was learning to understand life. By dealing with hatred, I could begin to comprehend the immeasurable richness of love. My experiences might have taken time away from my home and my marriage—but they were leading me into my own authenticity.

I felt a blanket of calm and certainty sweep over me. There was, in fact, nothing for me to defend. I finally had the answer to my husband's question. But without having lived these experiences himself, would Robert ever be able to understand? Or would my realization only cause his eyes to clinch a little more tightly shut?

I'd soon know. I felt the plane begin its descent, and my spirit begin to lift.

10

WHEN KILLERS ROAM FREE

In summer 1994, the national media was obsessed with one case. O. J. Simpson had been the "life of the party," but the investigation revealed a well-hidden dark side that only his wife had known. Just after Simpson's wife, Nicole, and friend Ron Goldman were brutally murdered, I received an inquiry from the office of the initial lead attorney, Robert Shapiro, but oddly enough, O.J.'s defense team quickly lost interest in their search for the killer.

In the weeks following the famous low-speed Bronco chase, reports of domestic violence in America skyrocketed. It wasn't the number of incidents that increased, but rather the courage on the part of battered spouses to report them. I watched news footage of Nicole and O.J., walking together and holding hands, him gazing at her with so much pride. But how had they gone from that kind of affection to the drama of a murder trial? The same question scared a growing number of women to pledge that just one instance of domestic violence would be one too many.

The topic was timely. Robert's self-esteem had hit an all-time low, and his outbursts an all-time high. With my becoming the breadwinner, tensions further sharpened. I listened to Nicole's 911 call played over and over on the news, and inside her fear, I could hear echoes of my own.

In a move I didn't want to make, I packed up my things and moved temporarily into a friend's guesthouse in town.

The September 1994 issue of *McCall's* magazine, which hit the newsstands during the first week of August, included a six-page article on my work. Although it was built around the investigation of the Justin Jones murder, one California reader recognized her own plight between the lines.

Her twenty-three-year-old son had also been murdered. The killing occurred in Huntington Beach exactly one week after Justin lost his life. After quickly releasing a frontal sketch of a suspect, local police claimed there were no other witnesses, although the murder happened on the main street of a popular tourist town. The case mysteriously disappeared from the local news, quietly and unnoticed.

Huntington Beach is a tourist area in full swing by early April. At dusk, Alice Sommer's son Kenny and his best friend, Mo Blanchard, a twenty-three-year-old father of a three-year-old, had stopped to order pizza, then stepped outside into the warm early-evening air to wait for their order.

A man in a trench coat and a ponytail walked up to them from the opposite direction, pulled a gun from inside his jacket, and opened fire at close range. Mo Blanchard died instantly. Kenny Sommer fell to the pavement. When he tried to crawl away, the murderer emptied his gun into Kenny's body, then calmly walked away.

Two dead. The suspect still at large. No known motive.

Alice didn't have the means to finance a search, but that couldn't stop us. By telephone, we started planning car washes and searching for foundations that might help with funding our expenses.

In between calls to Huntington Beach, my phone rang with a call from New York. *The Rolanda Show* was planning an hour-long episode on unsolved murders. They invited me to appear as an expert panelist on eyewitness recall, and the producer asked if I knew of any unsolved cases they could profile during the program. So happens, I did.

Even in the wake of her tragedy, Alice's high energy won over the producers, who flew her to New York to appear with me on the set. Their
plan was to delay our introduction until we were on camera, but I knew
her immediately when she walked in the door of the Loews Hotel.

On the set the following morning, Alice was kept across the stage in
makeup. We feigned a first meeting on camera, though in actuality, we
already had our case strategy well mapped out. After hearing the story of
Kenny's murder, Rolanda bounded down the aisle and announced on-air
that the program would pick up all our investigative expenses. We'd
found our miracle.

Alice and I left the studio after taping the show and wandered down
Fifth Avenue until we came to the Gothic spires of St. Patrick's
Cathedral. I walked through the cool, echoing silence of the church to
light a single candle for her son Kenny. Then I lit a second candle for
Justin, and one each for Angie Houseman and Cassidy Senter in St.
Louis, then one for Polly Klaas, and another and another . . .

Soon, an entire row of candles burned, one flame for each young life
lost, all swaying in unison to the gentle breeze of the opened door, their
spirits free following the anguished turmoil of their final moments.

That afternoon, we flew straight to L.A. to launch the search. While
Rolanda's purpose was a gripping story for her show, the camera crew
helped, not just by taping our movements, but also by working as our
unofficial security detail. If we got shot knocking on the wrong door, at
least they'd have it on tape.

Our digging stirred things up in Huntington Beach, but it also stirred
the interest of city hall. Kenny was an athlete who worked out every day,
avoided drugs, and was engaged to be married. But at the time of his
death, his dark hair was clipped so short for surfing that he appeared
nearly bald. After his murder, it had been "implied" to the press that the
killings were likely gang-related. Authorities made no move to correct
the misperception.

Two unexplained main-street murders in a town that thrives on
tourism was a chamber of commerce nightmare. But if labeled "gang-
related," the public would quickly turn their backs. Though Kenny
wasn't a gang member, the media bought the line and dropped the story.

Alice had spent months with no response to her calls for help. She

Murder victim Kenny Sommer.
(Photo courtesy of Alice Sommer,
Kenny's mother)

wanted two things: to find the killer and, just as important, to clear her son's name. She was promised an opportunity to speak at a city council meeting, which aired on the local cable channel, but the meeting was adjourned abruptly before her introduction. She pushed her way to the podium anyway, grabbed the microphone, and pleaded for her promised chance to be heard, but as she started to speak, the transmission light on the camera suddenly went dark. Weeks earlier, she'd convinced the city council to offer a modest and routine reward, but the gesture was useless if she couldn't get the story out.

She tried to conduct a fund-raiser, but that required a permit issued by the same city council. Her request was turned down without explanation.

Then came new hope. Frank DiBella, the chief executive officer of Planet Hollywood, offered to put up a sizable reward, but to make the offer public, he needed the cooperation and endorsement of Orange County officials—the same officials who controlled the liquor license for his Newport Beach restaurant. His offer was suddenly withdrawn.

The witnesses we found were all long shots. None had been closer

Left: Alice Sommer, mother of murder victim Kenny Sommer, distributes flyers with the suspect drawing on Main Street of Hermosa Beach, in the exact spot where her oldest son was killed. (Photo: Collection of the author) Right: The flyer was headlined PLEASE HELP A MOM FIND HER SON'S MURDERER and had this sketch and the following text: Murder suspect: Late 20s, early 30s, 5'3"–5'7", square jawline and dark brows, small "tail" in hair, dark cap, knee-length dark coat. If you have information, call 909-730-2601. All tips kept confidential. (Drawing by Jeanne Boylan)

than thirty feet from the site where the boys went down, and despite the frontal depiction of the killer released early on by the police, none had ever seen the killer from a frontal view. But two women had witnessed enough to help create a detailed profile image, and with that we at least had a fresh hook to push the story back into the news.

After hunting through my Rolodex, I got a hold of all the L.A. media contacts I'd acquired through the Martin Ganz execution case and invited them—along with the case detectives—to join us for the unveiling. We set up a tip line through Alice's business number, then spent a sleepless night at Kinko's getting media materials ready for distribution. We rented easels, audio equipment, and a beachfront-hotel meeting room to stage the press conference.

The case was five months old, but the press showed up en masse, though even the most wishful among us knew that the trail had grown stone-cold. I leaned forward and watched Alice, flanked by her family, as she used her own voice, unleashed at last, to clear her oldest son's name. This time, the cameras kept rolling.

But the truth was that we were likely dealing with too little, too late. Yet, someone had to know who murdered her son. Maybe one person holding the tip, the key to who took the lives of two young men, would look into the eyes of Kenny's mother and have the courage and the heart to pick up a phone.

I set my bags in the hallway outside my hotel room but had to check my Oregon voice mail just one more time. There was one call I was hoping for, and it wasn't work-related.

"Jeanne, my name is Beth Mallarky, Chicago FBI. Would you please call me right back? We have an urgent situation, a child killing, and we now think we have a witness. We need you here right away."

My hopes fell as I realized that it wasn't the message I'd wished for. I slid my return ticket to Oregon into the suitcase pocket, along with a stack of other unused return tickets, assuming I'd be heading east to Chicago instead. I dialed Agent Mallarky's number, but was put straight through to the case lead agent in Wisconsin instead.

"A serial child killer is loose in the three-state area that includes Illinois, Minnesota, and Wisconsin," he explained. "We think he has been operative for six years. The most recent victim appears to be a twelve-year-old girl who'd been out riding her bicycle."

Cora Jean Jones was kidnapped September 5 and found murdered five days later. When the scenario matched the serial profile, the FBI sent agents from the Serial Killer Unit to Waupaca, Wisconsin, to aid the local jurisdiction. On their arrival they learned of a woman who had survived a July 3 attack that strongly resembled the killer's MO in the Cora Jones case.

The difference was that the July 3 victim escaped alive and had a memory of the face of the man who'd tried to abduct her. The break in

the case was the first in six years. Two composites had been done from
the July 3 incident, but the living victim contested both, claiming neither resembled the face of her attempted kidnapper.

"Can you fly out here immediately?" the agent pleaded.

The South Chicago FBI field office sent a verifiable right-brainer
to pick me up at O'Hare. Beth Mallarky was a full-fledged agent
with none of the markings. Tall, pretty, and funny, when she'd tested for
entry to the FBI, they'd asked, "You want the good news or the bad
news? The bad news is you don't remotely fit our hiring criteria. The
good news is, we have need for people exactly like you. You're hired."

"We've got a live one for you," she said, laughing, as she backed out of
the tight spot in the airport parking garage. "We know you can draw, but
how great are your diplomatic abilities?" Mallarky pulled the blue Ford
van to a stop in line at the tollbooth.

"Why, what's this—another political bomb?" I asked. So many cases
revolved far more around politics, egos, and interagency wars than
around the crimes themselves.

"Oh, God, don't use that word *bomb* around here, you're in Chicago,
you know." Beth was also associated with the Unabom Task Force,
which took up a major section of the FBI's downtown Chicago office.

"No, no catfights, but we have a hostile witness. She told us what
happened to her in July and she is done with us. I mean, really done.
She does not want to be here or anywhere near anyone who even looks
like a federal agent. Sorry to do this to you, but you better pull out all
your charm to get through this one. This kid's tough."

As we darted through traffic, Mallarky juggled lane changes with the
somber business of the murdered child.

Three months earlier, the Chicago woman in her early twenties had
been with her family at their vacation home in the Wisconsin Lake
Country. Over the Independence Day holiday, she'd been out bicycling,
unaware that a killer roamed the Midwest roads in search of female
cyclists with whom he would intentionally collide, knocking the young rid-
ers to the ground and then kidnapping them from their position of weak-
ness. Once in his control, the endings were uniformly brutal.

Our eyewitness didn't fit the killer's usual criteria. Though youthful in appearance, with a long ponytail and not a hint of makeup, she was a decade older than his taste and strongly self-assured. When her ride through the rolling countryside was interrupted by a stranger who waved a map and asked for directions, she saw through his ruse and grumbled at him to leave her alone, then pedaled past him up the hill.

Just beyond the crest, the road dipped before the next hill. Her stalker's full-size car caught up, slamming her bike hard enough to send her flying thirty feet into a ravine. At the same time, an older man driving a van approached from behind, screeching to a halt at the "accident" site.

The attacker, obsessed by now with his prey, was unaware of the van and its driver, by then stopped only feet away. With his left leg wedged out of the driver's door, he steadied himself by keeping one hand on the steering wheel. With the other, he stuck his gun between the open door and the windshield and pointed it at the injured girl on the ground in front of him.

The van driver had thought the hit an accident, but when he saw the gun, he threw his transmission into gear and sped off. The suspect, realizing that he'd just been seen, jumped back inside his car and spun up gravel from the road's shoulder as he backed up onto the paved road and tore away.

No correlation was drawn between the July 3 attack and the previous murders until Labor Day weekend, when twelve-year-old Cora Jean Jones was kidnapped within a mile of the Chicago woman's encounter.

Cora was visiting her grandmother in a tiny village outside of Waupaca. Throughout Wisconsin, parents were afraid to leave their children alone even for moments, but the pastoral setting of the grandmother's rural house seemed far from danger. Cora left for a short ride. Her mangled bicycle was later found in the middle of a quiet road, only minutes away from her starting point. Hundreds of volunteers turned out to comb the area. The media plastered the news with her face, framed by long dark hair and a blunt cut of thick bangs. But no one found a trace of the twelve-year-old until September 10, when two deer hunters stumbled across her body posed in a ditch along a woodland road near the small town of Kempster, seventy-five miles from where her bike was found.

Cora had been sexually assaulted, beaten, and strangled. Then, as part of his grotesque ritual, the killer had stored and frozen her body before transporting and placing it in clear view for certain and quick discovery.

Immediately upon connecting the murder with the July 3 incident, the police contacted the older victim to obtain a suspect description, using a new computer compilation program to create a printout of pixels that formed a face with almond-shaped eyes, a long nose, and a big mole.

The picture was cartoonlike and peculiar, but under intense public and media pressure, the investigators went public with what they had. The face was released with a plea for help in finding "this man"—the man thought to have killed little Cora Jones.

The July 3 witness was astute and vocal, and when she expressed her stern discontent with the image, the task force decided to try again. This time they brought in a police artist, who used the standard visual aid format but oddly translated the selections into a profile despite the eyewitness's frontal views. The illustration showed a left-side view of a man with a full head of straight, thick, black hair, a glassy eye, and a deeply pockmarked cheek. The features were in direct opposition to the first sketch released.

Out of frustration, the witness stood up and walked out of the session. But, still under pressure, the police released the new drawing, asking for the public's help in finding "this man"—the potential killer of Cora Jones.

Within two weeks' time, the residents in the tri-state area had been presented with two vastly different images of the man thought responsible for not only one but a string of murders. They were terrorized, but didn't know what image to fear. Men who bore any resemblance to either face were stopped and questioned, but the "leads" led nowhere, and the killer roamed free.

The FBI teamed up with local and regional law enforcement to form a special task force and needed the public's support at the same time that public confidence in the faces for which they were searching was dwindling to near zero.

The July 3 eyewitness was by now openly hostile. Twice they'd failed

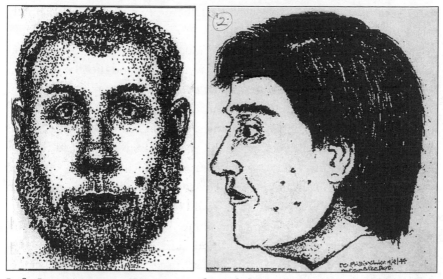

Left: Investigators in Wisconsin released the computer-generated image of a bearded suspect based on a description obtained from the survivor of a July 3, 1994, attempted kidnapping case. Right: A second hand-drawn suspect image was released by police. The eyewitness maintained neither image was in alliance with her recall of the suspect. Both were presented to the public as the suspect in the Cora Jones murder case.

to capture the image she held in her mind. Now she wanted only to be left alone.

In anticipation of my arrival, the FBI was temporarily holding her in their field office in South Chicago.

I needed to get her out of the bureaucratic setting and away from the authorities immediately. Mallarky drove us over to my hotel. I changed out of my beige suit and came out in blue jeans and a sweater, with no shoes on and my hair loose, then sat down cross-legged on the bed.

"God, these guys make me absolutely crazy," I said, and moved myself into a comfortable position to begin. My attempt to disarm her wasn't another subterfuge. I was sincere and beyond frustration at the series of mishaps in the case. The mutual discontent gave us common ground to break the ice.

I told her about Polly's case, about the Unabomber, and others where an original drawing had circulated first, before we were able to finally revise it to the witness's approval.

She relaxed and began to vent her thoughts about what the case had cost her in frustration, and in terms of pay, freedom, and the ill effects of a boss long out of tolerance. We talked for nine straight hours. At the end of the day, we emerged with a face radically different from the ones portrayed in the two composites already in circulation. One eyewitness, three techniques, three entirely different faces. But the witness was at last satisfied.

I wasn't. This time, even I was stumped. Typically, there was some common ground *somewhere,* but this was a face that would come as a total surprise to the investigators, as it had to me.

The new suspect face was surprisingly old. The hair was thin and gray, there was a faint mustache, lined skin, aged eyes. There was a weariness—a vacancy—in the eyes that was distinctive and recognizable. It was as if he were dazed and his actions were a matter of routine, like a janitor checking school doors at the end of a long, cold winter day. We produced him precisely as he was seen, not as a profile, but from her clearest and most frightened vantage point, which was at the moment she'd seen the gun pointing directly at her, his expressionless face angled slightly to one side.

Though we had an image, what we didn't have was my confidence in it. The witness had been shown hundreds of photos, even possibly over one thousand, by not just the artists, but by an overly zealous cop hoping to solve the case himself. It was highly possible that the witness was sublimating—unconsciously modifying her memories to align with what she'd since been shown and told. After all the missteps she'd endured, now I couldn't be sure of anything.

On a case of this magnitude, whether to release the drawing was an enormous decision. More than agency credibility was at stake—children's lives were at risk as well. If the sketch was wrong, it could mislead the investigators, freeing the killer to strike again and even further damaging the public's trust and faith.

But how had this kind of crisis happened again? The disregard for the hard-earned lessons of the nationally publicized Polly Klaas case prompted my request for a meeting with the head of the task force before I reboarded a plane home and I wasn't planning to mince words.

Within the hour, the arrangements were set. Early the next day,

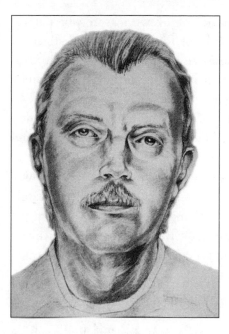

NOT FOR PUBLIC DISTRIBUTION was stamped on this suspect sketch. Although the July 3, 1994, incident eyewitness approved of the likeness, it was withheld from the public due to the task force's previous release of too much conflicting information. (Drawing by Jeanne Boylan)

Wausau FBI agent Ed Bruner picked me up in Chicago for the four-and-a-half-hour trip north to Waupaca, where the task force was based.

We drove slowly through the weatherworn town. Waupaca was built to withstand long, harsh Wisconsin winters, with tall, square homes fronted by long stairways leading up to second-floor front doors designed to open over deep snowdrifts. Gardens rarely had time to bloom before the chill of fall permeated the air.

After pulling up to an old public building with painted brown steps and worn metal railings, Ed Bruner led the way downstairs to the meeting room.

Agent Brian Manganello introduced himself. I expected we'd speak privately, but he held his hand up to stop me while detectives filed into the room.

"All right, you're on," Manganello said as he sat down in front. I looked around, suddenly aware that the one-on-one meeting had just turned into a full-blown presentation. My bravado immediately wilted. I couldn't do it. All longing to reprimand faded away as I looked around the room filled with weary eyes, each person working as hard as he knew how and each in his own kind of pain over the loss of this child.

Mistakes weren't intentionally made. They never are. There is no training in the psychological complexity of eyewitness recall, not for regional or state police detectives, and not for the FBI's investigators. Composites are still treated like little more than an elementary bureaucratic necessity—just a simple piece of artwork—and one more quick step to be ticked off the investigative list.

Instead of censure, I slowly and sadly explained why we couldn't release the newest rendition of Cora's killer, then, by necessity, I marked the drawing NOT FOR PUBLIC DISTRIBUTION.

After the meeting I took a long walk alone toward the heart of town. The smell of decaying apples and wet leaves drifted through air barely heated by the late-day sun. Posters of still another little girl were on grocery-store doors, gas pumps, and the back windows of cars. I'd never been to Waupaca before this day, but I knew I'd walked these same streets before.

The next night, the FBI staged an event in the high school auditorium under the guise of providing the townspeople with information on the latest developments, but the true purpose was to provide a magnet that might pull the suspect to the scene.

The psychological profile of Cora's killer led investigators to believe that he would revel in the chaos and terror he'd wreaked, and that he might enjoy showing up at public gatherings where he would gain some kind of perverted high over seeing firsthand the terror he'd caused. Children were excluded so as to fill as many seats as possible with adults in the suspect's age range.

First, an FBI behavioral scientist from Quantico would talk on the nature and actions of this criminal, then Agent Manganello would update the audience on the status of leads. Next it was my turn. Second to the eyewitness, who wanted nothing more to do with the case, the belief was that I would hold the best sense of what the suspect actually looked like. While I lectured supposedly on how to teach children observational skills, my assignment was to walk along the bleachers scanning the crowd for look-alikes to the killer. In the meantime, the agents outside were videotaping all cars entering and exiting the parking lot.

Afterward, as the crowd exited, I stood at the door in a makeshift receiving line ostensibly to thank people for coming. The passageway was purposely narrowed to allow me a clear vision of every person leaving the building. I shook hands and listened to thank-you's until one man reached forward and stopped, wrapping his weathered hands around mine.

"I'd like to introduce myself. I'm Cora's father." His touch sent his grief through me.

"I just wanted to tell you," he said with his wife looking on, "maybe you'll understand this. . . . You see, Cora never had any artistic interest or ability, but just before she died, the strangest thing began to happen. She'd become obsessed with the kidnapping case of another little girl in our area, talking about her fears day after day. During the last several weeks she was alive, she would sleepwalk. She'd take a tube of toothpaste or something, anything, to draw with and would create the face of a man. I'd come downstairs in the morning and look on the mirror or on the bathroom counter and I'd call to her, 'Cora, what the heck did you do here?'—but she'd have no memory of having drawn it. And the face was a lot like the one in your drawing that the FBI agents showed me. She'd done it all in her sleep. Did you ever hear of anything like this?"

The answer was yes. I'd seen a profound pattern of premonitions in cases, which were especially powerful in children. In truth, I knew of no exceptions to the rule.

In the late summer of 1993, for the two months prior to her abduction, Polly insisted on sleeping with the lights on in her bedroom because she felt certain that a stranger was going to come take her in the night.

Justin Jones had written elaborate poetry about his impending death over the months before he was murdered.

In California, an eighteen-year-old girl named Tara Moore became obsessed with her copy of *Messengers of Light*, a book about angels and the afterlife. She'd read her copy until it was tattered and the corners curled from carrying it with her everywhere she went. On August 15, 1992, she gave it to her sister Diana and explained, "Diana, I will always be your guardian angel."

On August 18, over dinner with her family, Tara suddenly asked her mother, "When you are through with your work on this plane, is it possible to move on to a higher plane to do work there?" Tara died in a car accident that night. When her parents returned from the scene, on the floor of Tara's room was a sheet of paper that had wafted its way across the room and landed faceup near the door. On it was a poem entitled "Now I Am an Angel." Her parents, Sandy and Kirk Moore of San Juan Capistrano, California, were so profoundly changed that they now dedicate their lives to publicly sharing their story with other bereaved parents to give them hope and faith in a higher purpose.

Elisabeth Kübler-Ross of Tucson, Arizona, a world-recognized researcher on death and dying, writes about spontaneous drawings, creative art, poems, and other statements made by children before their death. She explains that the families of these children often become aware of the hidden messages and symbolic language in these seemingly "insignificant" communications after their children have died.

Is there a universal subliminal knowledge that precedes death? With everything I'd witnessed, it was impossible to argue against it.

Cora's father listened intently, still grasping my hands while he absorbed the details of each story, searching perhaps to find a reason behind his daughter's fears and maybe even a basis for his own deepening faith.

The FBI asked me again if I'd release my sketch. Then they brought photographs of possible suspects to my hotel room and showed me which ones the victim had hesitated over during her initial interviews. The details were in close alignment, but the unavoidable question lingered: Had we actually captured the original image in her memory, or were we simply holding a sketch that was based on all the images she'd been shown following her attack? There was now no way to tell.

Maybe I could get a better sense if I saw the witness again. Manganello drove me to the Milwaukee airport where I caught a flight back to Chicago. Beth Mallarky and I met up again and drove to the victim's suburban home to give her a final view of the drawing. She endorsed it fully, even enthusiastically, but all within the space of a half-second glance, far too quickly for comfort. Was she now sure or was she just relieved? With such uncertainty and contamination, the risks of releasing it publicly were far too great, both because it would add further to the public's confusion, and also because it could be a gift to the defense and damage the case if he was caught and the answers were not the right ones. The water in this case had become too muddied.

A serial killer was still at large and roaming the back roads of three states in search of the next victim. Would he kill again? It likely wasn't a matter of if. It was only a matter of when.

With no way to untangle the answers, I packed up and flew home, with a heavy heart. But had I made the right decision? The Bureau had no more margin for error, and wolf had been cried once too often.

11

"GOOD-BYE Y'ALL, I LOVE YOU":

MICHAEL AND ALEX SMITH

'd left Rob as a temporary measure, to give him room and time to figure himself out, to soul search. So when men suddenly began calling me for dates, my friends formed a protective cocoon around me, inviting me out but always in the presence of a half dozen couples. Their company was safe, their examples inspiring, and the time spent in their company was precisely what I needed.

On Wednesday, October 26, I was scheduled to be guest number thirteen at a formal dinner party. In a rush to get ready, I picked up a bottle of wine and a card for the hostess, but had forgotten to check my voice mail before leaving the cottage. I dialed instead from the cell phone as I drove across town.

"Miss Boylan, I'm with the South Carolina FBI. There's been a carjacking in Union, South Carolina, and two children are missing. Would you please phone back as soon as possible."

I dialed as I circled back home, and an agent answered and added more details on the case. A young woman named Susan Smith, driving at night, two kids in the backseat, was stopped at a rural but well-lit intersection, when a man forced his way into her vehicle, pushed her out and took off in the car—the two little boys still strapped inside.

I scribbled notes on the envelope of the card I'd bought for the hostess.

"What's your availability?" the agent asked in his deep Southern drawl.

"Well, I guess I could leave now," I said as I looked down at my black dress and heels, a bottle of wine tied with a ribbon on the car seat beside me.

"Good. Can I get right back to you, Miss Boylan?" I assured him I'd stand by. But as soon as I hung up, the phone rang again immediately. It was Marc Klaas calling from his home in Sausalito.

"Jeanne, have you heard about the missing kids in South Carolina?"

Over the first months after his daughter Polly died, Marc established and served on the board of the Polly Klaas Foundation. In 1994, after growing weary of in-house politics and with grave concerns over board members' use of funds, he formed the independent KlaasKids Foundation to lobby for stronger laws to protect kids and to keep violent repeat offenders behind bars.

Marc was an emergency response team of one. He knew precisely how to organize volunteers, develop grid searches, help the police utilize media, and relieve the pressure that can overwhelm a desperate family in the midst of a crisis over a missing child.

"*American Journal* asked me to cover the South Carolina kidnapping for them," he said. "Are you going?" I told him the FBI was working out details. We both knew that the bureaucratic machine moved slowly and unpredictably, and that procuring approval and funding could take hours, often even days. I'd have to wait.

Within minutes he called back with word that the producers of *American Journal* were willing to foot my air bill if I'd leave right now and if I'd agree to an on-site interview upon arrival. I made another call to the FBI to let them know I was en route, then called Delta Airlines to book the first flight. The speedometer pushed eighty on the back roads to the Redmond airport and I just made it, last one on board.

In stiletto heels and with my business suit in a carry-on bag, I called the host of the dinner party from the Portland airport.

Marc Klaas has become a nationally known political activist and crusader in the fight for children's safety following the kidnap and murder of his daughter Polly. (Photo: Collection of the author)

"Chris, um, I have a problem. I was two blocks from your house, but I'm afraid a little something came up. I'm sorry, but I have to go to work. Rain check?"

I arrived in Charlotte, North Carolina, at 7:15 A.M., just past sunrise. After rushing to the nearest rest room to change into my trusty beige suit, I yanked a brush through my hair and ran to meet Marc's plane, scheduled to land just fifteen minutes later.

Marc stepped off the jet wearing faded red sweats bagged out at the knees, his hair standing up from sleep and static, and his puffy eyes redrimmed. He wobbled into the concourse like a child pulled out of a deep, short nap. I wrapped my arms around him and absorbed the sincerity of his return embrace.

American Journal hired a limo to drive us the fifty miles to Union, tucked in the foothills of the Blue Ridge Mountains across the border in upstate South Carolina. Union's population of 9,500—70 percent white and 30 percent black—took pride in their long-standing ability to get along.

Much about the place seemed straight out of the fifties. Shops looked like long-held family enterprises, right down to their lace curtains, chipped paint, and cracked sidewalks. A rare exception was the newer

Winn Dixie supermarket where Susan Smith's estranged husband, David, worked.

We went straight to the old brick courthouse in the center of town. At the top of the tall concrete steps, news reporters were rapidly setting up shop along the lawn while their crews were staking out positions for their equipment in the parking lot across the street. Marc and I hopped out of the limo and located *American Journal*'s camera crew.

AJ's producer/reporter, Katrina Daniels, had flown in from Florida the night before and was already familiar with the lay of the land.

I needed to locate my connection at the FBI. I left the news crew outside and made my way alone through the quiet hallways, but found no sign of my contact. By the time I walked back out the front door, Katrina and Marc were waiting in a van ready to roll.

Maybe there had been developments overnight and the FBI was at the scene or with the Smith family, I thought. I tossed my bag through the van's sliding door and jumped up on top of the camera equipment as the soundman sped off down the street. Katrina called out directions, consulting a map on which she'd already marked the route to Susan's whereabouts.

We wound over the rutted asphalt of the two-lane rural roads, past the faded grass fields and old fence lines to the home of the Russells— Susan Smith's momma, Linda, and her stepfather, Bev. Susan, David, and a list of their close and barely related kin were gathering rapidly and supposedly holed up inside.

The Smith family ties were a bit convoluted. When Susan was a senior in high school, two years before her marriage to David, she accused her stepfather, Bev, of molesting her. Later, Susan and her mother asked that the charge not be pursued, and an agreement was reached that all records be sealed. The details were murky, yet when asked where she wanted to go after the abduction of her children, Susan chose Linda and Bev Russell's ranch-style home, located on a large lot in one of Union's better outlying areas.

Randomly parked media vans already bordered the long, narrow lane leading to the Russell front yard, but there was no sign of the police or the FBI. Marc and I left Katrina and the crew just across the road and walked up the long concrete pathway to the front entrance. Before we were halfway to the house, a woman stepped out the front door, closing it securely behind her.

"I'm sorry. Susan's not interested in speaking with you." The words were delivered in monotone by a linebacker-like woman with a pixie haircut and tight spit curls barely springing off her chunky cheeks.

"We understand." Marc introduced himself and explained who he was, then explained why I was there.

"Jeanne is the expert, flown in here at the FBI's request to help Susan put a realistic face on the man who has her two boys."

The linebacker didn't flinch. "I told you, Susan is not interested in speaking to you." Her tone managed to flatten even further.

Union was a rural town in an East Coast state. It was possible that this robotic gatekeeper had never heard of either of us. On top of that, Marc and I were both aware of the suspicions that arise when a film crew is in tow. We'd just emerged from a news van, one of dozens that had parked along the same road before we had arrived. We just needed to deflect her concerns by letting her know who we were, why we were here, and how we could help her. Then things would be fine.

We regrouped near the van and dug through our things to throw together any press clippings either of us had on hand, to form a package we could funnel through to Smith's hands.

I was headed back up the sidewalk when the human roadblock popped out again. "I told you, Susan is *not* interested in speaking to you." There was no change in her facial expression, but she'd wound herself up enough to actually accentuate a word. That's okay, I thought, she just still didn't understand.

"No, you see, I am not a reporter," I tried to explain. "Please give this packet to Susan. I know that the FBI informed her that I was coming. I just flew all the way from the West Coast and I am certain she'll want to speak to me."

What woman wouldn't do all she could do to identify the man who had stolen her babies? I understood that she was afraid, but we also had no time for delays.

Back at the van, Katrina showed me the hastily prepared drawing of the suspect, just released by the FBI in the early hours and already showing up on posters all over town.

The basis of a manhunt: Hours after reporting that her two children had been abducted during a Union, South Carolina, car-jacking, Susan Smith selected facial features from provided photos to help a regional police artist compile this suspect composite. The FBI released the drawing and the national search for a black man ensued.

"What do you think?" Katrina moved over in the van's backseat.

The answer was easy. Susan had met with a regional police artist immediately following her reporting of the car-jacking. The resulting sketch was a profile view of a black man wearing a cap and sitting slump-shouldered, with no hint of facial expression. I looked at it and knew instinctively that something was terribly wrong. I shook my head no.

"Look at the scenario. If Susan Smith's car was broken into by an angry man entering through the passenger door, it's likely her first view would be of the man's full face, right? He'd be moving toward her. Her greatest moment of surprise and fear would have been at the moment when she saw him first enter her car. That's where we'd start. That fear would be our ally, so that's the vantage point we'd want to work off of. Then why this profile sketch? Makes no sense.

"If he's holding her hostage, why would he be in this stance? She's his captive. His focus would be directed at his own point of threat, which would be her. And think about this. What would *you* do if challenged by someone threatening to take your children. You'd look 'em in the eyes, right?"

Marc listened, convinced and concerned.

"She's young? Yes. Impaired vision? No. She had vision enough to drive, right? Her glasses were on, so why this lack of detail? Was she inebriated? No. Not from what we've each been briefed on. There was nothing to impair her vision. Yet, there is no detail at all in this drawing." Katrina agreed.

"Susan's viewpoint would have been across a front seat, twenty-four to thirty inches at most. According to the reports, street lighting at the intersection was good and the car was at a full stop when the suspect entered, so why aren't we seeing every line in that face? Based on the drawing alone, you'd think she saw him from a vantage point of thirty or more feet away, and in poor light at best. It's not right. In fact, something is very wrong here."

Marc shook his head and cast his eyes down at the floor. He'd heard those identical words once before.

"Look," I said, considering other elements, "she would have been in a state of excitement, and that's what would have helped to embed the image in her recall. But the *suspect* would have been at his height of fear, too. Or if not fear, then anger. Something! He'd be in attack mode, yelling orders to her. Yet look at this drawing. This guy looks more like someone about to nod off at the tail end of a Greyhound bus trip. Hardly the look of a person in the midst of a car-jacking, screaming orders to a terrified mother at gunpoint."

The sketch looked like a distant, sleepy, white-lipped smudge in a stocking cap. Nothing about it fit the scenario. Yet it had been released nationwide. Every network was running it now, and posters were being relayed to all police outlets in the region. Tips were already beginning to pour in, all based on the hazy image. Any black man resembling that drawing—and that was virtually any adult black male living within an eighteen-hour radius—now found himself in need of a good explanation.

Katrina directed the driver to pull into the parking lot near the courthouse. The sheriff's office's entrance was on the lower level and through a side door. I self-consciously jumped out of the *AJ* van and walked in alone. Marc Klaas had no political agenda and didn't care how he arrived at a case, just that he arrived to help, but depending upon the agent in charge, his affiliation with a television crew could be misread. It was too soon to bring him inside.

It wasn't the first time I'd been caught between two interests in the same story. This time it was *American Journal* who'd paid my airfare to circumvent the usual wait for the FBI's complicated funding process, and we all owed them for that. But I was on the case at the Bureau's invitation, and I couldn't make any move that might look as if I had aligned with the media instead. There was never a guarantee in any case that the two entities would end up on the same side.

The relationship between the police and the press could be called the classic love/hate. When the media were needed, they were really needed. Their power to disseminate information was like gold—if the release of the information was beneficial to the investigation. But there was another edge to that sword: they couldn't be used and then discarded. Once the media were in on a case, they were in all the way. Sometimes the facts they uncovered were ones the investigators preferred out of the public eye, which often left police spokespeople squirming.

Union's cramped county sheriff's office was lined with old wood-paneled walls cast yellow by the aged plastic coverings over suspended fluorescent lights. A parade of camouflaged searchers dipped their hands into a pile of hoagies set out on a folding table near the inside office door. Three women sat answering the continuously ringing phones, thanking people for calling and assuring them there was nothing for them to do. I was glad Marc wasn't listening. He'd have grabbed the receivers right out of their hands. There was plenty to do. Volunteer efforts, if organized, could *make* a case. It made no sense that such a strong resource was being wasted.

I was ushered inside and introduced to FBI agent Carol Allison. She had kind eyes behind her thin-framed glasses and had the easy manner of an old childhood friend.

"You're just in time," she said. "Come in. The sheriff's been waiting to meet with you." She signaled to agents down the hall and herded us all into a small office.

Sheriff Howard Wells, a tall, thin, handsome, clear-eyed man, sat calmly at his desk while others took windowsills, desk corners, or leaned up against walls. Carol closed the door behind them. The impromptu task force meeting was officially under way.

The atmosphere in the room seemed an extension of the sheriff's gentle demeanor. In spite of the media city that had sprung up outdoors over the hours, an uncanny calm reigned inside.

"Miss Boylan, we appreciate you coming here," the sheriff said slowly. "As you were briefed on the phone, we have a reported car-jacking with two young children missing. Do we understand each other that everything we are about to speak of in this room will be held in the strictest of confidence throughout this case?"

Had I ever known a case where I hadn't been asked to keep a confidence while the investigation was under way? The reminder was never necessary.

"Miss Boylan, do you also have ways in your interview techniques to detect fabrication?" he asked in his relaxed Southern drawl. "I want to know, could a person bluff their way through this kind of thing?" He pushed the suspect drawing across his desk to me.

"Yes and yes." Those were easy answers. "But what's far easier than to *detect* fabrication is to avoid aiding in the development of lies in the first place," I explained. "In this case, it may already be too late for that."

He looked at me and strained his neck forward to prompt a more thorough explanation.

"When Susan was asked to describe the face of the car-jacker, she was given police catalogs of facial photos to point to, correct?" Sheriff Wells looked puzzled and asked me to hold on for a moment while he made a telephone call to the supervisor of the artist who had prepared the suspect sketch. He turned back to the task force and verified that, yes, she had.

I continued, "You see, because that's the case, we now have no idea what image may or may not have existed in Susan's memory. Your victim had to produce *nothing*. Therefore, she would have had ample opportunity to lie without being caught, *if* that was her inclination. The visual-aid format of the interview is just that, an aid. It allowed her to focus on the photo choices, and to avoid revealing any neurolinguistic or body-language clues of lying that might otherwise surface in a straight face-to-face conversation."

To clarify the point I added, "In simple terms, think back to your college courses. If you walked into a course and were hit with a pop quiz for which you were unprepared, you always hoped it would consist only of multiple-choice answers, right?" I saw mouths curl into knowing smiles.

"When all you have to do is choose from the provided answers, you can easily bluff. And if Susan Smith is bluffing, she not only lucked out with a multiple-choice test, she also holds the only answer key, so she can say her responses are one hundred percent correct with no one else ever knowing otherwise."

"My God, that makes complete sense," Wells said. He shifted in his chair and looked around at the investigators in the room. "It's such a simple concept."

"I know"—I'd heard that many times—"but astoundingly, it's a concept that's seldom considered in police work. In this case, if she'd been subjected to the essay-test format, or to an interview that was based around her actual recall, if she'd been bluffing, you'd have known on the spot. The degree of detail she would supply wouldn't match up with the described crime scenario. Too much or too little information would have been a key to detecting fabrication. And if she tried to fabricate, her answers would likely have led to a drawing of a face that she already knew."

No one spoke. Investigators know that if a suspect is going to provide a false name, they usually provide either a variation of their actual name or all or part of the name of an associate. They're seldom so creative as to make up a new name out of the blue.

The same holds true when a person tries to fabricate a face. The result is typically a face that he or she is familiar with—that of a television personality, sports figure, or a neighbor, for instance—but the detail provided will be too great or too vivid for the described scenario. And the vantage point, the lighting, and the suspect's physical expression will clearly all be mismatched.

"Did she labor for answers? Did the degree of her labor match the described context of the crime?" I asked. "Did she exhibit the appropriate emotional reactions throughout the interview? And were the descriptions she gave consistent with the vantage point from which she had her sighting?" From the sketch itself, the answer was no. I paused for a question or any sign of disagreement, but there was none. The task force didn't have the answers. Instead all they had was a sketch.

"An interview—an unaided, nonsuggestive interview," I continued, "includes all these kinds of checks and balances as an ongoing part of the process. If she's telling the truth, it all falls into alignment, but if there's fabrication, everything will be askew." The room was silent. "These questions should have been considered and the answers analyzed long before any decision to publicly release a suspect sketch was ever made."

The sheriff drew his hands slowly across his forehead as if trying to iron out the signs of his stress. The drawing they had was being aired from coast to coast—and the manhunt was at full throttle.

I felt the energy discernibly shifting in the room. The release of the suspect drawing had created its own crisis of sorts. Not just because of the uncertainty over the image, or the dozens of men being detained and questioned based on a resemblance, but because of the race of the suspect depicted in the drawing. The sketch was fast becoming an emblem for racial unrest.

If it had been a mistake to release it, the mistake was developing its own life. Within the first day of its publication, protests sprang up in a number of Southern states against prejudice toward blacks in the criminal justice system.

The drawing itself was laden with its own problems, but whether those problems stemmed from a poor interview process or from a lack of truthfulness was still up for grabs. In Sheriff Wells's office, I could feel the conversation veering strongly one way—and it was not in support of Susan Smith.

I watched Sheriff Wells's lips move, but for an instant my mind flashed back in time. I heard Mark Mershon's words at the time the Polly Klaas case first broke: "We think the girls are lying." I forced myself back to the present and heard my own voice jump out in Susan's defense.

"Wait a minute, though," I cautioned. "What you don't know at this point is if the reason for the discrepancies is Susan, or simply the way in which she was questioned. Perhaps all these indicators never even had the chance to surface."

"Well, we might know." Wells leaned forward in his chair. "I'd like to tell you something, and as long as this investigation is open, I'd like it to stay within this room."

I nodded my agreement.

"We think Susan may be lying, that she may have the children hidden somewhere. When she submitted to a polygraph exam, she failed a portion of the test."

My heart went straight to the silent defense of Susan Smith. There is a reason that polygraphs aren't admissible in the courtroom. They aren't conclusive and they contain far too much room for error. In the Klaas case, Kate had failed a segment of the polygraph, although she'd never lied once throughout the case. The heightened state of Susan's emotions could have also skewed her test results.

Was I living this *again*, listening to a crime victim being proclaimed guilty until she could prove herself innocent?

The sheriff and task force members urged me to meet with Susan to learn all I could. They admitted that, by doubting her story, they'd severely alienated her. Because they had a shaky rapport, they recommended that I approach her as an entity separate from them to gain her trust and to have a higher chance of access to the Russell home. I listened, straight-faced, but inside I was already fighting a battle on Susan's behalf. I stood up, shook the sheriff's hand firmly in agreement with his plan, and walked out his office door.

Smith remained cloistered at the family home, dug in behind relatives, clergy, and Margaret, the designated bouncer. If Susan was lying, she'd have to stick with her story to save face with everyone inside. The task force believed that with my softer, uncoplike disposition, as they put it, I might be the one outsider she'd be inclined to confide in.

Carol Allison intercepted me in the hallway and mentioned a possibility of my wearing a wire to capture the words on tape should Susan decide to confess to me. I agreed to comply if that decision was ultimately made by the FBI, but I was less than comfortable with the idea of entering the home, gaining Susan's confidence, and then violating her trust by tape-recording her words.

By midafternoon, every major news network and magazine show in the country had generators running to support their equipment set up in front of the courthouse. I walked past the bright lights aimed at the

CNN correspondent doing a live remote from the front lawn. At the sheriff's suggestion, I rented my own car so I could come and go to Susan's house without any association with the police or media crews. Often my greatest asset to the investigative task force was that I wasn't one of them.

Rumor had it that Susan had done an interview with a program called *A Current Affair* and was displeased with the way she'd been portrayed. Ever since it had aired, she'd refused to talk to all reporters. In borrowed jeans and a jacket and ball cap from the *Inside Edition* crew's camera-man, I headed out alone and drove back out to the house.

"I told you, Susan is not interested in talking to you." Again, I was blocked from entry by the immovable Margaret, by now well-known among the media contingent. Margaret, the self-appointed family spokesperson, was reportedly also a media liaison for a neighboring county sheriff's office. She had the requisite poker face down all right—a face beloved by none.

The task force couldn't force Susan to comply—or they risked defeat from her attitude—so there was no choice but to bide time. Two little boys were missing, and every day, every hour, every minute, counted. Because Susan never emerged, it was impossible to know if the resistance was her own or that of a misguided small-town relative eyeing this as her own shot at the big time.

In the meantime, a big rumble was brewing within the media contingent. The daily press conferences had become routine announcements that consisted of two repetitious phrases: no news, no new leads. But something was terribly wrong.

Randell Pinkston, the CBS reporter, egged the other network correspondents on. "All right, whose gonna be first to call bullshit?" Not a little of the energy generated by a news story is due to the proximity of competing reporters. Though no one dared to go on record with his or her concerns, most thought it bizarre that the mother of two missing children wasn't reaching out, screaming out, for all the help she could get.

By the Union County Communication dispatcher's report filed at 9:12 P.M. on October 25, 1994, Susan Smith's burgundy Mazda Protégé was stopped at a red light on Highway 49 between Union and Lockhart when the black man who jumped in first told her to drive. But then she said he insisted she stop the car right beyond the sign marking the entrance to John D. Long Lake, and pushed her out the driver's side door. According to Susan's report, she was left standing in the middle of the road—with no other cars in sight—when the man pulled himself behind the wheel and drove off with her car, her two children still strapped inside.

But there was one catch in her story: the stoplight where Susan's car was reportedly abducted, supposedly with no other cars in sight, turns red only when a vehicle triggers the pad on the cross street.

Still, Marc and I were the last to doubt. We'd lived through the predictable course of investigators' practiced skepticism. We wanted to believe Susan, whose application for divorce from a philandering husband had been filed four days before she'd received a Dear Jane letter from her own boyfriend. Every aspect of her life was on the verge of falling apart the night she reported her two boys stolen.

Union is a close-knit community and few were unaware of her background—her charges against her stepfather, and more recently the separation from her husband. It seemed to make sense that she'd feel overwhelmed by her life, and then by the sudden onslaught of media crews, cameras, helicopters, police—all on top of the fear and loss.

All hotel rooms in Union were taken by reporters from networks whose travel divisions had called ahead for reservations. Marc and I ended up with the rest of the media contingent in accommodations a half hour away, in the neighboring town of Spartanburg. We used the daily round-trip to catch up on whatever progress we'd each made.

Marc managed to meet with Bev Russell, Susan's stepfather, who agreed to help, but couldn't force Susan to comply. Then Marc turned his efforts to David's father, who jumped at the offer to help. A meeting between Marc and David was set up. We needed Susan, but David was at least a way in.

The luck stopped there though. Marc showed up at the appointment with David only to be turned away again by Margaret, the person supposedly protecting the interests of the Smiths. "They're not interested in speaking to you," she said as she turned Marc away. David's father followed him down the steps with tears in his eyes, apologizing profusely.

Marc was writhing with frustration. We'd fought for two long months to get Polly back alive. It was incomprehensible to him that this mother of two wouldn't accept help. I watched him struggle to understand, once collapsing on a curb with pent-up emotion, yet still clinging to his determination to help her fight the ugly rumors that inevitably surround every family that endures this kind of nightmare. I couldn't share with him the doubts that the FBI had confided in me. I wanted to reach out to him, to assure him that chances were at least very good that the kids were alive. But I couldn't.

The media, for lack of any other angle, started preparing features around people who had endured similar traumas, both to fill their newscasts with human interest stories and also to use past victims to say the words that the media wanted to but didn't dare state themselves: "Something here doesn't add up."

Madeline McFadden, a friend as well as a reporter for *Inside Edition,* asked me to go with her to a nearby town where she'd uncovered a story of a woman whose own two sons were stolen in a car-jacking two years earlier.

The mother had dashed inside a convenience store, leaving her keys in the ignition and her two young sons in the backseat. When she came out, she saw her car, her boys still inside, exiting the parking lot. From the living room of her country home, she described the terror she'd felt on that day, the frantic race she'd undertaken to save her children by screaming, chasing the car, and even leaping through the air to grab on to the bumper as the thief drove away. He later abandoned the car with the two boys unharmed inside.

During the interview, the woman turned from Madeline toward the lens and said, "I heard her on television. She said that when the man drove off, she stood there in that dark highway and yelled to Michael, 'Baby, I've got to go, but you're going to be okay. Good-bye, ya'll, I love you.' But let me tell you, in that moment, when you see your boys being driven away and you can't reach them, no mother could ever—*ever*— find those words."

Marc and I headed back to Spartanburg after another hard day in Union. Marc had spent the day chasing leads, and I'd divided my time between the Russell home and the sheriff's office, on call should the family or Agent Allison notify me that Susan was ready.

Commotion marked the turnoff to John D. Long Lake. We could see aluminum boats floating on the murky surface while dredging equipment searched the muddy shallows along the shores.

It was late when we checked into our rooms. I was tired, but checked for messages before getting ready for bed.

"Um, Miss Boylan"—the voice was decidedly Southern, soft and tentative, definitely not the linebacker—"my name is Tracy Wright and I'm calling on behalf of Miss Susan Smith. Susan is ready to work with you on a caricature of the abductor." The message was left on my Oregon voice mail at 4:30 P.M. Pacific time. It was now 10:30 P.M. in South Carolina.

I slammed down the phone and raced down the hall to Marc's door. He cracked it slightly open at my frantic knock. He'd already turned in, and I waited outside while he threw clothes back on to head to my room so he could listen to the message himself. We played it back repeatedly, but decided it was too late to place a return call. We'd let Susan get a night's sleep.

In the morning, I'd schedule the interview, and later I'd also get Marc inside. Susan had only to be informed of who he was and how he could help her. Finally, we'd show the police that their guilty-til-proven-innocent theory was wrong again, and we could help to squelch the increasing unrest by the self-fueled skeptical media.

High on anticipation, neither Marc nor I could even think about sleeping. Instead we slid and rolled like two kids at Christmastime down the wet grass embankment that led to a restaurant next door. We planned how we would proceed the next day over a glass of Chablis.

Eight o'clock sharp, Marc walked down the hall with his coffee and hovered over my shoulder while I dialed. "May I speak with Tracy Wright, please," I asked when a sleepy voice answered.

"She's gone off to work already. I was just lying here in the bed, and when I woke up, she was gone," he said as slowly as words could be spoken without falling over, and never even asking who was calling. "But here's another number you can call."

I dialed the new number and waited through two rings.

"Hello." Oh my God—it was Margaret speaking. It was Saturday morning and I'd reached her at home.

"This is Jeanne Boylan." I blew up my cheeks with air to mock her appearance and shot Marc a frantic look to let him know who had picked up the line.

"Listen, I told you. Susan does not wish to speak to you."

Frustrated, I hung my head and Marc threw his hands into the air. There was no getting around her. No explanation would break down her barrier. Tracy Wright's name didn't seem to help. That I'd received an invitation on Susan's behalf was inconsequential to her. This was the last straw.

"Look, Margaret," I yelled suddenly, "I am fresh out of patience, girl-friend." Marc jumped back from the desk. "I have a message here from Tracy Wright saying Susan does indeed want to talk to me, and you need to know that she's looking very bad in the press about now, for refusing to help out. The media is milling around like sharks deciding who will be the first one to call her bluff. You're doing her no favors, Margaret." Marc clutched his fist in the air in support of the new atti-tude. We'd been kind to her all week and it hadn't done any good. It was time to change tactics.

Margaret was the problem. I no longer had a shred of doubt. She lived in the next county, had just answered her own phone, and had obviously not even been to Susan's home yet that morning. Marc and I were convinced that Susan was inside wanting all along to speak with us, but was being prevented from it by her barricading shirttail cousin.

I was out of options and due in New York City on Monday. Back in Union, Carol Allison, looking exhausted and resigned, met us at the sheriff's office entry, then walked Marc and me back to a hallway to talk privately.

"You two can go now," she said softly. "We've got all we need." The look in her eyes stirred mixed emotions. In a "read between the lines" conversation she made it clear that the FBI was now positive Susan was lying. It was just a matter of waiting it out to see how long she'd uphold her story.

"Oh my God, Carol, the drawing—"

"Yes, exactly," she interrupted. "It should never have existed. Looks like we owe a lot of apologies to a lot of folks. But we didn't know. We went with it. We just didn't know." She put her hands on her hips and stretched her neck toward the ceiling in exasperation.

Marc cupped his hands over his lips. I watched him and wondered which words he was physically holding back. He turned and walked a few feet away to contemplate the reality of what we'd been told, but quickly pivoted back around. "Wait," he said, "if she orchestrated the disappearance herself, she had to have taken her boys somewhere safe." The realization infused his voice with a sudden joy. "With her pending divorce, it makes sense that she would have been worried about having to give up her kids. She stashed them. Of course!"

Maybe Susan believed that with this cover story she could succeed in hiding them from their father, never imagining the ploy would launch her into the national spotlight. She'd be in serious legal trouble for years and was now guaranteed to lose custody in the divorce, but Marc and I left South Carolina with the comfort of knowing that, at least and thank God, Michael and Alexander Smith were alive.

I flew out Sunday morning, then spent a few nights in New York City for another *People* magazine photo shoot on a separate story. Flying back to Oregon early Thursday morning, I listened through the airline headphones as Susan Smith's voice suddenly filled the national news. Nine days after she'd reported the abduction of her two boys, CNN carried a news conference. David reportedly sat with his arm around Susan as she spoke.

"I would like to say that whoever has my children," she pleaded, "that they please, that they please bring them home to us, where they belong. Our lives have been torn apart by the tragic events. I can't express how much they are wanted back home, how much we love them and miss them."

Susan Smith stands alongside her husband, David Smith, and makes an emotional appeal for the safe return of their children as well as for the nation's prayers in a press conference held at the courthouse in Union, South Carolina, November 1994. (Photo © AP Photo/Mary Ann Chastain)

It wasn't the statement I expected. Susan had finally broken her silence, but I realized that neither Sheriff Wells nor the FBI had broken theirs.

The news update explained that Sheriff Wells had convened the media in front of the courthouse in Union for a case update. Following his announcement, Susan and David Smith had stepped forth to appeal one more time, speaking into the ocean of microphones.

"I just pray every day that you're taking care of them," Susan continued. David looked on, his face contorted in anguish.

It was pouring rain when I arrived home in Bend. Among the collection of messages was one from Portland's CBS affiliate, KOIN. I'd worked with the same news director on stories in the past and called him back right away.

"Jeanne, we know you've been on the South Carolina kidnapping case, and we want to know if we can get an interview. We'd like to fly a reporter and crew over to Bend right away." He was discussing logistics when suddenly he halted, "Wait a second, look at this—this is just coming over the wire. Union"—he paused—"South Carolina . . ." He started repeating each word as it appeared on-screen. "Susan Smith has confessed . . ."

I took a deep breath as I readied myself to hear what I already expected, that Susan had confessed to hiding the boys herself. But the news director continued, ". . . to the murder of her two sons."

"Murder?" I screamed out. The director explained that the story said the boys were found in John D. Long Lake.

"But that can't be!" I explained. "They were dragging the lake bottom when we were there, we saw the search teams in their boats. It's got to be a mistake!"

"Hang on," he said. "Let me verify this and I'll call you right back."

I punched the hang-up toggle and immediately dialed Marc in Sausalito.

Marc's recording prompted me to leave a page. I entered my number and switched on the television and radio.

The phone rang immediately. I picked up the receiver. Marc was speaking before the phone even reached my ear.

"Jeanne," I could hear him inhale before pushing out the words, "she killed them, didn't she?"

"I don't know Marc. CBS just called me . . ." The call-waiting interrupted our conversation. "Just a second, don't go anywhere."

The news director spoke softly. "Jeanne, I'm really sorry. It's true. She murdered both boys. It's confirmed by AP. They're at the bottom of John D. Long Lake. The car actually drifted over one hundred and twenty feet into the center of the lake, and last week apparently they'd only searched the areas along the banks. The reports say they're bringing it up now with the kids still strapped in the back in their safety seats."

I collapsed as Marc came back on the line. "Marc, it's confirmed. They found them. They're in the lake. God, Marc, they're still in the car—all this time, still strapped in their safety seats." My voice gave way as the news ripped through my heart.

Rain hammered against the paned glass, and the wind outside encircled the darkened cottage.

This had been even more than just a fight for Michael and Alex. For both Marc and me, this had been a chance to do for them what we were unable to do for Polly.

We held on the phone together, and wept.

Michael and Alex Smith. (Photo © Reuters/Melinda Wilburn/Archive Photos)

12

TO NEW BEGINNINGS

I still remember the time my father saw a man and his family circled round a car broken down on the side of the road. My father not only towed the car into town, he also put the man, his wife, and their four kids up in our home for seven days while they waited for the part they needed to get back on the road. This was the stuff I was made of. You didn't ask questions, you just did the "right thing."

Every time I boarded another plane and left my own plans behind, my father's lessons were the essence of my rationalizations. But one South Carolina housewife managed to shatter my twenty-year belief in altruism.

When a call came in from Stephen J. Cannell Productions in Los Angeles, telling me that they were ready to present scripts for both the movie and television versions of my life story, I was more than ready to turn away from kidnappings and murders. The FedEx package they sent contained a first-class ticket and a four-night reservation at the Roosevelt Hotel. No better place to escape real life, I figured, than Hollywood.

"Hello, you've reached the voice mailbox for Jeanne Boylan. Leave a message, or you can reach me at the Ro—" No, not this time, I thought. I hung up the phone and walked out the door, leaving no number at which I could be reached.

Cannell Productions had a Lincoln Continental reserved for me at LAX. I drove to the Roosevelt, just across the street from the legendary Mann's Chinese Theater and a few blocks down Hollywood Boulevard from the huge black-glass office building where the meetings were scheduled. I stepped over the inlaid brass stars along the sidewalk and past the giant statues of Emmys on the south side, then crossed the street to the office.

The project producers, Ann Gross and Marcy Westin, each grazed my left cheek with an air kiss as I walked in the door. "We are so excited, Jeanne. This is such a *fabulous* project. It's going to be just *fabulous*. Thank you *so* much for coming."

Then the executive producer walked in, flanked by the two young male writers they'd hired to prepare the "treatments"—the concepts that would be pitched to television-series executives and then to the movie-of-the-week departments at the networks.

This was the big moment, the "reveal" of their eight months of planning. The writers waved their arms around like boastful Italian mothers as they began to unveil their concepts. I grabbed a pad out of my bag and clutched a pencil, so I could write down every "fabulous" word.

"Well, you know," one began, "we needed to take a little artistic license."

Of course they'd have to employ some fiction in their writing—I understood that. They'd already told me that Kim Basinger was too old to play me, though she was born the same year I was, and that Heather Locklear was more the generation they had in mind. I edged out a little farther on my seat.

"You see now," he continued, "a single, intelligent, independent, articulate, ambitious, attractive female"—he paused, giving me just enough time to inhale the compliments, before adding—"will not sell. She won't be likable to the public, so, you see . . . we rewrote your character."

I was virtually speechless—and completely motionless, until I heard the thud of my pencil as it hit, then bounced, on the floor.

I remained silent while they detailed their pitch ideas. For the movie-of-the-week, my "character" was downtrodden, waiflike, dowdy, just fired from her job, living in the country, and afraid to be alone. A soon-to-be parolee sends her segments of a description of himself, daring her to piece together a drawing of her own would-be killer, announcing that he will come to get her when he gets out of jail. Then the local sheriff takes pity and comes to her rescue, at which time they, of course, fall in love, although she and the killer running off together might have made for a more intriguing plot.

It was a silly story, and I couldn't see anyone sticking with it after the first feminine-product commercial. But—there was more: they also had another idea they planned to pitch to the network series department.

In the weekly series, I, or she, was to be a forensic psychologist who lived above the train in Chicago. To supplement her income, she drew a weekly cartoon for the city's newspaper, into which she wove facts about her daytime criminal cases. A disgruntled retired detective was her reluctant cohort, and would hang over her shoulder reviewing her cartoons, grumbling over discrepancies, unintentionally helping her to perfect the strip until the real-life crimes were solved.

"So, Jeanne," one of the writers asked, "what do you think?" I looked into their youthful and optimistic eyes. They looked like two panting puppies begging to be held. I didn't have the heart to tell them the truth. I took myself out to see *Pulp Fiction* that night just to brighten up my day.

The next morning, we walked into the office of Donna Cooper at NBC Studios in Burbank. She stood up, grabbed my hand, and shook it like a water pump after a two-year drought.

"I've heard so much about you. I've read about you, and I am absolutely fascinated by your work."

She sat us all down and began asking intelligent and spirited questions about my experiences. We were well into a fast-paced conversation when I glanced over and saw the look in one writer's eye.

A network "pitch" appointment was hard to come by—the networks accept new ideas only on occasion, and this was the writers' twenty-minute window. I took the hint and stopped midsentence to turn it over to the boys. Behind Donna was a bouquet of helium birthday balloons, one severely deflated. Before they wound down their pitch, she began to strongly resemble the silver one with the slow leak. When they finished, she stood, extended her limp hand, and politely said good-bye.

My sentiments matched hers. One down, I thought, two to go. We were finished at NBC, and ABC was, thankfully, taking no more ideas for the coming season. I cringed through a repeat performance at CBS. Our last appointment was with Fox TV.

It was five o'clock on a Friday afternoon when we pulled up to the yellow brick building on the Twentieth Century lot off Pico Boulevard. Paul Nagle agreed to take the last-minute meeting. I took the most distant seat in the back of the room, hoping to disappear into the thick cushions of his down-filled sofa.

Red-haired Paul rapped the eraser of his pencil on his desktop like a drummer on speed and interrupted the writers midway through their spiel. "Wait a minute, wait a minute, let me understand something here," he said, extending his milk white hands into the air. "If anyone would have told me that there was a common denominator—a single common thread—between every major, high-profile, and publicly recognizable case in this country in the last decade, I would never have believed it. Yet you've got her sitting right here. Why would you embellish?"

I felt my vertebrae snap into line, then threw both hands straight into the air, stood up, and released an involuntary operatic note in a range I hadn't even known I could reach. I brought my hands to my heart, looked into the eyes of Paul, and said, "Thank you."

For all practical purposes, the Fox meeting ended at that moment. The buyer wanted truth, the seller was stuck on "artistic license." I knew that no network with a grip on reality would be buying the two treatments. Thank God. I could rest easy, although I knew I'd never view the words "based on a true story" in the same light again.

That evening, I dressed up and took myself out to dinner on the outdoor patio of my favorite Beverly Hills restaurant, then window-shopped under the canopy of white lights that wove through the trees on Rodeo Drive. I stared into the windows of the Ferragamo store trying to read the prices in the heels of the Italian men's shoes, looking for the pairs I might recognize from my husband's closet.

It was late when I got back to the hotel. With my high-heels dangling from my fingertips, I walked down the long, plush Roosevelt corridor and slowly turned the crystal knob on the hotel door. The scent of the roses sent over by Cannell still permeated the air four days after their arrival. I turned on the bathroom light, unpinned my hair, started to run the bath-water, then looked at the phone and wondered, Do I dare call him?

I slowly dialed my old home number. The phone rang only once. Robert answered just as I'd decided to hang up, but it was too late.

"Rob, hi. How you doin'?" I'd caught him off guard.

"Oh my God, Jeanne. It's great to hear your voice. I miss you, where are you?"

I exhaled in relief at his response. Our marriage had been a perpetual cha-cha-cha. When I moved toward him, he withdrew. And when I pushed away, he wanted me closer. It was a pattern that had to change.

At the end of the hour long call, I told him that I needed more time to rebuild the trust. We agreed that I'd come home as soon as I had made my decision about the marriage, and that decision, he insisted, would then be final, no matter what.

I needed to find a neutral place to unravel things, to sort out my feel-ings. Bend was too small, and it would be too tempting to see him. I glanced over at my suitcase and all the unused return tickets, the rem-nants from so many midtrip diversions to other cases. I calculated the frequent-flier miles represented by all that travel, and had a sudden idea. I pulled the laundry bag from the hotel closet and threw in my walking shoes, toiletries, and a few pieces of clothing. After a quick shower, I packed my business clothes in my suitcase and rolled it out through the lobby to a Mailboxes, Etc. store just a few blocks down Hollywood Boulevard. Twenty minutes and $71 later, my suitcase was on its way to Oregon without me. En route to the car I picked up an $11 Vietnamese backpack, a pair of sandals, denim cutoffs, and then drove the rented Lincoln back to LAX.

After giving the ticket agent my frequent-flier number I asked, "How far can I go?"

"You have enough mileage to go anywhere you want," she said.

"Enough for Costa Rica?"

I landed at the San José airport at dusk. It took six hours in the back of a vinyl-upholstered cab to get to the Península de Nicoya on Costa Rica's west coast. It wasn't high season yet, and rooms were plentiful.

The warm white sand of Tamarindo Beach was exactly the respite I needed. I spent days walking on the quiet beaches, even signing up with a local softball team to get a little exercise and clear my mind. I planned to stay away until I felt intuitively that it was the right time to go back.

Two weeks later, we'd just finished a ball game near the Flamingo Beach Hotel. I expected few calls since I'd left no forwarding number on my service in Oregon, but walked over to the hotel's pay phone to check in anyway. The first words I heard brought great news.

"Jeanne, hi, honey, this is Lisa, Lisa Dahl." She delivered her words in stilted half sentences. "Jose Avina was sentenced today for Justin's death. The judge gave him sixteen years to life."

Sixteen years—possibly out in four—but at least Avina was behind bars for now. The two case inspectors had shown up for the trial, likely at Angela Alioto's "suggestion," but they'd at least made the effort to make amends with Lisa for their absence throughout the case. Lisa and Andrea could finally begin their own journey toward healing. I could already hear a budding peace in her voice. She'd finally found justice for Justin.

With every case I worked, the same lesson surfaced over and over: nothing mattered more than family. Not work, not money—in the end, relationships were all that mattered. I began to feel a restlessness to get back home, back to my husband and to my marriage.

The next morning, I walked to the phone to move up my reservation and checked my messages one more time. But this time, my in-box was jammed with calls from reporters from Chicago, Minneapolis, and Milwaukee.

"Ms. Boylan, I'm calling from the *Chicago Tribune*. We'd like to know what you think of the remarkable likeness between your drawing and the suspect arrested in the Cora Jones case. Would you call me back with a comment?"

Cora's killer had been caught? Each reporter's message told me more.

A man named Spanbauer had been arrested while attacking a woman during a home invasion. The reporters said his face was a perfect match for my drawing, and the media wanted an answer as to why the sketch hadn't been released earlier. The calls were already a day old. It was too late to respond, and I could tell by the sound of the reporters' voices that they weren't asking for information, they were issuing demands.

I spilled the contents of my wallet on the ground while searching frantically for the number of Agent Ed Bruner. Ed answered and filled me in on the details.

"Jesus, Jeanne, where have you been? I've been trying to reach you. What did you do, leave the damn country? The press has been all over this thing. Your drawing is right smack on the money, but we're catching hell. The press is digging for reasons why it was withheld."

"Didn't you explain?" I asked. "We couldn't release it, Ed, not after the fiasco the case had already been through. You had two faces out there that weren't even near what I'd come up with. Your credibility was gone. It was a mess!" But I was preaching to the choir.

"I know. But this guy hit again, this time an older woman in her own home. Nothing even similar to the other cases."

On December 8, 1994, David F. Spanbauer, fifty-three, was caught committing another attack. Upon his arrest, he confessed to the murder of Cora Jones. He was then confronted with and confessed to the kidnapping and murder of twenty-one-year-old Trudy Jeschke and the kidnapping and murder of ten-year-old Ronelle Eichstedt, the same little girl whose case Cora had worried relentlessly over prior to her own abduction.

Spanbauer's confession came on Cora's thirteenth birthday. "Maybe this was our present to her," Cora's mother told the media.

The headlines were rightfully incisive. Papers throughout the Midwest ran Spanbauer's arrest shot alongside my drawing, with headlines that blasted the FBI for withholding the eerily accurate sketch. The public wanted answers.

AUTHORITIES WITHHELD SKETCH IN MURDER CASE

DRAWING RESEMBLING SPANBAUER WITHHELD

ARTIST'S DRAWING DESCRIBED AS "DEAD RINGER" FOR SPANBAUER

SKETCH WAS SEEN AS UNRELIABLE

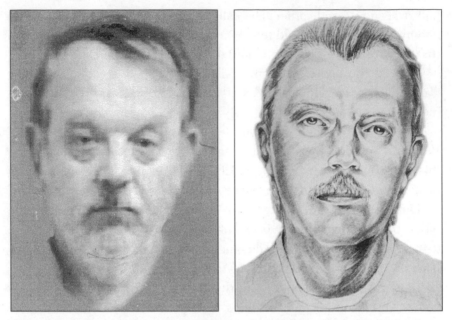

Following the December 8, 1994, arrest of David Spanbauer (left) for the murder of Cora Jean Jones, media throughout the Midwest demanded explanations for why the suspect sketch (right) had been withheld from the public. (Photo courtesy of the FBI; drawing by Jeanne Boylan)

The county sheriff issued a statement declaring that it had been withheld because "state and federal authorities feared the drawing would generate too many leads." They added that "the drawing had not been deemed reliable."

I nearly took Ed's eardrum out. "What? Not reliable? Too many leads? What were they thinking? The sketch was not the problem, it was what took place on the local level beforehand—*that* was the problem. So they tried to put the onus on me? And what's this about too many leads? That *is* the point of a drawing, to produce leads. Did the media actually buy that explanation?"

The problem was that the authorities knew that the real reason for withholding the sketch wasn't going to make them look too good.

I hadn't been available to respond to press inquiries, so the sheriff's office deflected the heat off themselves. The FBI didn't argue, although they were bearing the brunt for a decision that was neither made by them nor necessitated by their actions.

Now we all had to live with the question of whether Spanbauer might have been arrested before his latest attack had the sole eyewitness's memory been protected and handled well from the beginning.

The story unraveled an even longer history, with tentacles that had devastated even more lives. A woman named Carol Grady had been a victim of Spanbauer clear back in 1960, when he broke into the home of her aunt and uncle, where she was baby-sitting. He brutally attacked Grady, then shot and killed her uncle on his return home. For his crimes that night, he received a seventy-year sentence, which Carol Grady had interpreted as life in prison. She was shocked and infuriated to see his name and photo released as the Midwest serial murderer.

"Can you imagine the horror and betrayal I felt when I found out that David Spanbauer had been released after serving eight of a seventy-year sentence?" With that question, Carol Grady began her fight back, immediately launching a petition-gathering effort to support a truth-in-sentencing law.

The messages on my voice mail continued, each offering more proof that all of my outstanding cases were moving toward closure as if divinely synchronized.

Updates on the Susan Smith case told me that she'd been placed on twenty-four-hour suicide watch, and her attorney was considering an insanity defense, which would likely include unsealing the records on the sexual abuse charges she had claimed against her stepfather years earlier.

My heart was beginning to open up again. I could feel it. I'd even managed to feel the first pangs of empathy for Susan, maybe not forgiveness, but a glimpse, at least, at understanding the source of her own deeply buried pain.

The release of my anger and bitterness toward her coincided with a sense of forgiveness for Robert, too. None of these lessons had come easily. But after undistracted effort and a lot of prayer, I felt I'd finally found the peace—and renewed faith—that I'd fled to Costa Rica in search of.

In the village, I bought a small, hand-carved sculpture symbolizing

faith and trust. It was created from white marble with two abstract figures, arms linked together in unity, and perched on a solid base. It was
the perfect Christmas gift to symbolize our new beginning. I wrapped it
carefully and slid it into my cloth backpack before traveling to San José
to catch the flight back.

I'd surprise Robert with my arrival and with my answer.

It was time to go back home to my husband, my family.

Without either of us knowing it, Robert and I passed each
other going in opposite directions in the Portland airport, same
day, same half hour, same airline, same concourse. Not until I got back
to Bend did I find out he'd just left for Hawaii to help a friend on a construction project.

For the two weeks he was away I worked out, read books, waited. My
energy was high and my resolve solid. It was almost Christmas, and my
husband and I would be back together in time for the holidays.

On December 22, I called but the phone rang endlessly. The answering machine didn't catch the call, which meant he was finally back in
town. I picked up my wrapped gift and drove the faster back roads over
to the house, then careened into the driveway, but had to maneuver
around a huge truck parked in front of the house. My car hardly fit
alongside the giant rig with its extended cab, fender flares, oversized
wheels, and darkened windows. Robert had friends who used their rigs
to pull horse trailers, and I figured one must have come over to welcome
him home.

Minuscule silver flakes were suspended in the cold night air. I walked
around the front of the long truck and crunched through the dry snow
on the walkway, tucking his Christmas gift under my arm, even nervously running a last-minute brush through my hair.

I stopped short as I reached out to grasp the metal door handle.

An odd light was pulsating from inside. I heard noises: first, a
woman's voice, then Robert's. Then came stronger sounds and more
words, words I'd heard before—though never from the other side of a
closed door.

I'd come "home," but it was as if I'd been led by the hand to face reality before making a wrong decision. I stood still just long enough to imprint every detail of the moment: the chill of the air on my cheeks, the grains in the snow on the porch, the light spilling down the siding, the cold glow of the moon, the pulsating light inside, their voices, and the sounds . . . the unforgettable sounds.

I raced back to the car hurling Robert's gift into the darkness, cranked on the ignition, and backed out onto the road. As the car turned, my head-lights caught the truck's custom license plate. It read, "WLD-WMN."

It didn't take long to get the divorce papers in order. I signed away the past.

I found a winter rental and moved from the tiny guesthouse to new, expansive surroundings. It was a starting point: fresh place, high ceilings, clear mountain view, a virtual hospital room for my soul.

Our old log house had sold to the first person who toured it, and the new owners even took Dillon. Every part of our dream was gone, but still, I felt an optimism rising inside me, a chance to start over, to build something even stronger, better.

On the day the divorce was final, a torrential spring downpour soaked my hair as I ran across the Bend street to a restaurant for a celebration on that Monday night.

"This is to you," my friend Pat said, raising a champagne glass high in the air. "Today you are finally free from your marriage and the emotional demands of your work. Here's to a wide-open future. May it all begin for you right now, as of this day, April 17, 1995!"

13

SWIFT, CERTAIN, AND SEVERE:

OKLAHOMA CITY

"Terror is emanating from America's heartland. A truck bomb ripped through the Oklahoma City Alfred P. Murrah Federal Building this morning at 9:02 central time. Hundreds are feared dead."

My heart nearly stopped at the rare sight of Tom Brokaw interrupting the regular morning programming. The network news sound track beat rhythmically under his familiar voice.

It was Wednesday morning, April 19, 1995. Snow still clung to the shady sides of the giant red rocks on the steep hillside encircling my patio, and fresh deer tracks surrounded the feeders I'd left outside. I'd just walked in the door from a morning workout, tossed the rolled-up paper on the counter, and flicked on the television set, when I caught the breaking news.

Along with the rest of the world, I stood immobilized, dropping my keys and newspaper on the floor and watching the horror unfolding on the screen. Rescue workers were frantically searching for survivors, carrying lifeless bodies from the rubble. Children were streaked with blood,

One match, one two-minute fuse, 169 lives.
(Photos: Collection of the author)

and wounded victims sat dazed in the streets. Smoke blackened the morning sky, cars burned, sirens wailed.

Dozens of dead bodies had been unearthed, including twelve children from a ground-floor day-care center. Hundreds more were believed to be still buried under the debris.

The investigation was already moving with lightning speed. The first piece of evidence—a truck axle—had fallen out of the sky within seconds of the explosion, spinning like a boomerang and smashing onto the hood of a maintenance man's car parked blocks from the site of the blast. FBI agents quickly surmised that the metal part had to have been directly under the origin of the blast to have acquired its unusual trajectory. Amazingly, the vehicle identification number, or VIN, on the axle's centerpiece survived intact—like a small toy left unscathed in the eye of a hurricane.

Before the sun set on the bomb scene, the Bureau's bomb specialists had traced the axle's VIN to a Ryder truck rented two days earlier from Elliott's Body Shop in Junction City, Kansas, 270 miles north of Oklahoma City. Agents sped to canvass that area's motels in search of Unsub 1 and Unsub 2, FBI jargon for the two unidentified subjects reportedly seen by the owner and two employees in the Ryder franchise.

By midafternoon the day following the blast, the networks announced that Junction City's Dreamland Motel had hosted a guest in Room 24, registered for four nights under the name Tim McVeigh and who, the manager recalled, had driven a yellow Ryder truck. That truck had been rented a few miles down the same highway at Elliot's Body Shop, and its VIN matched the VIN on the axle from the blast. The leads began to snap together in perfect order.

But who was Tim McVeigh?

Federal investigators tapped his name into the National Crime Information Center computer base and discovered that he had been pulled over near Perry, Oklahoma—eighty-eight miles from the blast site—only ninety minutes after the bombing. No connection was made to the blast at the time, but an astute state highway patrolman had noticed a missing rear license plate on his 1977 Mercury Marquis, and when the trooper also found a concealed weapon, he arrested McVeigh on traffic and firearms charges, then held him in jail pending a court appearance.

FBI agents immediately contacted the county jail. They learned that McVeigh was, at the very moment of their call, being accompanied by a deputy sheriff on the way to court for a bond hearing, with almost certain release to follow. Agents raced to the courthouse. Within thirty-six hours after the blast, Timothy James McVeigh was placed under arrest, charged with the bombing of the Murrah Federal Building and the largest mass murder in U.S. history.

Finding the axle that started the chain reaction of rapid discovery was a textbook picture of investigative genius by the FBI's alert bomb squad.

A drawing of Unsub I had been released on the day following the bombing, but because the link to McVeigh was so rapidly made by the hotel manager, who recalled the short-haired guest with the yellow Ryder truck from the motel's parking lot, McVeigh's identity was uncovered quickly the sketch immediately faded from the news. McVeigh's face proved to be as simple as the sketch itself, overtly lacking a single outstanding feature. The alleged bomber had the look of any generic Midwestern American boy.

To calm the rising tide of speculation about foreign involvement, authorities put McVeigh on display in a globally televised "perp walk," allowing the world its initial look at him as he was escorted from Perry's Noble County Courthouse in handcuffs, shackles, and orange coveralls. Crowds screamed "Baby killer!" in the news footage background.

McVeigh's registration at the Dreamland Motel included an address in Decker, Michigan, on a farm owned by brothers James and Terry Nichols. The authorities immediately tracked down James, and by late April 21, Terry turned himself in after hearing his name on televised news reports. Both were held as material witnesses, though James was later released and only Terry was charged.

Still, authorities felt that at least one other suspect was at large. The staff at Elliott's Body Shop in Junction City had reportedly seen another man in the background when McVeigh, using the name Robert Kling, rented the Ryder truck on April 17. The FBI released a sketch of the other man, prepared by an in-house Bureau artist. With McVeigh already in custody, every network led with the drawing of the wanted suspect, then dubbed John Doe II.

Hundreds of look-alikes—John No's as the press alternatively named them—were detained for questioning all across the country. NBC's *Dateline* ran a piece on the frenzy surrounding the John Doe II sightings. One scene showed traffic stopped in both directions as a man who resembled the drawing was held spread-eagle on an Arizona highway at gunpoint, then taken into custody and interrogated for ten hours before being released. The same drama was being repeated in every state as tips flooded the switchboards of the FBI and the major networks.

Thank God, I thought, at least there were direct witnesses and the face was on paper. The drawing depicted a man with a head of thick, dark, wavy hair combed back, with a square jaw, heavy jowls, full lips, an upturned pug nose, and an intense gaze. The eyewitness clearly had face-to-face contact with the suspect.

Attorney General Janet Reno made clear that while McVeigh and Nichols were under arrest, the investigation was by no means closed. "John Doe Number Two remains at large," she said sternly. "He should be considered armed and dangerous."

With the nation reverberating from the most deadly terrorist attack ever on American soil, an international manhunt was immediately launched. President Clinton announced that a crisis management team had been dispatched to Oklahoma City. An FBI command post was set up in a dilapidated former phone company building, a nondescript, unsigned center where, in Clinton's words, "the world's finest investigators" were being gathered.

"Let there be no doubt—we will find the people who did this," the president said, his voice low and determined, his eyes penetrating the lens of the camera. "When we do, justice will be swift, certain, and severe. These people are killers, and they must be treated like killers. I ask all Americans to pray."

Artistically, the John Doe II drawing being flashed all over the news channels looked excellent, though the caliber of the artwork could never guarantee the accuracy of the information it represented. And in this case something, the bombing task force commander explained, was apparently wrong. His phone call to me the day after the bombing came as a surprise.

"Ms. Boylan, would you please keep your availability open and stand by for further instruction?"

I packed a bag, placed it in the trunk of my car, and as promised, stood by. A day after the commander's request, I watched CNN break in with a story that the FBI would be releasing an updated drawing of John Doe II, but I still hadn't received the call to go. When the sketch appeared on camera, the host looked at the audience in confusion. The FBI had not released a new sketch at all, but just a muddier version of the original John Doe II drawing, the only alteration being the addition of a baseball cap over the identical face.

For three more days I stayed near the phone, on alert as ordered. The phone rang nonstop, but with questions, not instructions.

Reporters from coast to coast, friends, family, even strangers, were asking one question: "You going?"

On Tuesday afternoon, April 25, at the request of the Oklahoma City task force, I boarded a plane to Oklahoma City.

———

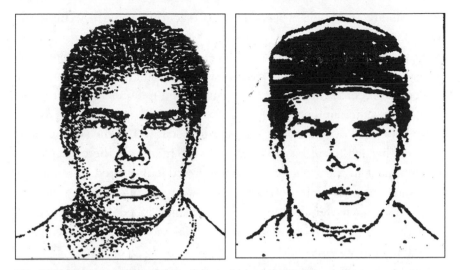

Two FBI-produced sketches—one with and one without a cap—were released as part of the search for John Doe II, suspected of accompanying Tim McVeigh to the Ryder franchise where the truck used in the Oklahoma City bombing was rented. (Drawings courtesy of ABC News).

In the Portland airport, then again while changing planes in SFO, I walked past rows of newspapers, all featuring the obliterated north face of the Murrah Federal Building alongside the existent John Doe II sketch. People strolled past the headlines, disconnected from the reality I was about to head into.

As the plane descended into Oklahoma City, I pressed toward the porthole, trying to see the blast's crater through the breaking sun. At the gate, the two agents assigned to escort me stood waiting.

To coordinate the task force effort, Attorney General Janet Reno had sent in the FBI's special agents in charge, the highest-ranking agents, from most of the neighboring states, backed by more than four hundred law enforcement agents from all branches of federal investigative agencies.

There was concern that the bombing was a direct attack on the government. While the FBI didn't have an office in the Murrah Federal Building, thirteen other security agencies, including the Secret Service and the Bureau of Alcohol, Tobacco and Firearms, did. With an ongoing series of postblast bomb threats being called in to hospitals, schools, and government buildings, and at least six calls from people claiming responsibility on behalf of Muslim sects, security around the blast site was on its highest alert.

As we approached the task force headquarters, we were stopped at each of multiple military checkpoints where our identification was scrutinized and recorded before we were authorized to enter farther into the heart of the command center.

I followed my drivers up the long outdoor stairwell to the second floor. We were headed toward a private area in the middle of the center when all movement in the frenetic surroundings suddenly halted in a national observance of a two-minute silence in memory of the bombing victims. Phones rang unanswered. Heads dropped. Hands stilled. Voices silenced.

It was 9:02 A.M., Wednesday, April 26. One week to the minute since the lethal blast was detonated.

I glanced around the frozen scene at the long rows of computer terminals, and the family photos that were near each, the assurance to the operators that their own families were still safe and real. Only the boxes of Kleenex around the room outnumbered the personal snapshots.

On one wall was a bulletin board papered with funeral notices for the relatives, colleagues, teammates, and lovers lost in the tragedy. Ads were posted for counseling services and dial-a-prayer numbers were torn from the yellow pages and tacked onto the board.

SAC Danny Coulson from Dallas, Texas, opened the door to the command center's Red Carpet Room. Devoid of carpet, the only red I saw in the room was in the weary eyes of the commanders.

This was the pulse point of the operation: Direct telephone land lines were linked to the offices of Attorney General Janet Reno and Director Louis Freeh of the FBI. Enlargements of the suspect drawing were interspersed with handwritten notes taped along the walls. Chairs were scattered and trash cans brimmed with remnants of fast-food lunches and styrofoam coffee cups.

Coulson swung a folding chair around, sat down knee-to-knee toward me, then pushed up his wrinkled dress-shirt sleeves. Though he was in the center of unimaginable pressure, he smiled at me as he slowly sighed.

"I've heard a lot of good things about you, young lady," he said with his slight Southern drawl. In the midst of all the chaos, Coulson made me feel as if I'd just sat down in front of a weekend barbecue pit with my favorite uncle. "Tell me about this famous interview process of yours that I keep hearing about," he continued, though he was distracted from my answers by a nonstop string of phone calls.

I could overhear that news of my arrival was being conveyed and decisions about what was in store were pending. He broke from conversation long enough to pass instructions over the phone to SAC Tubbs from Kansas City, who was heading the command post set up at the Fort Riley Military Base just outside Junction City, Kansas, where McVeigh had rented the Ryder truck.

"Jeanne, we'd like you to go up to Junction City," Coulson said as he hung up the phone and then swung his chair around backward to sit back down again. "The primary witness is at a place called Elliott's Body Shop, where McVeigh was reportedly accompanied by another man when he rented the Ryder truck. We've got trouble. You see those desks out there?" He motioned toward the two cavernous rooms, lined with desks and manned computer terminals, that I'd passed through on the way into our meeting.

"All those phones ringing off their hooks are delivering leads. Supposed sighting reports are pouring in from people who think they've seen Unsub 2, or John Doe Number Two as the press calls him. We're dispatching agents to follow up in every state. It's costing time and it's costing money, a lot of money. We still have no suspect and there's a strong chance that these ye-hoos might hit again.

"We'd like you to go up and talk to our eyewitness. I hear you have the ability to uncover additional information and find out what's wrong with these damn drawings. All we know is that something isn't right. We have a Learjet ready to take off at Tinker Air Force Base, and we have agents waiting to meet you in Junction City."

As background, he told me that in fact three witnesses had reported seeing two men in Elliott's Body Shop on April 17, and all had seen McVeigh, who stood at the counter and completed the paperwork under the name Robert Kling.

When it came to identifying the man with him, though, recollections got magically hazy. Owner Eldon Elliott said he was distracted by other business and noticed little more than that another man, "a little shorter than me," was waiting while the man with the long, thin face and military haircut rented the truck. Bookkeeper Vicki Beemer said she was focused on the contract and hardly looked up, except to discuss "Kling's" birth date, which he stated as April 19. They discussed his upcoming big day, though at the time Beemer didn't comprehend his hidden meaning.

The third witness, Tommy Kessinger, a mechanic, was our best hope. On a break in the chair inside the office when the truck was rented, he had little else to do but observe.

I started adding up the prospects. There had been no immediate trauma in the context SAC Coulson described. The truck was rented two full days before the bomb was detonated, so there was no particular reason for Kessinger to have embedded the image in his mind.

The three coworkers had never been instructed not to discuss their memories, and they had been interviewed together, so the chance that they'd homogenized their recall was high if not guaranteed. Plus, Tommy had been subjected to the facial-identification catalog by the Bureau artist brought in from the Special Projects Section in D.C. Tommy had already seen nearly a thousand images during the context of assimilating the image of the suspect.

My heart sank one more time. The only bet I was willing to place was that the odds at this point were not in our favor.

En route to Tinker Air Force Base, the drivers drove by the blast site. I watched the rescue workers carry empty stretchers into the inner security ring. They walked more methodically now than when I'd seen the first day's televised footage, evidence that they had abandoned hope of finding anyone else alive, though the mass grave still held the bodies of more than a hundred people. Flowers and wreaths were woven through the chain-link fences, and American flags flew from every floor on which the body searches were complete.

We drove past blocks of shattered glass and boarded storefronts. Prayers were printed on banners that hung on the sheets of plywood, the building owners more concerned about the grief of others than for their own misfortune.

When we arrived at the air base, the aircraft was waiting for takeoff. I stepped into the customized Learjet and looked around at the polished brass fixtures and powder-blue leather upholstery. Multiple telephones sat on the floor and the end table. The pilots, from the Drug Enforcement Administration, explained that the luxurious plane, confiscated by the government in a drug deal gone bad, was now used by FBI and DEA to shuttle commanders cross-country when discreet air travel was needed quickly.

I strapped into the executive seat that backed up to the cockpit, squeezed my drawing case between the seat and wall, and retrieved the *Newsweek* magazine I'd picked up on my way to Oklahoma. I turned past the cover photo of McVeigh in manacles, being presented by agents for the world's first look at our latest mass murderer, then opened the magazine to the photo of a grimy firefighter tenderly carrying the tiny, bloody, lifeless body of year-old Baylee Almon from the ruins of the blast. The next page folded out to form a three-panel poster of the gaping hole in the Murrah Building.

At first sight, the shot seemed like a hard look through a journalist's eye—an effort to provide a glimpse at the full physical effect on the building. But as I looked longer, I saw something more. On top of what was once the building's roof was one man, his body intact, a white towel placed over his face. He had survived the blast intact, but he had then taken a step out onto what once was the floor, probably in shock and confusion, and had fallen to his final resting position onto the building's concrete roof.

Before seeing that photo, I'd comprehended the death toll only academically. But something about the dark blue buttons on that man's shirt pulled my attention away from the death tally, to the sobering truth of the individual lives lost. Each person pulled from or still buried within the bomb rubble had a separate and distinct life, a history, hopes for the future, a family. Each one had gotten up, buttoned buttons, drunk coffee, and perhaps kissed a spouse good-bye on that ordinary Oklahoma morning.

A wave of grief rose through my body, deeper and more powerful than I imagined it could be, and I waged a losing battle with my own feelings. I wanted to be the consummate professional in front of the DEA agents, to hide all emotion. I gritted my teeth and tried talking myself out of it, but nothing worked. I leaned forward to let the tears fall in a straight line to the floor. As I kept my head down, I studied the frayed edges of my weathered art bag, full of nothing more than a child's school supplies: watercolor paper and handfuls of half-used yellow No. 2 pencils. How in the world had I ended up in this seat? I was just a kid from Montrose, Colorado, who liked to doodle in notebooks. Here I was, under orders from the attorney general and the FBI, alone in the cabin of a Learjet, being flown to interview the primary witness in the biggest terrorist attack in U.S. history. I thought of the responsibility—and then I thought of the odds.

I squeezed my eyes shut and began to pray.

The copilot reached back and tugged on my elbow. "Jeanne, you okay?" He took off his left headphone. I sat up without turning my face toward him, knowing even a glance would give me away.

"Is it your ears?" he yelled.

"Yeah, my ears, they'll be okay, thanks," I answered, never looking his way, then pulled myself together as the Learjet taxied down the runway.

The FBI had a car waiting on the tarmac to drive me to the command post. As the pilot unlatched the jet's door, the copilot turned around in his seat and gently touched my arm. "Wait a second," he whispered. "Jeanne, it's okay. We lost five from our office. I understand."

The rings of security were no less stringent at Fort Riley. I signed in at the last checkpoint and stepped into the old wooden barracks. SAC Tubbs popped out of his corner office and introduced himself. He invited me inside and a small group of agents joined us to devise a plan. Tubbs gave the instructions for me to conduct my preliminary interview with Kessinger and to call with a report before I proceeded further.

An assigned driver delivered me to Elliott's Body Shop, its exterior already familiar after a solid week in the news. Vicki Beemer sat behind the rental counter, as she had when McVeigh had come into the shop on April 17. Tommy Kessinger was waiting inside owner Eldon Elliott's private office.

I'd been forewarned about Tommy, told he was less than worldly, and not well-spoken or educated, but that he was—"unfortunately"—the best they had.

Tommy was caked in what looked like a perpetual coat of body-shop dust that lingered on his eyebrows and lashes. His large belly tested the strength of the aged threads in his turquoise Harley-Davidson T-shirt, and his nails were bitten down to the quick.

Tommy was a shop mechanic with a good heart, in the wrong place at the wrong time. He hadn't asked to be the primary witness in the nation's biggest case. One look into his eyes revealed his anguish, yet it was clear at a glance that he was trying with everything in him to be the best help that he could be.

The magnitude of the death toll was certainly within his understanding. The exact attributes the investigators had seen as an obstacle might in fact be our greatest asset when it came to his ability to remember exactly what he'd seen.

Whether he was highly educated had no bearing; education has more to do with opportunity than with innate intelligence. Yes, Tommy's world was small. But precisely because his boundaries *were* so limited, if there was anything askew, Tommy would be likely to notice.

He explained to me why he'd so vividly been able to describe John Doe I, Timothy McVeigh:

"He was standing there, and he had these two wads of chew under his lip, you know? Now when a guy chews, he tucks the chaw over to one side or the other so he can talk, know what I mean? But he doesn't divide it in two. This guy standing at the counter had a long, thin face, blue eyes, this short flattop hair like an army guy, and two puffs, like two plugs of chew, one tucked over on each side of his bottom lip. Funniest damn thing I ever seen. I just got fixated on looking at his face, I tell you. I couldn't take my eyes off him, trying to figure it out."

"Tell me more, Tommy," I urged. As eyewitnesses go, this case was blessed to have had Kessinger on a break, sitting exactly where he had been when McVeigh walked in.

"Yeah, I seen a guy kind of lurking over there by the door," he said, pointing out the octagonal office window, past the rental counter to some company posters hanging on the wall near the front entrance.

"But I tell you one thing," he said, leaning over the desk and lowering his voice to a whisper. "Sheez, I don't know why they got that damn picture out there of that John Doe II guy, 'cause this much I know. That picture ain't *nothing* like what I seen at all."

His words ricocheted in my mind and I reeled at the substance and gravity of what he'd just said, but I sat still and expressionless as he went on.

"Shit, you know, they sent this artist guy in here and he was real nice and all, but I told him what the guy at the counter looked like, I mean, I knew exactly about him down to his damn eyelashes, but then when he asked me about the other guy, I told him it wasn't as clear. I was fixated on the guy at the counter, see. So he got out this book with a bunch of pictures in it. He tried to tell me to pick out the first guy's face, but I didn't need no damn book to do that. I know what I seen—exactly. But then on the second guy, it was more hazy and so he stuck that book in front of my face again, and, hell, you know"—Tommy lowered his voice further—"when the FBI tells you to point, well, damn it, you point."

I silently reran the NBC *Dateline* footage through my mind: I could still see a man held spread-eagle at gunpoint on an Arizona highway because he resembled the FBI's wanted poster of John Doe II. Other supposed "suspects" who'd been fingered as look-alikes to the sketch had lost jobs and fought with employers and neighbors who'd turned them in. Their lives had been blasted apart after agents had shown up at their homes and places of employment following up on "dead-ringer" tips flowing through special phone lines in two full warehouse rooms of the command center.

"That's okay, Tommy, no big deal," I said placidly. "Maybe we'll try again, and this time, we'll just go from what you *did* see."

When we finished the first stage, I asked to use the phone to call Tubbs. Tommy sat outside.

"SAC Tubbs? I finished the preliminary interview with Kessinger."

"And," he said, awaiting my report, "what do you think?"

Tension flooded into every muscle as I anticipated his reaction to what I needed to say. "Well, we have a problem." I repeated Tommy's exact words, and I could feel the staggering implications ignite the commander's fury. The unprecedented manhunt had been under way for a full week, there was a threat that the terrorists responsible for the tragedy might strike again, and agents around the globe had been detaining people based on a sketch that the primary eyewitness was saying was not what he'd seen at all.

Tubbs's infuriated voice lowered to the level of a slow, drawn-out hiss. "How . . . did . . . this . . . *happen?*"

I swallowed hard. "All I can tell you is that the right questions were never asked. Kessinger was told to point pictures out from a book of facial features. He did exactly what he was told to do. Unfortunately, the book contained nothing he'd actually seen." I kept it simple. I didn't dare bring up the word *contamination*.

"The photos were all frontal views, while Kessinger had seen only a profile. The angle, the time frame, the level of emotion and encoding, the context of his sighting—none of those elements were taken into consideration. Any options for the true answers to surface were eliminated in the interview. Kessinger hadn't done anything wrong—he'd done precisely what he'd been instructed to do."

Early on the mechanic had tried to tell the authorities that the resulting sketch was wrong, but with the pressure to get a face in front of the American public, the Bureau had released the full-frontal, thick-black-haired, jowl-faced, pug-nosed image of a man who was never seen by any eyewitness from the front, who had never been seen without a hat on, with whom the witnesses had had no eye contact or voice contact, and who had exhibited no association with the man at the counter now known as Timothy McVeigh. For all we knew, Unsub 2 could have been bald and could simply have been a prospective customer who had walked in and out of the office with no more than a passing interest in renting a Ryder truck.

Because of the lack of overt trauma in the Unsub 2 encounter, even the time frame could not be established with certainty. Or at least with no more certainty than a person could give if, say, he was asked one week later to describe who it was he saw on a single given day at lunch, if he frequented the same restaurant daily.

Trauma consolidates the information into a single context or frame as it's encoded into recall. The detonation of the terrorist bomb was a national trauma, but it took place two full days after the truck was rented. Without trauma at the time of the sighting, there was no chronological boundary around the perceived image. One day's memory could easily bleed into another, making it all the more important that witnesses not ever be interviewed together, and that they be instructed not to discuss among themselves the fragile memories of what each believed he or she saw.

Once the possibility was introduced that a second man was with Tim McVeigh on the day the truck was rented, and then when that idea was validated by the Bureau's international release of the official John Doe II wanted poster, a John Doe II existed—not just in the eyes and minds of the witnesses, but in the minds of the American public as well.

During the first week, when Tommy persisted in his protest over the image and explained that it was not what he'd seen, the FBI hurriedly withdrew it. That was when they initially called me with the request to stand by. But wanting to keep the mistake manageable and in house, they faxed it instead to the original Bureau artist, by then back in D.C., who simply made the quick addition of a ball cap to try to appease the witness and correct the errors.

Then, during a perplexing national press conference, the "new drawing of John Doe II"—cap added—was put into circulation. Viewers scratched their heads in confusion, but Tommy continued to protest. That's when a solution to what was perceived as "Tommy's problem" was sought through the creation of a brand-new drawing. But the truth was, it had never been Tommy's problem.

An FBI agent, at Tubbs's instruction, took me to a Junction City hotel where I was given the order to check into a room while the task force developed a plan to deal with the crisis. I was told not to leave the room until further notice. I flipped between CNN and network-news updates, watching continuing coverage of the rescue efforts and listening to senators on talk shows speculating about the political motives behind the terrorist's bomb.

Hours later, Tubbs called with news that two agents were on their way to the hotel to question me about my interview with Kessinger.

The sun was setting. I was going on thirty-six hours without sleep by the time the agents introduced themselves and sat in the two available chairs. I sat on the edge of the bed prepared for an interview, but what I experienced began to take more the form of an interrogation.

They wanted to know at what points in the interview Tom Kessinger inhaled, when he exhaled, at what point did he lean forward, when had he spoken rapidly, when had he looked away. I held my hands up.

"Hey, wait a minute. Remember, you invited me here. I'm on your side—why are you talking to me like this?"

They lightened up a bit, but something odd was going on. They packed up their notes and left me with another directive to stay in the room until further notice. "Keep the phone line clear."

It got dark within the hour and it became increasingly apparent that I'd be spending the night in Junction City, without a toothbrush or a change of clothes. I'd noticed a Wal-Mart nearby and was contemplating running over to make a few purchases when a heavy hand rapped on my hotel door.

"Ms. Boylan?" It was one of the two agents who'd just left an hour earlier. "The information you produced this afternoon"—he paused and stared directly into my eyes—"does not exist." He remained frozen for a moment, stone-faced and motionless.

"Wh—what information?" I asked, stunned and still confused.

"Very good." He gave a single nod, then turned abruptly and walked away.

I closed the door, then walked over to the bathroom mirror and placed my palms down on the counter's surface, looked myself in the eyes, and began humming the theme from *The Twilight Zone* with my added lyrics: "Now they're going to have to kill you."

I lay awake all night long. At seven A.M., the two DEA pilots arrived to drive me to the military base airport where the Learjet was waiting.

Not a word was said about a reinterview with Kessinger.

Flying back to Oklahoma City, the DEA copilot invited me to trade places and sit in his seat. We were cruising at twenty thousand feet when the pilot's voice came through my headphones. "Jeanne, go ahead and bank it." He pointed to my controls and I turned the yoke in front of me slightly.

"No, really—go ahead and bank it," he said again, watching my tentativeness. I turned it again, a little harder. "No, really," he insisted. This time he reached over and yanked the wheel a full half turn. The plane cut hard to the right with a power that surged through my hands and up both arms. I let out a high-pitched shriek of excitement. He laughed.

"Now take it up," he said. I pulled the wheel gently toward me. He issued the identical look. "No—really." That was all he needed to say.

"Okay!" I yelled back, and forcefully jerked the wheel toward me as hard as I could. In seconds flat, the plane kicked up to twenty-three thousand feet. The wail of the engines won out over the sounds of our laughter, but all three of us were, at least for a moment, relieved from the pressure of the reality we were living through.

If the information I'd produced in Junction City "didn't exist," I wondered, should I report it to the SACs at the command center? Did it "exist" within the FBI but not outside the ranks? I decided I'd disclose my instructions to SAC Danny Coulson as soon as he got off the phone, but there wasn't time. Instead, Coulson hung up and explained that there had been breaking news overnight. A new witness had been uncovered and deemed highly reliable through a preinterview—not by a Bureau artist this time, but by a trained FBI agent. My drivers took me to the home of Debbie Nakanashi, an employee at the post office branch located near the Murrah Building.

Debbie recalled that on the morning of April 17 or 18, McVeigh and another man had come up to her window, not to buy stamps but to inquire about where they might find federal job applications. She remembered the exchange because the question struck her as odd: they were clearly in a post office, and the Federal Building was in plain view across the street. Also, she'd found the second man at her counter attractive and their interaction had bordered on flirtatious.

Her impression was that McVeigh was submissive to the other man, that McVeigh stood silently in the background, almost as if he were the "driver," and that the second man, whom she described as looking like an American Indian or Pacific Islander with darker skin, bigger bones, and a more muscular body than McVeigh, was more like the "boss."

Debbie's face was still covered with abrasions from where the glass from the post-office windows had grazed her skin. She had purposely not watched the television news to protect her young daughter from associating her mother's injuries with the commotion being telecast, so the information she revealed was not distorted by prolonged exposure to news reports.

At the end of a six-hour interview, we'd produced a clear illustration of her impression, but it was not quite strong enough for public release due to the passive context of the sighting. It was, at least, suitable for use as an internal aid to the investigators.

Debbie's sighting was corroborated by a coworker at the neighboring counter window, who had just begun to walk away when the olive-skinned man approached. The coworker had had a protective interest in Debbie and didn't care for the seductive tone of the conversation he was overhearing, so he paid attention to both men. Independent of her account, he also identified Tim McVeigh as the person standing by quietly in the background.

Following the meeting with Nakanashi, the agents drove me outside the city to her coworker's brick home. Because of the lack of discrepancy between their descriptions, I decided not to create a separate rendition, so as to avoid adding ammunition for the defense's case. The risk outweighed the potential gain.

That night, I finally reunited with my bags at the Oklahoma City hotel, but again there was no time to sleep. I had only a few hours to clean up the work I'd done with the postal workers and prepare for my early-morning report to the SACs at the command center. I was on night number three with no sleep. To keep myself awake while I worked, I turned the television on and the volume up.

The broadcasts replayed the week's events, not as thirty-second news items but in documentary style. Periodically, when a search order had gone out for total silence at the bomb scene, all activity had instantly ceased. Cellular phones snapped off, helicopters flew away, and hammering and sawing—even breathing—was silenced as much as possible while listening devices monitored the still air for sounds and heartbeats.

At one point, a whimper was heard through the silence, which led a team of firefighters down into a basement under a pile of rubble, where they found twenty-year-old Dana Bradley pinned under a five-hundred-pound concrete wall. She was in an area so unstable that the remaining structure threatened to cave in at any second.

The woman had been pinned for more than three hours when volunteer Dr. Gary Massad crawled through to help. The buckled walls above her rumbled and her blood pressure was dropping into the danger zone, but the material over her couldn't be budged. The hole in which she lay was so small the doctor couldn't even maneuver enough to inject a needle into her body.

Several times while trying to help, building vibrations and additional bomb threats forced the rescue team to race for safety. Dana Bradley, bordering on shock, begged them not to leave. Finally, the rescuers had to get her to safety, and to do so she had to be cut out from underneath the wall that imprisoned her.

The amputation took ten grueling minutes. "You cut, pull back, clamp. Cut, pull back, clamp," Dr. Massad said. "I'll never forget the sound of it. My greatest fear was that I would be ordered to leave the building, that I would have to leave her trapped there. I would have carried that to my grave." Dana Bradley survived, in critical condition for weeks, only to learn later that her two children and her mother had died in the blast.

Moments before the explosion, she recalled seeing an olive-skinned man, who she said had stepped out of the passenger side of a Ryder truck, but her injuries were so severe and the emotional toll of her loss so extensive, that her family rightfully protected her, allowing no more interviews. The commanders talked of bringing me in again when she was able to speak, but the week after the bombing was just too soon.

I looked down at my drawing board, at the face on the drawing board in front of me. Exhausted and weary, I looked away and toward the television, then stood up to shake myself away from being emotionally consumed. The haunting eyes in the drawing seemed to follow me as I paced across the room. Fatigue had taken over my body. I dialed Marc Klass's California number. The deal we had was that we would call each other whenever we needed each other. Marc hung on the line with me as I explained the horror of the days now imprinted forever in my own memory. But even after being strengthened by his support, each newscast only brought greater heartache.

Edye Smith felt the explosion from her office in the IRS building. When smoke started filling the skies, she followed her colleagues out into the street to see what had happened. There she saw bloodied children tottering, crying. Involuntarily, her feet flew from underneath her, running toward the federal day-care center where minutes earlier she'd left her sons, Chase, three, and Colton, two. She studied every child's face she passed as she ran down the street.

When she saw the Murrah Building, with nine stories of debris crushed on top of the day-care center, she began screaming the names of her babies into the dusty, smoky ruins of the safe haven where she had last told them she loved them. It was hours before her brother, an officer with the Oklahoma City police, finally found his sister's sons. He assumed the grievous task of identifying the two tiny, ravaged bodies of his own nephews—one in the temporary morgue near the former day-care center and one at the medical examiner's office.

An office supervisor had sat down with a cup of coffee and called a Wednesday nine A.M. meeting to order. Seventeen people had filtered into the room, all with coffee and notepads in their hands. Two minutes later, only the supervisor and her desk remained, perched tenuously on a ledge.

All seventeen others were dead.

Two dozen children lost both parents. Two hundred children lost one parent. Nineteen children lost their lives.

It was almost four in the morning. I was dizzy from the news coverage. I felt myself teetering on an emotional wire when again, by necessity, I picked up my hotel phone.

It was nearly three A.M. In Colorado and I could tell from my mother's voice that I'd jarred her from sleep. "Mom, I'm in Oklahoma City and working on the bombing. I'm really scared. I need your help. Bodies are still trapped under tons of concrete and glass, and at least one of the bombers is still loose. I'm working hard, but I don't know how much I can really do." Tears started rolling, hers and mine. "There has to be something more. Will you please pray with me right now?"

I held on to the phone while she spoke. Her gentle words soothed my heart and gave me strength. "Would you do me a favor?" I asked when we'd finished. "Would you call your prayer chains at the church in the morning and ask them to pray for these families?"

I knew she would. We said good-night. I finished my work and had just enough time to shower and dress before the agents knocked on my door to drive me to my meeting at the command center. After a review of the interviews and the sketch from the postal worker's sighting, SAC Coulson told me that I had orders to return immediately to Junction City. Headquarters in Washington, D.C., had decided I was to continue the interview with Kessinger. Another private plane was waiting for me at the air base.

Agent Scott Crabtree, who in addition to the Bureau's artist had also interviewed Kessinger the day of the bombing, drove a car onto the Fort Riley airstrip to pick me up. We went first to the command post and through the intense security checkpoints before being allowed in the front door. I signed the needed papers and walked into the old building again. SAC Tubbs greeted me and asked if I was ready to go, if I'd yet eaten lunch. I hadn't eaten since a small snack on the flight from Oregon—I'd actually forgotten to.

Stopping for food seemed like an indulgence given the pace we needed to move at. Tubbs ordered me to wait while he sent an agent out to get lunch. I tried to insist on getting straight to work, but the commander hadn't phrased it in the form of an option. "Sit down. Take your time," he insisted. "Everybody needs to eat."

Soon, a huge hamburger, fries, and a milk shake were placed on the table. I leaned forward over the desk, folded down a portion of the wrapper covering the burger, and began to take my first bite. Then I stopped, paralyzed by the face that appeared before my eyes. Pinned on the wall in front of me was a military photograph of suspect Timothy McVeigh. But in the photograph with him, among others, was a smiling, muscular, olive-skinned man. Right age, right height, right build. He matched the description from the post office sightings perfectly. I dropped the hamburger onto the table and jumped up, motioning frantically for a nearby agent to come look.

The door to the corner office closed quickly after the agent passed on my comment to the commanders. Within a moment, he returned and told me with certainty that I should now wrap the burger and take it with me. After all, the witness was waiting.

Scott Crabtree took me straight to a room in the office area of the Fort Riley post, where Tommy was already seated. This time, on instructions from Director Freeh in the event that additional information should surface, as it so often did in my interviews, Agent Crabtree stayed with me, taking a seat in a corner chair. He rested his right ankle over his left knee, while his right knee restlessly shook at a rate of roughly four beats per second. I'd had no chance to brief him on how slowly and calmly I liked to work. I also hadn't had the chance to explain that he wouldn't be a part of my conversation with Tommy.

From my preinterview, I'd gathered insight into Tommy's world. I moved him onto talk of motorcycles and topics of life within his thirty-mile comfort zone to help keep him relaxed. I knew it was going to take work to excavate beyond the faulty sketch that had by now been seared into his mind. I cautiously began periodic prompts within the conversation.

"Well, did he have a mustache or what?" Agent Crabtree urgently interjected, meaning only to speed up the process. But with his interjection, thirty minutes of intentional diversion flew out the window and I now needed to overcome the suggestion of the characteristic Scott had just introduced. I smiled and flashed him a subtle admonition to remain silent. Thankfully, he picked up the cue.

A direct question such as Crabtree had asked would cause Tommy to "try" to remember, which was the worst thing he could do. It would cause the shift from a subconscious to a conscious level of recall, or to the most recently embedded image in his memory. The misinformation in the first John Doe II sketch was our main obstacle. If I couldn't move him beyond that image, we'd end up with nothing more than a description of what had been encoded in his mind from the existent wanted poster. This interview needed to move slowly and seamlessly to reach the latent image of the person he'd previously seen.

After several hours we had the finished profile drawing. The face was dramatically different from that described by Debbie Nakanashi of the man with McVeigh in Oklahoma City. It was also a different face from the one on the current John Doe II posters. Tommy Kessinger was relieved, and his contentment, witnessed by Agent Crabtree, was now on record.

The next challenge was to erase the thick-haired, pug-nosed frontal face not just from the news but from the nation's memory. If we could.

———

Back in Oklahoma City, my hotel's registry was made up of rescue workers from around the country, most in their twenties or early thirties. As an expression of appreciation, management offered an "all you can eat" shrimp dinner on the house. When I walked into the crowded room, an older man stood up and offered his chair.

As we spoke, I learned that he'd been involved in the Lockerbie, Scotland, Pan Am Flight 103 crash investigation, as well as that of the World Trade Center bombing. He introduced himself as FBI Agent Dave Williams.

"Have you been down to the site?" he asked. I told him that several agents had walked me through the rings of security up to the final fence at the foot of the building.

"But have you been *inside* the building? Meet me in the lobby at six o'clock tomorrow morning and I'll take you through it."

I delayed my flight home the next day and waited for him to pull up to the hotel front door. He handed me a card. Williams, quiet and unassuming, turned out to be the head of the Explosives Unit at the FBI Lab, entrusted with the responsibility of the entire forensic investigation in Oklahoma City.

He explained how the disaster crew had worked meticulously floor by

A reinterview with witness Tom Kessinger in Junction City, Kansas, resulted in this profile sketch of the suspect dubbed by the investigation as John Doe II. (Drawing by Jeanne Boylan)

floor, forming a human chain to pass buckets of debris down to ground level. At the bottom of the chain, each bucket's contents were sifted through a fine metal screen, like one a gold miner would use, in a gruesome search for body parts, bomb fragments, and identifying jewelry, any tiny piece that might be linked to one victim or one suspect. Rescue workers had spray-painted GOD BLESS AMERICA in ten-foot-high letters across the building's crater in testament to their determination to fight back against the terrorists.

"That parking lot"—Dave pointed across the street—"was filled when the bomb went off. Eighty-seven cars. It was just after nine in the morning. Most were still arriving at work and died before they ever stepped out of their cars. It took the Jaws of Life tool to extract them. We had to tag them with their vehicle identification numbers—their bodies were burned and mangled beyond recognition."

Directly beneath us was the fresh gravel-filled crater.

Once the surface of a busy city street, the blast had left a gaping hole thirty-five feet wide and eight feet deep.

Beyond the horrifying sights, what seethed into my senses most was the distinct aroma. The sounds of the heavy equipment forced us to nearly yell to be heard, and every massive piece emitted diesel fumes. No matter the camaraderie, the goodwill, and the outpouring of sentiment in the form of flowers and ribbons on the chain-link fence around the bomb site, there was the unforgettable smell of diesel combined with the stench of corpses decaying underneath the tons of debris.

We walked down the street to the Evidence Unit, in a former mechanic's garage. Brown bags, numbered and standing along the floor in ordered rows, contained painstakingly rescued dust-sized particles that accounted at that time for 65 percent of the Ryder truck rented by McVeigh. In the middle of the warehouse sat another Ryder truck, identical to the one rented from Elliott's on April 17. Thirty-five-gallon tanks filled one-third of the truck's cargo bay, replicating the surprisingly small mass of bomb material that created so awesome an explosion.

Williams opened the door of McVeigh's confiscated car. It had been processed for evidence and sat eerily isolated on the shiny concrete floor below the low, dull fluorescent ceiling lights. Dave nodded for me to go ahead and look more closely.

FBI Special Agent Dave Williams takes time out from his duties as evidence supervisor of the bombing sight to comfort and counsel rescue workers, April 1995. (Photo: Collection of the author)

"It's all right," he assured me. "It's already been processed." I slid in, balancing my weight on a single knee while wrapping my fingers around the steering wheel.

I looked through the windshield and over the hood, trying to imagine what could have been going through McVeigh's mind the moment the bomb went off. By the FBI's calculations, he was only eight blocks away and just entering the freeway at the time of the blast.

A feeling of sickness seeped through my limbs and heart: to be so close to that degree of evil, to touch what he had touched, to look through the glass he'd been sitting behind at the time that the bomb went off.

Dave walked me outside the building for fresh air. The exterior was purposely unmarked. This inconspicuous mechanic's garage housed every shred of crucial evidence needed to convict the mass murderers.

There was more than one day-care center in the tragedy. The first, called America's Kids, was on the northwest side of the second floor of the Murrah Building. The other, operated by the YMCA, was in a building across the side street, but in a direct line of the bomb blast's trajectory. We walked in past the guards at the front door. I steadied myself on

A breeze brings momentary relief from the mixture of diesel fumes and decay at the sight of the Oklahoma City bombing. (Photo: Collection of the author)

a pile of demolished furniture and stared at the walls where names still labeled crib sites: Justin, Madeline, Kimberly . . .

Along the lower walls were the remnants of the toddlers' bloody handprints, left as they'd tried to grope their way out of the darkness after the blast.

Dave knelt next to a toy slide. Fragments of human tissue were embedded by shards of glass that had literally pierced through a child before lodging into the bright orange plastic. He explained that some of the toddlers who were near the windows at the time of the explosion were now blinded for life.

One hundred and sixty-eight people died, but the number of those in the psychological wreckage might never be fully tallied. Estimates were that from the moment of the detonation, the explosion—then the implosion—lasted eight seconds. Count again, I thought as the car turned the corner to the airport. The explosion left scars on this country that would last forever.

14

JOHN DOE II:

THE POWER OF SUGGESTION

When I stepped off the plane at Denver International, I walked directly into an ambush of reporters. But I'd flown out of Oklahoma City on a last-minute reservation, so how had they managed to find me? What flight-schedule database were they tapped into?

I edged my way past the cameras. When working for a family as an independent contractor, I had the freedom to comment to the press if it would benefit the case. When local or state police agencies were involved, they'd often bring me in specifically to resurrect the interest of the media. But for the FBI, the rules were very different: comments had to be filtered through a single source. In the case of the Oklahoma City bombing, that source was SAC Weldon Kennedy.

Our new John Doe II image was revealed at a press conference in Oklahoma City a few hours before my arrival in Denver and was now a top story on the networks' broadcasts. Explanations about the subtle nuances that make a face identifiable could make a highly useful sound bite for the evening's news, but I didn't dare risk it without the approval of the FBI. I hid out in the ladies' room hoping for the reporters to disband.

I had less than twenty-four hours to get back to Bend to vacate my seasonal rental, and the last thing I had time for was a three-hour Denver layover. Later, I exited the ladies' room cautiously, dodged into a shop, and spun a display of postcards. Among them, one card seemed to be out of place.

The photo was of a woman, alone, soaking in the sun in a corrugated metal horse trough. The angle was from behind her, as if she didn't know anyone was near. Her long blond hair spilled out from under a black cowboy hat, and only her shoulders and elbows were visible over the back of the metal tub. Her perfectly manicured feet were resting on the far ledge of her makeshift spa. Faded denim clothes hung from an old, weathered fence post, and her horse grazed nearby. In front of her was nothing. Just vast open space, foot-high golden prairie grass, and clear blue, cloudless sky. I turned the card over to see where the shot had been taken, but there was no caption.

The smell of diesel fumes in the airport only revived the horrid memories from my time in the Murrah Building. Yet the sight of that postcard photo bathed me in a sense of immediate peace every time I looked at it.

I bought four cards, one for each of my sisters and one to keep for myself.

On the flight back, I starting scratching out a list of the things I needed to do in the one day I had home before the move: house hunt; clean carpets; rent a truck; buy boxes; get cleaning supplies. I looked out the window as we taxied to the Portland terminal, and as usual, it was raining. My plane to Bend was always in the last slot on the small tarmac of the commuter concourse. The question was never *would* I get wet in the Portland rain, but, how wet would I get?

I walked quickly up the jetway from the 757 into the main Portland terminal and right into another press ambush. Bulbs flashed and microphones aimed at my face. Passengers pushed around me to escape, while I tried to muddle my way through the chaos.

"Could we get comments on your experiences in Oklahoma City?"

"Any news on the whereabouts of John Doe II?"

"Do you think McVeigh was part of a bigger group?"

"What do you know about a cover-up, Ms. Boylan?"

"What was it like being at the bomb scene?"

But I had no freedom to answer.

"Let me make a call and I'll be right back, I promise," I interrupted, then ran over to a pay phone and hid behind a partition.

Bart Gory was the FBI public spokesperson in Portland. I knew the office number by heart and was relieved to hear him pick up the line.

"Bart, I am *so* glad you're there. This is Jeanne Boylan. I'm in Portland trying to get back to Bend. The press tracked me down between flights in Denver and again here. CBS News, *Inside Edition,* the newspapers— they all want comments on the new John Doe II. What shall I do? Can I send them over to you?"

"Jeanne," he said without hesitating, "we trust you. Say whatever you want. You're a professional. You know how to handle 'em. After all, you've been doing this public relations stuff for years. Just let me know if you want any help."

We trust you—I loved those words! I hung up and returned to the reporters. But when I finished explaining the details in the new image, they followed me on up the concourse. *Inside Edition* and CBS began to battle it out for rights to an interview I hadn't consented to. My eyes alternated between them as if tracking a tennis match. The CBS producer prevailed, explaining that she wanted me to postpone my flight and spend the night at Portland's four-star Alexis Hotel so the station could do a "sit-down interview" outside the noisy airport termi- nal.

"The Alexis?" I asked.

At home I had chaos, a refrigerator full of two-week-old food, and a list of chores I couldn't start until morning.

"And a massage?" I added, kidding.

"Okay, sure, and a massage," she relented, to my surprise.

She waited until I got checked in at the hotel counter before shatter- ing my dream of a restful night. "Oh, but we won't be using your room for the interview. By the way, did I mention that you'll be going live with Harry Smith?"

"But Harry Smith is in New York." I was about to hear the catch.

She knew she'd reeled me in. "That's right. So we'll need you at the KOIN-TV studio by three-fifteen A.M."

Two other news crews had entered the hotel behind us. They'd ingeniously let CBS pick up the hotel tab and simply tagged along. I was cornered.

The last crew members packed up and left the room after one o'clock in the morning. I had ninety minutes to get ready to leave for the CBS studio. There was no point in lying down. I'd finally hit the stage of fatigue where sleep didn't even matter anymore.

I took a hot bath and wrapped my hair in a towel, then dialed my voice mail by the low, gentle light of the fireplace. It was jammed with media calls and messages from distant relatives who'd seen the airport clip on the evening national news, but one call, from Tony Ferreria, was flagged "urgent."

Tony was the head of the Portland Police Bureau Bomb Squad. I wondered if "urgent" meant urgent enough to call at this time of night. Tony wouldn't use the word lightly. I dialed.

"Yeah, Jeanne, hi, I'm glad you called."

"Tony, what's up? I haven't talked to you in at least a year. Everything okay?"

"Listen to me very carefully, sweetheart." He spoke slowly and in a low, deliberate tone. "I want to tell you how to recognize a mail bomb."

"What? Are you serious?"

The sound of his words shook me into full alert. Tony was an old friend. Three years earlier, I'd entered the Portland Police Bureau parking structure after work one day to find him lying underneath my car in what turned out to be an investigation of a bomb threat on all PPB detectives. Tony was the best in his field, and if he spoke, I'd listen.

"Watch out for packages that are stamped and not metered," he warned. "A bomb will have a little weight to it, enough so that a normal person would take it to a counter and have it weighed for postage. But a bomber won't let himself be seen. He'll put his own postage on the package, and it will require a lot. It will look odd.

"Look for a return address you don't recognize, even if it looks like some harmless organization. You'll know who should be sending you things and who should not. And if you've gone that far, never open the package in the predictable way it would normally be opened. Most packages are opened from the right-hand upper corner and torn downward. That's where the detonator will be wired. If you think it's safe, even if you are sure it is safe, poke a tiny incision into the opposite corner and peer in to see what's inside. Even that's no guarantee. The bomb could be bound in a book or another package.

"Jeanne, your best bet is if you have *any* doubts, call me, or take it to the airport police, identify yourself and explain the situation, then have them x-ray it for you. Are you listening to me?"

"I hear you, Tony. But why are you telling me all this?"

"Just remember what I've said. Okay, kiddo?" He spoke sternly. "Do you promise me that?"

"Yeah, okay, thanks. Good night, Tony." I dropped the phone into the cradle and sat still in the quiet of the firelit room.

The KOIN tower was silent at three-fifteen in the morning. The sounds of my shoes echoed in the hallways as I walked into the freezing studio for the remote interview with CBS in New York. I searched for something warm to wrap my fingers around—coffee, tea, hot water—but even interns didn't show up at this insane hour. The interview was to take place at four o'clock in the morning, airing live at seven A.M. on the East Coast.

"Have a seat," a producer's voice boomed from some speaker in the ceiling. I couldn't see his face. I couldn't see anyone's face.

A half hour later, a huge robotic camera began circling like an unmanned dental X-ray machine closing in on me, then adjusting angles, moving farther back, and whipping around to my side, undoubtedly searching for an angle that best hid my lack of sleep.

"Good morning, Jeanne, thanks for joining us this morning." The large monitor lit up with Harry Smith's face, as if he were sitting across the set instead of across the country.

I sat up a bit in my chair while he ran through an accounting of various cases I'd been involved in. Then the topic turned to the bombing.

I described the details of the new drawing without explaining why there was one. Just as in an eyewitness interview, you don't discuss what it is you're hoping *not* to reinforce. But how do you diplomatically say to the public, "Never mind what we've already shown you, what we really meant was this" without explaining the reasons why? We successfully dodged the issue, and by four-twenty, I was through and off the set.

The producer walked down the hallway with a light step and a smile. "Sleep well?" she asked as she held her fresh cup of hot coffee. I could see that *she* had.

"Yeah, great, thanks."

"You don't mind staying for a live interview at seven A.M.?" Producers do that. They use an upswing on the end of a sentence as if they're posing a question that they never intend to actually ask.

It was 8:30 A.M. before I settled into a town car for the ride to the airport—another whole night without sleep. I'd lost count of how many in a row. I leaned against the back window into the warmth of the morning sun and laughed at my own innocence as it finally occured to me. I'd never received that promised massage.

A t eleven A.M., I pulled up the steep, juniper-lined drive to my house. Two pickup trucks and a Jeep lined the driveway, and beyond them I could see into the open garage. Boxes were stacked in neat rows.

Tentatively, I edged up the steps and peered guardedly through the open door. On the counter was a vase of long-stemmed roses surrounded by a spread of food.

I rounded the corner into the kitchen only to find a line of friends in ball caps and blue jeans ready to load their borrowed trucks for my move. Carpets were cleaned, windows washed, everything on my list had been done. One had even made arrangements for a place I could move *to*, since I'd had no time to house hunt. It was their remote contribution to the Oklahoma City cause.

A mutual friend owned a ranch that had been on the market for a year, with an airstrip, horse arenas, a secluded setting, and best of all, the massive estate was protected by electronic security gates. The keys were mine for the time being.

I'd barely settled in to the privacy at the ranch when Marc Klaas called from Los Angeles. He'd opened that morning's *L.A. Times* only to discover an article written about the Oklahoma City bombing.

He read the headline first, then added, "Jeanne, it's written by you."

"No, it's not, Marc. I didn't write any article."

It seems that, inadvertently, I had.

When I'd called my mother from my Oklahoma City hotel room and asked for her prayers, she'd responded by relaying my request to every church in Montrose, Colorado. The local newspaper had then run a story asking the whole town to add their prayers for the victims in Oklahoma City. In response, I'd sent a letter to the editor, thanking the town for their support. The Associated Press wire service had subsequently picked the letter up not as an editorial, but as a feature article.

The headline read "Good Emerges All Around," In it, I'd shared my firsthand impressions of how the very event that had the power to destroy us if we dwelled only on the evil, also had equal power to lift our spirits. By focusing on the limitless efforts of volunteers, rescue workers, the Red Cross, and the prayers of an entire nation for the Oklahoma families, the national tragedy was able to fortify us as a nation and bring out the very best in us all. Unbeknownst to me, the letter meant for my hometown was picked up and published in newpapers from New York City to Seattle.

I no sooner hung up from Marc's call, when the FBI task force in Oklahoma City called again. They'd received a report from a man acting out of self-proclaimed "civic duty." He'd seen the arrest photos of McVeigh and Nichols on the news and realized he'd seen those faces before, along with that of a third man who had visited his real estate office in Cassville, Missouri, the prior November. The location roughly fit McVeigh's known travels, which made the sighting more than a remote possibility.

Under task force order, I left immediately, flying into Oklahoma City to join up with Special Agent Bill Teeter for the drive to southern Missouri, where the witness, retired sergeant major Bill Maloney, was standing by for our arrival.

On the day of his November 1994 sighting, Maloney and his associate, Joe Lee Davidson, were in Maloney's one-car garage that had been converted to a realty brokerage office, awaiting the arrival of a man who had called in response to an ad for a remote piece of property. The sergeant major confirmed the caller's name. "McVey, like the street here in Cassville? M-c-V-e-y?" he asked.

"Close enough." the caller said, and hung up. But McVeigh wasn't one of the two men who showed up for the meeting. One man, who Maloney said was Nichols, sat quietly, passively, during the meeting. The other man was dark-haired, clean-cut, muscular, and olive-skinned. The realtor remembered him as jovial, talkative, and seemingly "calling the shots." His skin was taut and his hair cut in a military style. His jaw was square and solid, neck short and thick. He identified himself as "Jacks," spelled, he explained, "like it sounds."

The property the two wanted to look at was in a hollow, or ravine, in the Ozark Hills. The ad described it as being "in the middle of nowhere," on land where there were caves. Joe Lee found a topographic map and unrolled it on a table so the men could see the location. The secretary stepped in briefly to deliver papers, then left, noticing little beyond the presence of the two men. Maloney sat back and watched from his desk twelve feet across the room, using the observation skills he'd acquired in the military.

He'd taught his men to do the same. From one day to the next, he'd move a single item in the room and then grill his troops over the change to teach them to take notice of the smallest details. Observation was his pastime, but in this case, he also had a personal interest. The muscular man had ethnic features, and his look aroused memories of an unpleasant experience in his distant past. Though six months had passed and there had been no trauma around his sighting, between his phenomenal visual skills and the emotional connection to a distinct memory, there may have been enough reason to encode the image into his recall.

We used the hospitality room of a rural hotel for the interview. Teeter sat in the back of the room, out of Maloney's vision, a lesson learned from the interview with Tommy Kessinger. Teeter positioned himself just enough within my sight so that he and I could communicate non-verbally.

The interview moved swiftly. Maloney recalled vivid details right down to the pattern on the soles of the shoes the muscular man was wearing, visible as he'd kept one ankle positioned over his left knee.

Teeter and I continuously bounced glances off each other in astonish-
ment at his degree of precision. In military terms, Maloney explained
that "the man's gig lines were not askew," meaning that everything about
him was in order from his shirt collar button to his belt buckle and the
creases in his pants. The profile of the man's nose ended in a sharply
chiseled point, and the back of his neck was so thick and rigid that
there wasn't even a hint of indentation.

As a witness, either Bill Maloney had fallen from the sky as a pure
gift from the heavens, or he was completely certifiable. We didn't know
which. But there was no gain in it for him, except his satisfaction as a
patriot—a good man doing the right thing. I believed him. So did Teeter.

He explained that when the real estate meeting was nearly over, the
door opened and a third man, whom he was "one hundred percent certain" was Timothy McVeigh, walked in and asked what was taking so
long. As McVeigh looked down, his eyes landed on a bronzed bullet on
Maloney's desk.

"Oh, I just use that for shootin' coyotes when they come on the property," Maloney said. McVeigh, who laughed in response, tilted his head
back and momentarily exposed a darkened right eyetooth.

I snuck a look at Teeter, to ensure he'd heard the comment. This was
big. McVeigh was in custody and the FBI could obtain his military dental records and easily verify a root canal or injury that could have caused
the discolored tooth. If we could substantiate that, I could proceed with
confidence with the rest of Maloney's extraordinary recall.

When it came time to reveal the drawing, the sergeant major nodded
with approval, then pulled a telescoping pointer out of his pocket and
targeted tiny areas where he felt "the angle of the nose was two degrees
sharper," the forehead "an eighth inch deeper." And then we were done.
Teeter and I looked at each other, poker-faced but inwardly ecstatic.
Now it was up to the FBI to protect the image carefully while they
searched for Tim McVeigh's associate and possible accomplice—the
man who called himself Jacks.

Next, Maloney's partner and secretary came for separate interviews.
Both corroborated Maloney's recollection, but Joe Lee's rendition differed slightly from Maloney's: he described a man with bulkier features
and a slightly older face, even more ethnic in appearance, and heavier,

with thicker hair and thicker skin on the cheeks and under the eyes.

Since two descriptions should never be homogenized into one, and each witness is always correct in his own perceptions, we faced a choice. Due to his observational expertise, and his emotively based reason for recalling, the sketch based on Maloney's perspective would become the official rendition for release to the task force. Teeter and I wrapped up the meetings and headed through the thick foliage of the northern Arkansas hillsides and back to Oklahoma City.

"You've got to get me those dental records, Bill. Please don't forget," I pleaded. Heading into a meeting with the task force SAC, I'd have paid anything to get my hands on that information to know how much credence to put in Maloney's account. But it would take time. I'd have to leave it in Teeter's hands.

After the long drive back to Oklahoma City, I entered the commander's office alone to report in.

"There are some similarities but also many dissimilarities among the descriptions," I explained to SAC Bob Ricks. "The dark-haired man sighted in Elliott's Body Shop by Tommy Kessinger was described as muscular, with no reference to skin tone or ethnicity. But the dark-haired man in Missouri was described as darker-skinned and ethnic, as was the subject sighted in the Oklahoma City post office one or two days prior to the bombing."

The SAC interrupted, "What if I were to tell you that we believe we've now identified the Junction City subject? And he's a ringer for your sketch."

He explained that a man named Todd Bunting had been in Elliott's Body Shop to rent a Ryder truck. He walked in, stood precisely where Kessinger recalled seeing him, and was wearing the same hat as the one described in Tommy's interviews. But his visit to the shop was on April 18, one day *after* the day that McVeigh came in. He *was* with a second man, who was also a military man, but that man was army sergeant Michael Hertig, who had stood at the counter and completed a Ryder rental contract exactly as Timothy McVeigh had done the day before.

Like McVeigh, Hertig was tall, fair, and had military-style, short-cropped hair. Both transactions occurred in the afternoon—but one day apart. Todd Bunting was the right man, right description—wrong day.

The implications were huge. The description of the second man, the now infamous John Doe II, had been released to the networks immediately after the bombing and published in newspapers worldwide. It had resulted in a manhunt of monumental proportions costing massive amounts of money and investigative hours and creating havoc in the lives of hundreds who resembled the erroneous image. At one point, the task force reported processing eleven hundred leads a day based on the release of the original drawing.

Once that drawing was in circulation, the well-documented power of suggestion took over. The idea of a second man at the Ryder counter who was linked to the bombing permeated the minds of not just the public, but more importantly, also of the eyewitnesses involved.

How had an error of this magnitude happened to begin with? Without trauma—and we knew from the beginning that the three Elliott's eyewitnesses had experienced none—there was no chronological boundary, no reason for the mind to enclose and encode detail into a singular context, a fact that should have been considered during the initial interview. Had it been considered, questions could have been devised to determine the full context of the witness sighting. But questions of chronology were never addressed.

Then, to further embed the error, the "reality" of a second man had been revalidated with every viewing of the ceaseless airing of the John Doe II poster which even after the release of the corrected image, the media continued to use in their coverage. The problem, once created, perpetuated itself.

The mistake had never been that of the eyewitnesses, but rather the lack of understanding on the side of the investigation of how recall is encoded in a non-traumatic scenario. The right answers were in the psychology of how the memory functions, not in how artistic or aesthetically good the drawing turned out to be.

As Tommy Kessinger so aptly explained, "Well, hell, when the FBI tells you to point, damn it, you point."

Thus, the legend of John Doe II had been born.

In total, seven witnesses described an olive-skinned man who accompanied McVeigh on the days leading up to the blast.

Two were the Oklahoma City postal workers, who saw McVeigh and

After the devastation of the Oklahoma City bombing, the building was leveled, and plans were initiated to create a memorial for the 169 people who lost their lives. (Photo: Collection of the author)

the darker-skinned man on either April 17 or 18. A third witness was a Tulsa bank executive caught in traffic four blocks from the Murrah Building a half hour before the blast. He reported pulling up alongside the Ryder truck and a car matching the description of Timothy McVeigh's Mercury Marquis. From their hesitant behavior, the banker deduced that the out-of-state travelers needed directions, but when he offered to help the driver whom he identified as McVeigh, he got only a "steel-cold stare." The passenger who accompanied McVeigh fit the description of the olive-skinned man, but the banker saw only a partial profile, and the task force decided against pursuing a drawing based on his sighting.

A fourth witness was bomb-blast survivor Dana Bradley, who reported looking out the plate-glass window of the social security office a few minutes before the explosion and seeing a yellow Ryder truck pull into the driveway. She caught a side view of an olive-skinned man leaving the passenger side of the truck. Seconds later she became a victim of the blast, and the critical condition in which she lingered for weeks precluded an interview.

The fifth, sixth, and seventh witnesses were the three Cassville, Missouri, residents, two of whom could provide descriptions of the confident and talkative dark-haired man they say accompanied Terry Nichols into their real estate office in November 1994.

The infamous and legendary John Doe II, sought by the investigation from its earliest hours, was accurately identified as Private Todd Bunting, a coincidental visitor to Elliott's Body Shop—and completely unrelated to the bombing.

The discrepancies between the Junction City "sighting" and the seven other Oklahoma City and Cassville descriptions at last made sense.

Now the legend of John Doe II could finally die *if* the media and the public would allow it. But the new mystery became: "Where is the muscular, olive-skinned man who called himself "Jacks," the man for whom Timothy McVeigh acted as his driver? Who is John Doe III?

John Doe III: Consistent with the reports of several eye-witnesses and based on the extraordinary recall of a retired veteran in Cassville, Missouri, this sketch depicts the face of the man seen with Tim McVeigh over the days and hours preceding the bombing of the Murrah Building in Oklahoma City. (Drawing by Jeanne Boylan)

15

THE COVER OF *NEWSWEEK*

With a letter to the *San Francisco Chronicle* on June 27, 1995, the Unabomber was back in action. Hell hath no fury like a terrorist upstaged. First he threatened to blow up an airliner departing out of Los Angeles. Then the next day, in a second letter sent to the *New York Times,* he claimed his threat was only a ruse. "Since the public has a short memory," his letter stated, "we decided to play one last prank to remind them who we are." Prank or not, the nation listened.

LAX was put on full alert, followed by tightened security measures at all airports. New public-address announcements cycled warnings that cars couldn't be left at curbside and that passenger bags had to be tended at all times. Departures were delayed while checked baggage was correlated with passenger boarding records. Airport security had changed forever—and the Unabomber was the reason why.

I'd been home for a full week, with my mind off all cases. I'd gotten good at acclimating. Within an hour of pulling my suitcase through the door from the Missouri trip, it had been as if the entire other half of my world didn't even exist. But, the FBI wasn't going to let me linger for long.

In late June, the Bureau had found a possible witness in the case of a bank-robbery ring. In seventeen incidents over six states, a group of robbers had taunted the FBI by committing blatant and dramatic armed robberies, during which they called each other by retired FBI agents' names. In some cases they wore masks with the insignia FBI in bold letters across the front. They dared to be captured and left behind signature smoke bombs at every robbery scene.

No one had yet seen a face.

Then, in late June the task force received its first big break. A getaway car had been recovered, and the person who had sold the car remembered the face of the buyer.

For once, my layover in Chicago was a productive use of time. While waiting for the connecting flight to Wisconsin, I was jarred to a stop by a newsstand display. Staring at me from the cover of *Newsweek* magazine were the piercing blue eyes of accused Oklahoma City bomber Timothy McVeigh. He was posed under studio portrait lighting, his face turned at just the right angle to capture the look of innocence in his plain farm-boy eyes. On an inside page was a horizontal bank of three close-up photos, taken in succession like the instant snapshots from a booth at a street fair. In the first, he rubbed his temples, as if he'd somehow been inconvenienced by this disruption to his otherwise normal day. In another, he posed in profile, looking serene and contemplative. But in the center shot, he looked straight into the lens and smiled broadly. On his right-hand side, second from the front, clearly visible, was the distinctly darkened tooth.

I fumbled through my wallet for Teeter's card.

"Teeter, you rat!" I yelled, skipping any introduction. "You didn't get back to me on that darkened tooth! Have you seen the July 3 *Newsweek?*"

He laughed. "Yeah, in fact I just did. I was going to call you, but I kept getting yanked out of here on leads."

That Sergeant Major Maloney was correct in his description of the darkened tooth of the driver who'd entered his office that November day meant one thing: the image we had captured on paper of McVeigh's accomplice was likely the clearest vision yet of the unidentified olive-skinned man.

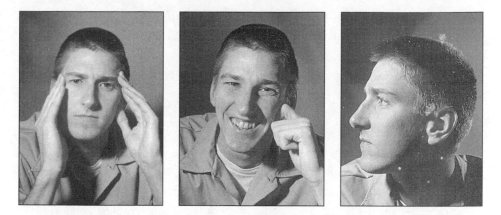

The needed clue: Oklahoma City bombing suspect Timothy McVeigh, photographed during a post-bombing jailhouse interview. One photo (center) revealed a darkened eyetooth as described by an eyewitness in a November 1994 sighting in rural Missouri. The dark tooth corroborated descriptions by witnesses of three men who had inquired about a remote parcel of property for sale. A second man was identified by a witness as Terry Nichols. The identity of the third man, who called himself "Jacks," remains a mystery. (Photos © Eddie Adams/Corbis Outline)

Since the beginning of the Oklahoma City case, I'd been running from one case to another nonstop. I hadn't had a chance to think, much less act on anything called a personal life. It was time to slow down before the summer completely passed by unnoticed.

One August night, at a barbecue at a friend's hand-built adobe home just outside of Bend, I sat watching a beautiful high-desert sunset. The aroma of juniper filled the early-evening air.

"Hey, by the way," he called from his open door, "did I tell you that I saw your drawing of the Unabomber in *Newsweek?*"

A year earlier I'd pleaded with Agent Max Noel to instruct the task force not to publicly release that sketch. With the time lapse between the sighting and the interview, and the high degree of witness contamination, the probability of accuracy was low. It was far too long a shot.

I figured he might have meant he'd seen a photo deep inside the magazine of the task force at an oblong conference table, perhaps with a small copy of the sketch pinned on the back wall of some conference room. But as he walked toward me, the actual full-size Unabomber drawing flashed at me from the magazine cover.

"Oh my God," I gasped, "this was never supposed to even be released!" Worse, underneath the bomber's face my signature was clearly legible.

What was even more of a shock was that the bomber's face sported a mustache. The witness had been emphatic that there had been no facial hair. She'd never agreed to its being in the first drawing and was displeased with herself for not voicing her discontent more strongly at the time. It had been a primary feature that we'd corrected in the 1994 reinterview. Yet there on the cover of *Newsweek* was the corrected version of the Unabomber's face—with the added mustache.

In order not to create a discrepancy between the first drawing released in 1987 and the amended drawing, the task force elected to release the mustached version of the new sketch to the media, so that it would more closely align with the sketch they had previously circulated.

The Unabomber image, not intended for public release, broke on the cover of *Newsweek* and went on to become the most widely circulated composite in investigative history. (Drawing © Jeanne Boylan. Cover © 1995 Newsweek Inc. All rights reserved. Used by permission.)

The rationale must have made sense at the time: The decision meant one less issue to explain to the press.

A simple mustache might seem insignificant, but it was in fact a psychology in itself. It represents an attitude, a visual statement of ideas and beliefs—not unlike a headband. It signifies lifestyle, status, occupation, politics. It's worn with consistency, and those who don't wear one never would. It is a statement entirely apart from the wearing of a full beard.

Something about the phantom image of the Unabomber eerily caught the imagination of the public as well as the press. It was ghosted behind articles in newspapers and magazines and used as a backdrop for network nightly newscasts. It held a kind of mystery behind its hidden eyes, a symbol of the unknown, and the representation of how someone, anyone, as ordinary as a next-door neighbor could quietly dispense terror into all of our lives.

The next morning I hit the speakerphone as I opened the living-room drapes and listened to the previous day's voice mail.

"Hey, girl. What's up? This is Beth Mallarky, Chicago FBI. Remember me? I can't get you tickets to *Oprah*, but then, hey—no one can get tickets to *Oprah*. But how about a round-trip ticket to Chicago anyway? We need you. It's a biggie. Here's a number I want you to call right away. I'll see you soon."

"Jeanne, this is Max. Long time, kid! I have a favor to ask you. We have a little Unabomber case mini-crisis brewing and could use your assistance with it. Not urgent in itself. In fact, I'm embarrassed to bother you with it, but give me a call when you can. Soon, okay? I've got some reporters breathing down my neck."

"Hey. Gordon Recht here. I know *Dateline*'s been after you for a year to do a piece on your work. I want to produce it. Call me."

"This is Rachel, Paul Nagle's assistant at the William Morris Agency in Los Angeles. Would you please call him back."

I let out a sigh of relief. Nothing but good news and no new cases, thank God. Not yet anyway.

I dialed Agent Max Noel first. Ever since our dinner in Park City, he'd ranked high on my list of all-time favorite agents for his devotion to his wife. I hadn't forgotten that. He'd set a standard for me that had been no small factor in the decision I'd made as I examined my own marriage in the year that followed our first meeting.

"Hey, Max, it's Jeanne. Got your message. What's up?"

"Hi, hon. Good to hear from you. You know, your drawing hit *Newsweek.*"

"Yeah, I saw that—the full cover, Max!" I said as I cleared my throat, hoping he'd offer some explanation.

"Well, seems we've upset the artist who did that 1987 rendition. You know, the one yours replaced. Seems you stole his claim to fame, and he's not at all happy about it."

"What? I didn't steal anything, Max—I never even wanted my drawing to be published. Remember?"

"Well, get ready for this bit of news. This guy called his own press conference and is claiming that the face you drew was not that of the Unabomber." Max laughed with disbelief.

"Excuse me? May I ask then, exactly whose face might it have been?"

"Well, sit down for this part. This guy is claiming that the face you drew was in reality *his* face, that the eyewitness was simply describing him based on her recollections from their interview together in 1987, and he's released a photograph—Jeanne, I'm not kidding you—of himself to the media. We need this like a hole in the head."

"Are you serious?" I could just imagine the Bureau's reaction. But the man had gotten involved through a local agency long before the case ever reached national magnitude and now they had no control. To try to recoup the attention, he'd gone so far as to release more drawings of what he construed the Unabomber to look like without the disguise, a legal *disaster* if that were to ever end up in court. It was akin to saying, "Well, we don't have the suspect's actual fingerprints, but we think they might be something like these." Speculation, about any characteristic, is not done for sound legal reasons. A courtroom is no place for guesswork, and a case of this caliber could afford no errors.

"It's a real mess," Max continued. "Look, we are just getting this investigation back on track here, and we need to get the public consolidated and behind us in our efforts. We need to be a team on this. Would you mind doing a little press to help us get this problem off our backs?"

"Sure, what can I do?"

"We have media calls coming into our office. This guy has even written letters to newspapers on this thing, filled with accusations and innuendo claiming to know things we don't. We can't actually order him to stop—it's a free country. But can we just send press calls up to you? Let me give you two numbers right now that have been calling here all morning long. Here's *Inside Edition,* and would you mind calling back the *L.A. Times?*"

I followed up with the *L.A. Times* in an effort to quickly dispel the frivolous story, and *Inside Edition* finalized their plans to fly in a crew from L.A. for an interview the same afternoon. In the meantime, the return call to Beth Mallarky delivered better news.

After the release of the *Newsweek* cover, the Unabom Task Force in Chicago received a peculiar contact. After several letters and calls to get through, the caller finally fell into the hands of Mary Bustamonte, a young conscientious lead agent who paid attention to what the caller had to offer.

The informant was a mathematics professor who remembered a man who had milled about at Northwestern University near Chicago years earlier. He was socially awkward and only approached the professor after the enrolled students had cleared out of the lecture hall. He had a "manifesto" he carried, which he wanted the professor to read. It wasn't professionally polished, and the professor suggested he find someone to assist him in editing it before he tried to get it published. In the meantime, they had several conversations.

The professor had felt a discomfort for many years over the encounter and had drawn a correlation between the author's political views and the actions of the Unabomber. The locations, the connection to the wood industry, the contents the professor recalled in the manifesto—all of it had added up, and for years, all of it had haunted him.

Often, he'd been tempted to call. But he'd hesitated because the young man he remembered, he explained, didn't look like the first sketch that had been in circulation all those years. When the new drawing was released, the similarities were strong—strong enough, he felt, that it was time to make the call.

Still, he almost hesitated again because the man that he'd met all those years earlier had extremely staunch political views that he'd ardently voiced in their conversations. And "those political views in that era," he stated, "would never have supported the wearing of a mustache." Only the strength of the remaining features had finally triggered his decision to reach out.

The timing was perfect. The FBI wanted me in Chicago eight days later, which gave me time to keep two media commitments in Los Angeles later in the week.

I was scheduled to appear first on a *Leeza Gibbons* show, as a member of an expert panel along with Marc Klaas concerning child safety issues, and then to go on to San Francisco for the taping of *Dateline*'s piece on the murder of Justin Jones.

Leeza Gibbons had become one of us. She was an ally and a crusader for justice and victims' rights. She had a gentle demeanor on camera, but she also knew how to shake up a case when it needed it. Investigators who had stamped a case "filed" or "suspended" jumped to open up cases again if it meant having to answer questions on national

Leeza Gibbons (left) became a champion of victims' rights, calling attention to unsolved cases on her network talk show, *The Leeza Show*. In the center is producer Debbie Alpert. Los Angeles, 1995. (Photo: Collection of the author)

TV. With her warm smile and patient diplomacy, she made police departments feel honored to be under what was, in fact, an inquisition.

As a result of Leeza's efforts, fresh leads were generated, and families rediscovered hope. Whenever her staff called, I moved earth to help her on a case. Leeza could pick up where agencies left off, and with the power of television, the end result was that she got things done.

Immediately after taping her show at Paramount Studios, I joined the *Dateline* crew for the first day of interviews in my Marina Del Rey hotel suite. The second day of shooting would follow at the crime scene in San Francisco.

Maria Shriver began by interviewing Lisa Dahl about Justin's life and death. From across the room, I sat watching the power of tragedy work its inevitable transformation in yet another life. For years, Lisa had been a successful shoe rep in the West Coast retail world. The lucrative field supported her well but it never touched her real passion. Her partner Andrea was a chef, and together, they dreamed of opening their own restaurant in some exotic locale outside the city. Maybe, she'd said, she'd even sing to her customers someday.

After my interview, Lisa returned to her suite and Maria stayed to talk while the crew packed up. During the taping, she was focused and serious, but once the cameras shut down, her eyes softened and her manner relaxed. As we moved from the weighty subject of the piece, she began asking about my lifestyle and my personal story. I grabbed the chance to turn the tables. Jokingly, I unclipped my mike and pinned it on her. Maria was married and had children, yet spent as much time on the road as I did. She'd not had to give up one for the other. How had she managed it?

"My husband," as she so succinctly phrased it, "would never have been interested in anyone whose universe was not at least as large as his."

"Then that's it, that's the key for me!" I laughed. "But Tom Brokaw is happily married. There's Matt Lauer on the *Today* show, but he's a little young. How about Peter Jennings? He's single!" I laughed, but the simple logic in what she had said hadn't escaped me. I didn't need to make a choice. I only needed to broaden my vision to see those whose boundaries were not unlike mine.

I knew that Maria had a place in Sun Valley and asked about the lifestyle there, what it was like. It was on my list of potential places to move to next.

"You can just do that?" Her eyes opened wide. "You could just decide to move and then just, just move? Like that? Just like that? Just *go?*" Watching Maria Shriver reeling over such a simple concept was somehow amusing to me.

"Yes, I guess I can. I can go anywhere I want, I suppose," I answered, "any country I want. Truly, I've never been so unencumbered."

She gasped, threw both hands over her chest, fell back in her chair, then lunged all the way forward and said breathlessly, "*Unencumbered—* what *is* that word? What does it mean? Just tell me, please, *what* would that be like?"

The grass, they say, is always greener.

MacKenzie Green met Maria and me the next day in San Francisco. The NBC camera crew followed us along Haight Street where Justin was murdered and then to the Tenderloin district to Chicago's room. Chicago had been not just the primary witness for the drawing that led to Jose Avina's identification and arrest but also the star witness at the murder trial. The man deemed by the case inspectors "not credible on the witness stand" had proven them dead wrong.

Reunited with bounty-hunter MacKenzie Green (left) on the streets of the Haight-Ashbury district in San Francisco for a taping of NBC's *Dateline,* August 1995. (Photo: Collection of the author)

I walked down the familiar flophouse hallway and cracked open Chicago's door. The room was bare. As expected, he'd moved on after the trial. I wondered where he'd gone, if this case had changed his life, too. The dresser top was cleared of the remnants of his fake drugs, and his red-stenciled letters had long since been washed off the wall. Maria and the camera crew followed us in with tape rolling, but nothing about the place was the same.

"Hey, look," MacKenzie said in her low, raw voice, "the bastard even took his fucking television."

Of all of us involved in the case, only Mac's world remained unchanged.

The crew finished taping and was loading up the van when Maria kissed me on the cheek to say good-bye. "Where you off to now, Jeanne, another big case?"

"Well, yeah, to Chicago, on Unabomber." I felt the word move out of my mouth like a smoke ring in midair and cringed in horror. Over our two days in Los Angeles and San Francisco, Maria had become almost a friend. But I was on my way to a highly confidential meeting with a highly confidential witness in a highly confidential location on the most notorious terrorist case in the country, and I'd just named it before a member of the national press. *What* was I thinking? I wished to inhale the word back, but it was too late.

"Oh, yeah, right." She laughed, thinking I'd cracked a joke. "I guess if you told me, you'd have to kill me, right?"

"You got it." I smiled and began to breathe again.

"Oh, and Jeanne, by the way"—she stopped in traffic midway across the street—"I'll keep my eyes open for a great guy for you. How about a great film director? Or a photographer? Maybe a writer? Someone your type, creative and adventurous, but"—she sped back up as she shook her head—"a definite no on Peter Jennings."

16

A SUSPECT REBORN

Agent Beth Mallarky promised a night out in Chicago following my late-afternoon flight from San Francisco. I cashed in frequent-flier miles for a first-class upgrade and dressed for dinner before boarding so we'd waste no time, but upon arrival, she met me in full business dress. Girl's night out was off—the professor was anxious and wanted to get started right away.

Following the FBI's advice, my room reservation was under an assumed name and the hotel location was intentionally far from the professor's home to minimize the chance that he might be tailed to the meeting. Because so little was known about the Unabomber's method of selecting targets, all precautions were taken to protect the informant's identity as well as to conceal our location. The initial evening session ran well into the night. We resumed work early the next day.

The time frame of the professor's recall was eerily right. Two bombs associated with Northwestern University were linked to the Unabomber. The first device was in a package found in the parking lot of the engineering department of the Chicago Circle Campus of the University of

Illinois on May 25, 1978. It was addressed to a professor of engineering at the Rensselaer Polytechnic Institute in Troy, New York, and carried as a return address the name of an engineering professor at Northwestern's Technological Institute. The Northwestern engineering professor didn't recognize the package and turned it over to the university police department, where it exploded in the hands of a police officer.

Less than a year later, a sealed box left in a common area at the Technological Institute exploded when a graduate student attempted to open it.

The Chicago press, responding to a leak, had recently run a story speculating that an unknown Northwestern University professor had called in a Unabomber suspect lead. Faculty members had begun E-mailing him, asking if he was "the one," and the media was hot on his heels.

The man he remembered was thin with dark eyebrows and brown hair combed down onto his forehead, then swept back in a kind of pompadour, James Dean style. He was painfully shy and would wait until the math classes were over before making his way to the front of the room with material he referred to as a "manifesto" in his hands. He wanted the professor to read his manuscript, which elaborated on the dangers of technology.

At one point, the man accompanied the professor into his office and sketched out a map of where he lived. He included a major cross street, a forest preserve, and a freeway. The man also mentioned living with his mother and one brother, although he'd never made mention of a father living in his home.

Even more deeply embedded in the professor's memory were the man's demeanor and mannerisms. He'd hunch his shoulders up a bit and often tilt his head to one side. He spoke softly and expressed his staunch antitechnology sentiments and political viewpoints only through his writings, which he carried guardedly in his hands.

With its misspellings and periodic misuse of words or phrases, the manifesto was in need of academic polish, which was not an area of the mathematics professor's interest or expertise. He remembered the paper as "somewhat amateurish," but referred its author to engineering professors at both Northwestern and at the Chicago campus of the University of Illinois.

That wasn't the last the educator would see of him. When the engineering professors rejected the manuscript out of hand, the man returned frustrated, even angry. "He never raised his voice," the professor recounted, "but there was rage and he was visibly trembling." The man's ringing words upon departing the professor's office were "I will get even."

Five weeks later the first bomb exploded at the University of Illinois in a parking lot by the engineering department—the same area where the young man had been sent for assistance with his manifesto.

The professor's dedication to our task made my work a pleasure, but the intensity of his interest was based on more than the desire to benefit the overall case. He was working to identify a man who, if aware of the professor's involvement, could in fact become his own killer.

In total, we spent twenty-three and a half hours drawing out different aspects of the professor's recall. In the end, we'd produced a precise image of the face he remembered, and in our hours together we'd also become friends.

Though the agents warned us both not to be seen together, the professor had an idea. In bringing forward the detail of the man's appearance, we'd also revived his memories about the composition of the map the man had drawn.

When we were done he laid out a Chicago area map he'd carried in from his truck.

"I think I can narrow it down to this area," he said, pointing out where the criteria of a forestry center, freeway, and a certain street all appeared in the same quadrant on the map. "You game?"

We delayed the call to the agents to inform them that we were finished. He left through the stairwell and I took the elevator and the hotel side exit, watching carefully in case any press had followed, then I slipped into his old pickup truck when he was ready to pull off the lot. We were able to isolate the neighborhood to roughly forty square blocks and slowly drove along every street looking for a home that would fit the scenario of either a woman or an older couple living with two young men.

"I'll apply mathematical probability to correlate their likely economic status with property values," he said, "and you use your gut instincts, your gift of intuition."

Why not? I thought. Cases had been solved with far less sophisticated methods.

By nightfall, we ended our search and noted all the possibilities we'd found. Then he drove me to the various campus locations where the bombings had taken place. By midnight, we arrived at his home in an upscale area near Northwestern University. His wife was waiting with a fire burning and a nightcap of sherry already poured. She brought out the copy of the Chicago headline story which all but named the professor as the source of the lead.

I listened while they talked of a possible move to escape the danger. As I sipped the sherry, I watched my two hosts through the cut crystal of the upturned glass. The splintered image seemed an accurate rendition of the chaos that had just come into their lives.

Within weeks of our interview, the professor moved his family to Denmark out of concern that the press would formally break the story. But during one trip back to the United States, a well-dressed man sat next to him in the first-class cabin. An hour or two into their conversation, the man began to ask questions—first as if out of general curiosity, but then moved into more pointed inquiries specifically about the Unabomber case.

Once the professor's suspicions were aroused, he said no more, but he reported the incident to agents upon his return to Chicago. His skepticism panned out. Investigators learned that the passenger was in fact a network TV plant assigned to prod him for information on the case.

There was no safe place for the family to hide. The press had their ways, and if they could so easily find him, the professor reasoned, then so could the bomber.

He and his family would live hiding from the phantom until the day the killer was caught.

An FBI agent picked me up the next morning for the drive to the downtown-Chicago office to address the task force. As I entered the conference hall, agents began arriving for the briefing.

I studied every face as the Bureau employees methodically moved into the room.

In the early 1980s, I'd been recruited to join the Bureau after being flown to the FBI's Behavioral Sciences Center at their training academy near Quantico, Virginia, to consult on a new compositry course they were creating for use in training police. While there, I had an FBI agent roommate whose specialty was foreign counterintelligence, known within the Bureau as FCI. Prior to becoming an agent in her late twenties, she'd worked as a professional tailor.

Her assignment was to get close to a suspected Middle Eastern terrorist living in the eastern United States. As a pretext, the Bureau had set her up with her own tailoring shop, complete with a storefront and an employee. Daily she'd go to her shop and take in work, but she spent evenings in her arranged apartment, located in the same building and on the same floor as the apartment of the suspected terrorist. The two shared a washer and dryer.

The ruse was intended to allow her to monitor the daily life of the suspect and to learn more about his social contacts, his beliefs, and most importantly, his plans.

For two years, she lived with a lover whom she would kiss good-bye each morning as she went off to work. Even he could never know the truth—that she was an FBI operative or a UC, the term for an undercover agent. She described to me the events of one ordinary day that first put her into the crawl space of an attic, and then onto a train traveling cross-country, all in an effort to shadow the suspected terrorist's cohort. At day's end, she was relieved by another agent so that she could catch a plane and get back to her apartment at her normal arrival time.

When she walked in her door at night, she described to her partner only the suit she was supposedly making for a client. She was never completely convinced that her lover himself wasn't a plant, sent to romance her in order to uncover her own ploy. She could trust no one. As I listened to her stories, I pushed the Bureau application materials a little farther away from me on the dormitory desk.

During round-trips between Quantico and Washington, D.C., I

became friends with her FCI classmates, who I'd met in the cafeteria on Friday evenings, when the hall became a social center, with the lights dimmed and beer served. On their last Friday night in Quantico, I pulled a camera to my eye to snap a picture of them all together. Instantly, chairs tumbled and people scrambled to move out of the shot. I understood. Something as simple as a class photo could make these agents identifiable, which could at some point in their careers cost them their lives.

Even with all the pitfalls of working for the most powerful investigative agency in the world, every agent in that room had wanted and competed for the right to be there. They'd all chosen and pursued their careers, but through one small twist of fate, it seemed my career had chosen me.

After the Chicago briefing, Beth took me to the airport and insisted on walking me not just to the counter but to the gate, even sitting with me until my plane departed.

"What are you doing this for?" I asked her. "Don't you trust me not to run down to the *Tribune* or sell my story to the tabloids? Have to make sure I get out of town?"

"No," she said laughing, "I wanted to walk you. I know what it's like traveling on business. You're always alone, never anyone to walk with you to a gate or greet you when step off on the other end. It can get lonesome. Don't forget, I'm your Chicago family. After all, we're sisters in the brotherhood, right?"

For the first week back at the ranch, I defiantly refused to check my voice mail messages.

Tex, the ranch's Labrador, was dozing near me in the sun and I'd just opened up a novel when the phone's ring drew me back inside.

"Can you please hold for Paul Nagle?" his assistant requested.

Paul was the bright executive at Fox Studios in Los Angeles who had seen through the ridiculous treatments that had been pitched at him by the television writers. I assumed that he was calling to make sure I knew that Fox hadn't purchased the project, a fact I think I'd once mourned with a glass of champagne.

"Hi, Jeanne. Paul Nagle. Listen, I've been trying to get in touch with you. Where have you been? I've left several messages. I want you to know that I've left Fox. I am with William Morris now in Beverly Hills. I know your option expired with Cannell Productions, so let me just tell you this: I've been waiting patiently for you to be free again. I think there is a story here—a real story. That Cannell missed it is our gain. This is perfect material for a television series, but I think that it would also work if developed into a screenplay for a feature film, and Twentieth Century Fox is very interested in talking to you.

"Oh, and Jeanne, they have an offer ready and an impressive list of writers they'd like you to interview. One's a top writer from *NYPD Blue,* and a couple are very well-known feature writers. I'm going to send you this contract material. These are A-list writers here, and one I like very much. He writes strong feature-film female-protagonist roles, unlike the television experience you had." He laughed. "His name is Ron Hutchinson."

I dropped down in my desk chair.

In all my dealings with Hollywood, I'd always remembered the psychic's words: "I see them wanting to make a *film* about you and what you do . . . There's a manuscript in the hands of a man named Rod, or perhaps *Ron* . . . this work will *never* let you go . . ."

"Jeanne, hello—are you still there?"

Up until now, the fact that television uses tape and not film had given me my last reason to believe her premonition might be wrong. It wasn't much to hold on to, but every other prediction had materialized.

After hanging up, I reached across the desk and picked up my cherished postcard of the woman in the secluded desert tub. The idyllic photo seemed perhaps set in some remote part of Arizona, miles from the nearest crime scene, I thought. All I really wanted was to find that same tranquillity. Somewhere, it had to exist. Somehow, I had to find it.

My next decision took only an instant. I dialed the airline and booked a nine-day trip to Phoenix. Bend was only a month away from winter. I could find a place like that, get back in time to load up a truck, and be gone before the first snowfall. The timing was perfect. I'd just run away.

———

A woman at peace. (Photo © David R. Stoecklein)

landed at Sky Harbor Airport in Phoenix in late afternoon on October 10 and spent a few hours just driving through Scottsdale to drench my senses in the warm desert air. I passed outdoor cafés, art galleries, and streets lined with cactus and palm trees wrapped in coils of tiny white lights. It was only a few states away but somehow it felt like another world. I knew no one in Arizona. Nothing truly bad had ever happened there, right? After all, when was the last time I'd heard anything about Arizona in the national news?

Before leaving Bend, I'd run an ad to hire a personal assistant to take over the mail and screen my messages after I left. If I kept the same local Oregon number and mailing address, no one would even need to know that I'd gone, and if no one realized, no one would try to find me. They'd assume that I was away working on cases as usual, and I could quietly slip away into my new peaceful reality. I took a room at a Scottsdale hotel and called my voice mail to check for any response to my ad.

There was only one message. The voice cut through my calm like jagged glass. "Ms. Boylan, we need to know your availability," an FBI agent explained. "We've got a train derailment involving potential terrorist involvement or sabotage." I fell into a seat.

Eight of twelve cars on the Miami to Los Angeles Sunset Express had left the track, killing one Amtrak employee and injuring more than a hundred passengers. Early indications were that the tracks may have been tampered with.

"We don't know much more yet—it just happened last night—but in the event we come up with eyewitnesses, where exactly are you? Call me and let me know. We might need to get you on a plane to Phoenix."

PHOENIX! I set the receiver down slowly and reluctantly turned on the news. Just over an hour outside the city, in a desolate stretch of desert, an Amtrak passenger train had left the tracks, killing one man.

The message, however, said that they didn't have witnesses . . . yet. It was possible that they would never find any, and that the investigation would run its course with no need for a sketch. I'd stick with my original schedule and leave, as planned, the next morning.

My method of choosing a town to live near wasn't exactly scientific. I'd locate a nonfranchise café, nurse a cup of coffee, and absorb the conversation of the locals while trying to gather a sense of the personality of the place. Then I'd let instinct dictate. First, I headed northeast to the mountain town of Payson, too big; then Strawberry, too high; Pine, too remote; Sedona, too commercial; Jerome, too cold; Prescott, too big; down to Patagonia, too flat; Tombstone and Bisbee, too dusty; and on the last night of the nine-day trip, I found a tiny adobe artisans' village near the Mexican border called Tubac, population 1,067. It was just right.

I drove the side roads through the mesquite trees and arid canyons in search of anything resembling an empty house. Just at dusk, under the brilliant yellow-and-pink-streaked Arizona sky, an abandoned adobe appeared amid a remote grove of mesquite trees. I knocked on the door of what seemed to be the main house.

"Excuse me for bothering you. I was just wondering if the empty casita on your property over near the ravine is a rental?"

The bearded man invited me inside his spacious brick home. Double French doors opened to a large lighted pool in the backyard.

"No, it's not. I don't like having anyone on my property," he answered, seemingly referring to me. The old man looked like a recluse, someone more likely found in a remote mountain hideaway than an upscale artisans' retreat.

"Well, thanks anyway. I was just looking for a quiet place to be alone and do some writing over the winter. Sorry to have bothered you." I turned away.

"Hey, wait a minute, wait a minute." He shook his finger around in the air. "I know you, yeah, that's right, I know who you are!"

No, he didn't, and he was scaring me. I started to plan my escape route out the front door.

"Yeah, you're that, that lady who—well, look here." He bent over his coffee table and opened the *Arizona Star*. In the October 15 Sunday edition, was a half-page article that contained a three-by-five photograph of me standing at a podium in front of a horde of reporters at a press conference regarding a serial-rapist case I'd recently worked on in Palo Alto, California.

I stood, stunned, with my eyes fixed on the Associated Press piece on his coffee table. I could run from this work, but I could not seem to hide.

By the time I tuned back into what he was saying, he was holding a key in his hand. He led me across the acreage to the empty house and

October 1995. Speaking at a Palo Alto press conference regarding the California serial rapist case that appeared in the *Arizona Star*. (Photo: Collection of the author)

switched on a light. Saguaro cacti out front, mountains in the back, seventeen miles from the Mexican border and at the tail end of a dead-end road. It was perfect.

"Just get here when you get here!" he yelled as I disappeared down the long gravel driveway, my new house key clutched firmly in my hand.

When I returned to Oregon, I hired Jennifer Moe to take over my mail, pay bills, screen all calls, and to contact me only in the event of an emergency—no cases, period.

O nce settled in Tubac, I tuned the world out, listening only to Mexican radio stations so I wouldn't understand the news. I worked out, meditated, read, and hiked the warm canyons at sunset. The only threat came from the javelinas—the wild pigs—that would steal the pink petunias from my clay pots around the deck at night. The locals warned me that they could be dangerous and would attack with their sharp tusks if confronted. The oldest, ugliest, fattest, and most aggressive of the pigs, I nicknamed WLDWMN.

Just before Christmas 1995, Maria Shriver's *Dateline* piece on the Justin Jones case aired on NBC, but beyond that interruption, I had finally succeeded in breaking all ties with work.

In the quiet, I wrote daily. I wrote to educate investigators about the complex process of memory. Maybe somehow attention to the topic could be opened up, maybe even spawning a long overdue change in an antiquated system.

The limitless Arizona sun and the isolation were healing all remnant wounds from my broken heart. As the months passed, I felt emotionally centered, spiritually healthy, physically fit, and finally, divinely at peace.

In early April, only to honor a commitment made to an old friend a year earlier, I flew to Bend to be key speaker at a statewide firefighters' conference. As consolation, I took along my skis.

I told Jennifer I'd check my own voice mail for a few days. An average was six, maybe seven calls on a given day, but what I was about to hear on my telephone line that day was unprecedented.

"You have twenty-nine unheard messages: Ms. Boylan, I'm calling from the *Washington Post,*" the first message began. "We'd like to get your reaction to the arrest of the Unabomber."

"This is CNN. Would you please call us back with your comment to the suspect's arrest in the Unabomber case?"

"This is ABC News in New York. Ms. Boylan, we'd like to schedule an interview with you in regard to the arrest of the suspect in Montana today. Would you please call back as soon as possible?"

They couldn't all have it wrong, yet it was impossible to believe the words. It had to be a media leap of faith at a false alarm on a slow news day. The big story tomorrow would surely be about the ruse.

I called back an old friend first, a producer from ABC's *Prime Time Live* in New York, "I'd love it if you'd only talk to us for a day or so, okay?" he asked. "We've just accessed a driver's license photo of the man arrested, someone named Theodore Kaczynski. If you'll tune in tonight when we air it, we'd like to call you afterward for your response."

I sat nervously on the edge of the couch as the *Prime Time Live* program aired.

The piece showed a dilapidated cabin in rural Montana, then scrolled through the chronology of the bombings. Suddenly, a driver's license photo of the man named Kaczynski filled the screen.

The image flooded my mind with excitement first, and then with shock. I didn't recognize the face. I needed to see more, I needed to see him without the facial hair and from the angle seen by the eyewitness. Most importantly, I needed to see what he looked like at the time of the actual encounter—nine years earlier.

Over a restless night, the press proved their usual resourcefulness, and by morning, all networks broadcast older photographs of Kaczynski. In a 1969 Berkeley photo, his face was shaven and at the precise angle as in the eyewitness sighting. It was the shot I'd needed. Theodore Kaczynski was indeed the same man seen planting a bomb in Salt Lake City in 1987.

After seventeen terror-filled years, the serial killer had at last been dragged out from behind the infamous disguise. The protruding jawbones, the underbite, the way the lips were pursed and tight, the straight lip line, the jutting chin, the facial width, the skin tone, the texture, the dull brown hair, and the thickened nares of the nose—all of it was present in the older

Unabomber suspect Theodore Kaczynski is unveiled from behind his long-held disguise of a hooded sweatshirt and sunglasses after his seventeen-year reign of terror. (Left: Drawing © Jeanne Boylan; right: Photo © AP Photo)

photos. The Salt Lake City secretary's memory was finally vindicated.

Kaczynski had aged radically since the 1987 sighting. His new arrest mug shot bore almost no resemblance to his earlier photographs. As the story continued to unfold, the rugged toll of his wilderness existence easily explained how and why his amazing metamorphosis had taken place.

The day's phone calls were filled with congratulations from friends, news producers, and FBI agents, but there was also an extraordinarily sad undertone to the excitement.

Since the public release of the Unabom manifesto, published jointly on September 19, 1995, by the *New York Times* and the *Washington Post,* similarities between the document and the writings of a family member had plagued the conscience of David Kaczynski. His older brother, Ted, lived the existence of a recluse in the Montana woods. But the chronology and the locations of the bombing incidents began to form a picture of a frightening possibility that David and his wife, Linda, tried but were unable to wish away.

In an unimaginable gesture of patriotism and heroism, David Kaczynski, his wife, Linda, and mother, Wanda, made a difficult and pained decision to turn over to the FBI years' worth of letters and an essay written in 1971, all penned by Ted Kaczynski. The bomber's insistence that the manifesto be published was, ironically, the final link that had led to his capture.

I had to call Max Noel. He'd be euphoric. As a principal case agent,

Max was in Montana and had been one of three agents who'd taken Kaczynski out of the tiny cabin in which he'd spent the harsh Montana winters with no electricity, no telephone, and no plumbing, and in which he manufactured his bombs. The cabin would become a gold mine of evidence, even including the old manual typewriter on which the manifesto was created. Remarkably, agents also found a hooded sweatshirt and sunglasses, perhaps those that had launched the ghostly image of his face into international infamy.

I thought the breaking news of the arrest would move the media's fascination away from the drawing, but calls continued flooding in—from as far away as England, Germany, Australia, Brazil, and Italy.

I was finally ready to hit the ski slopes of Mt. Bachelor when one more call came through. This one, I thought, was surely a prank.

"Ms. Boylan, this is Vic Walter of ABC News in New York, senior producer for *Brian Ross Investigative Reports*. Could you call me right away? I'd like to talk to you about the Oklahoma City bombing."

I figured it was Max Noel calling back as a joke, but it was in fact Vic Walter of the investigative research department of ABC News.

ABC was planning a one-year anniversary special on the Oklahoma

FBI agent Max Noel (left) assists in escorting Unabomber suspect Kaczynski from a remote cabin in rural Montana. (Photo © Gamma Liaison/Derek Pruitt)

City bombing case. In their research, they had discovered a witness who had been interviewed but whose perceptions were inexplicably discounted by the Bureau's investigators.

ABC wanted to follow up as part of their retrospective, with me conducting the witness interviews. They also planned to reinterview Tommy Kessinger, who had been so maligned in the year since he first attempted to provide the John Doe II description.

The Oklahoma City bombing case defense and prosecution teams were working at full throttle, with enormous pressure to contain eyewitness descriptions. The prosecution wanted witnesses to remain speechless, adhering to their original stories through the trial. The defense wanted to rock the boat by discrediting or influencing the eyewitnesses to alter or deny their original stories. ABC News wanted to find the truth, no matter which side would benefit. Anything being swept aside in the case would make for breaking news.

"Can you give me overnight to think about this?" I asked. What ABC was asking me to do was reinterview one witness I'd already interviewed on behalf of the FBI a year earlier. There were legal and ethical considerations, not to mention my allegiance to the Bureau's case.

But something the producer said kept rolling over in my mind: "an eyewitness whose perceptions were discounted by the Bureau's investigators." After all, I'd seen it happen with Tommy Kessinger. If it happened to the primary eyewitness, could it have happened again? What if there were still more people involved in the bombing and the information was being overlooked?

According to ABC researchers, an eyewitness claimed to have seen a tall man with collar-length blond hair with McVeigh in the Dreamland Motel two days prior to the bombing. The witness was clear that this unknown man was *not* Tim McVeigh, *not* the olive-skinned man, and *not* Terry Nichols.

Who then was he? Could there have been a John Doe IV?

FBI agents told him repeatedly that he was mistaken, that the man he saw was in fact Tim McVeigh, but he'd remained adamant that it was someone else. What if he was right?

I looked at my skis and poles standing in the hallway. It was a brilliant blue-sky day, sixty degrees in town, just over thirty degrees on Mt.

Bachelor, with clear skies predicted to last three more days. This was my only chance to ski all year. The sunlight streamed across the counter as I reached back for the receiver and dialed.

"Vic Walter? Jeanne Boylan. I'm in. Where shall I meet you?"

I checked into a Kansas City airport hotel late that night and, after dragging my ski gear across the lobby, met up with Walter and his crew the next morning.

"I hear the best downhill runs are in Kansas," he said, laughing as he extended his hand.

Vic Walter was a seasoned investigator for ABC News. His behind-the-scenes work laid the foundation for in-depth and often controversial reports for ABC's *Nightline, 20/20* and *Prime Time Live* programs. With his partner and correspondent Brian Ross, they worked as if choreographed, each man at the highest rung of his professional career. Each of their names was synonymous with multiple Peabody and Emmy nominations.

The television crew loaded a van with the masses of network-caliber equipment and followed us to Junction City.

The first witness, Jeff Davis, would meet me at our motel. While I began the preliminary interview, Vic and the crew planned to head out to begin the reinterview with Kessinger. According to press reports, Tommy had begun to change his story. But had he, really, or was he simply saying what he'd been trying to voice all along?

I heard and felt the rumbling of a specialized muffler through the motel's cinder-block walls. The racket stopped, a door slammed, and a stocky, redheaded man labored his way up the concrete-slab steps.

Jeff Davis had worked for the Hunan Restaurant in April 1995 and delivered an order of moo goo gai pan and egg rolls to McVeigh's room in Junction City's Dreamland Motel. But he maintained that another man had opened the door to accept the order, while McVeigh sat on the bed clearly in view in the middle of the room. The small talk extended beyond just the cash transaction—not on any topic of significance, but enough to keep Davis's eyes firmly fixed on the man's face long beyond a glimpse. Though he'd been interviewed on multiple occasions by the

FBI, Davis was firmly told by the agents that he had a mistaken impression.

"You sure it couldn't have been McVeigh?" the FBI would ask.

"Yes, I'm positive," he'd answer.

"But it could have been McVeigh."

"No, it was not Tim McVeigh. Tim McVeigh sat visible to me in the middle of the room on the bed, and this man came to the door and spoke with me. I saw them both, and the man I spoke with was not Tim McVeigh."

"It probably was Tim McVeigh," the agents implied repeatedly. And so it went, Davis refusing to recant what he so vividly recalled. His aggravation and sense of indignation would be key elements in sustaining his impression, and the best news of all, his recall hadn't been contaminated by post-event visual aids.

When Vic and the camera crew arrived at Kessinger's small rural home, Tommy opened the screen door several inches wide but didn't invite them in.

"Tommy," a woman called from inside the house, "you ain't supposed to be talking to nobody." He rolled his eyes and kept talking anyway. "Tommy," she yelled again, "I told you, you ain't supposed to be talking to nobody!" Her voice grew increasingly hostile, but her warnings suddenly stopped, to the audio man's relief as he readjusted the sound level on his equipment. Suddenly, a yellow pickup truck came barreling around a corner and down the country lane, swirling dust trails behind it. Tommy's tiny house was one of few on the long country road, so the truck's destination was not in dispute.

"Shit!" Vic yelled to the camera crew. "Let's go! Protect the tape!"

They tore back into the news van, followed by three men assumed to be FBI agents in the cab of the truck. The cameraman careened along back roads and around blocks and alleys through town, finally losing the pickup long enough to get back to the motel.

Vic hurled the door to my room open and yelled, "Grab your stuff!" With one stroke of his arm he swept the table clear, dumping my supplies into a bag, which he thrust into my hand.

"Let's get out of here. Fast!" He grabbed the extended handle of my suitcase and bounced it down the long concrete stairwell. Jeff Davis, who'd taken a security-guard position at a military camp, savored each second of the melodrama.

"I'll keep up," Jeff yelled as he jumped into his own car. I leapt into Vic's car and the crew took the van. As we sped toward the freeway, Vic noticed the truck on his tail again. I hunkered down. If indeed it was the FBI, I couldn't let them see me inside the car with a news crew, although I had done nothing to violate their trust.

Vic sped through traffic and skidded down off-ramps, taking side roads until we reached Topeka. Jeff pulled in behind us at the old stone Senate Hotel, his red face still glowing with joy from having eluded the authorities.

We set up for taping in the historic hotel's barely heated basement. Jeff Davis finally offered his full story, determined to be heard, almost angry in his delivery at not having been listened to. The drawing we produced would support his claim that the person he saw was someone other than Timothy McVeigh.

The man he'd spoken with in McVeigh's room at the Dreamland Motel had blond, straight, longer-length, disheveled hair, large, light eyes slightly sunken in their sockets as if from fatigue, an inverted chin, and a large nose with a convex bump on the bridge.

Other than for height and a light hair color, there was no resemblance between the man he described and Timothy McVeigh. But who was he? The man Jeff Davis had seen in the Dreamland Motel room that April day had to be . . . John Doe IV.

When the cameras finally shut down near midnight, it was time to make good on a pledge to Jeff. Network news divisions cannot pay for information, but they were allowed to feed the man, and in return for having dragged him away for hours and for causing him to miss a shift at his night watch job, they had promised dinner following the interview. Jeff loved food, and he'd challenged Vic to raise the bar, extracting a promise not just for dinner, but for a lobster dinner.

If they rushed, the crew had one last shot at making a late-night flight out of Kansas City to make it home in time to spend Easter morning with their families. I offered to take Jeff out while they packed up their gear. But what I hadn't considered was that at just after midnight on Easter in Topeka, broiled lobster tail was not an easy find.

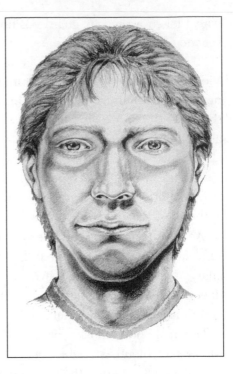

John Doe IV: Jeff Davis, then a
Chinese restaurant employee,
recalls this as the face of the man
who opened the door of room 24
at the Dreamland Motel two days
before the Oklahoma City bombing. (Drawing by Jeanne Boylan)

We drove around the slick streets for a half hour looking for an
upscale restaurant, then later looking for any restaurant at all, until
finally we found one still open. Jeff looked up at the neon sign, but the
disappointment was written on his face. It was a corner biker bar named
Jerry's in an otherwise pitch black end of town.

We sat at the smoke-filled counter and yelled to be heard over ZZ Top
music and the sound of cue sticks striking balls on pool tables around
the room. The haggard bartender handed us two sticky plastic-coated
menus and Jeff ordered a burger. I put my hand over his menu and said,
"No, Jeff, you don't understand. After what you've been through, they
owe you."

"You're right," he said. He called the bartender back over and added a
cheeseburger, onion rings, the Philly steak sandwich, cole slaw, and one
pastrami on rye.

Jeff Davis had been through a solid year of hell being interviewed,
reinterviewed, doubted, coerced, embarrassed, and denied, yet he had

held true to what he'd seen. All he had wanted was to be listened to. Now, in what would be a nationally televised interview, his story would finally be heard.

No, Jeff Davis wasn't dining on broiled lobster—nor was I on the ski slopes of Mt. Bachelor—but we'd achieved something pretty important together. It was Easter morning in Topeka, Kansas, and something had been reborn.

17

SISTER DIANNA ORTIZ

Jennifer sounded a little harried for an Easter Sunday afternoon. "I signed up as your personal assistant, not your press agent," she joked over the telephone. "What am I supposed to do with all these media calls? Don't answer. First, I should tell you, I've already accepted one request for an interview."

I looked at the open trunk of my car in the driveway. "Jennifer, I just walked in my door from the airport!" I plopped onto the Pendleton blankets of my bed. "I haven't even carried in my bag yet."

"See, then, you're ready to go. This one is for the *Today* show. They even have some big-time hotel booked for you on Central Park." I could hear her two children crying in the background. "If you don't go, I swear to you *I'll* show up instead and just tell them I'm you."

The *Today* show wanted to highlight the likeness of the Unabom sketch to Ted Kaczynski's photo, and I guessed I could use the precious national airtime for a few minutes of sorely needed education on the issue of eyewitness recall. After all, ignorance wasn't bliss on this topic, and every outlet helped. If even one investigator finally got the message, the trip would at least be worthwhile.

I dialed the NBC producer to plead for at least one solid night's sleep in my own bed before boarding another flight, but she took her offer a step further. In exchange for my promise not to do any other network's morning news show, she agreed to push back the interview by a day and offered me not one, but two nights at the Essex Hotel in New York.

That was a deal.

I arrived in New York twenty-four hours later and, from my room overlooking the park, ordered a four A.M. wake-up call. The next morning I dressed in reliably chic New York black and met the driver in the hotel lobby. The NBC limo wound through the quiet streets, dropping me at the front door of the Rockefeller Center studios long before daylight. Bryant Gumbel, originally scheduled for the interview, had to leave for the funeral of Commerce Secretary Ron Brown, who had died along with thirty-two others in a plane crash outside Dubrovnik during a mission to Croatia. Brian Williams, coanchoring in Gumbel's absence, would handle the interview instead.

An intern ushered me from the greenroom into the interview area and to my seat in the cream-and-black-striped chair. For years I'd been fascinated by all the different hands that had run their fingers over the armrests of that same chair. I'd watched everyone from Hillary Clinton to Bette Midler to Henry Kissinger to Paul McCartney speak from that very seat, never dreaming I'd be sitting in the same place one day.

Brian Williams stepped onto the set and sat in the facing striped chair, without looking up. I leaned forward to check out the scripted questions he was studying on the list in his lap.

"You know what?" I pointed to a question on the sheet. "May I suggest you not ask that second one?" I knew that most television interviewers refrain from conversation until the camera light goes on, so that the synergy is fresh and the audience meets the guest at the same time the host does, but this time I had to speak up. "That answer will take up all our time and it won't deliver anything of substance, really." It was the dreaded "How did you get started?" question, which required a pointless five-minute answer.

Williams looked up at me slowly. "Well, these are just the producer's suggestions." He turned the list over. "I ask my own questions," he explained as he moved the list out of my sight.

"Okay, but one thing I must say: please don't ask me my personal opinions about Kaczynski's guilt or innocence. You can ask things like how I arrived at the face, or about the methods of interviewing that enabled me to recover the image, but the FBI doesn't need personal opinions as they're forming their case, so please"—I smiled—"whatever you do, do not ask me if they've got their man."

Katie Couric listened from her seat at the anchor desk. The stage manager stepped near the front of the cameras. "Four, three, two, one." He flung his arm out to a rigid point and quickly stepped out of frame as Williams began.

"The Unabomber investigation is the longest in the history of the FBI," he said, looking squarely toward the lens. "Everyone has their own opinion. The *New York Post* says you nailed it dead on." He shifted toward me in his seat. "Other people say, 'I don't know how they think the guy in the hood and glasses is the bearded guy they picked up.' How do *you* think you did?"

I took a deep breath and fought my ambivalence between answering literally or being politically correct. After all, it was a strange question. The *Today* show producers had just spent $1,400 on an airline ticket to get me to New York, which they wouldn't have done had they thought I'd missed the mark, so why was Williams spending priceless time by putting me on the defensive?

"We had so very little to work with," I started out diplomatically, then tried to maneuver toward points that might do some good. I explained the nature of the split-second sighting in 1987, the long seven-and-a-half-year lapse before my interview, how the eyewitness's memory was left badly contaminated by the first drawing process, but how that same frustration over its inaccuracy had actually helped to fortify the original image in the witness's mind.

Surprisingly unimpeded, I managed to squeeze in the crucial point that, contrary to popular belief, the answer to retrieving accurate images lies in the psychology of how memory functions, not in the art, as police agencies believe.

"Let's take a look," he said as he turned toward the monitor on the wall behind us. "We're looking both at your drawing and the suspect photo." I nodded.

"Now we can merge the two electronically," he said as the square-jawed, hooded man in my drawing morphed into the week-old arrest mug shot. Despite a control-room blunder, which resulted in use of the 1996 arrest photo instead of the correct older photo taken near the actual time of the eyewitness sighting, the technological melding of the two images was astonishing. The lower jaw and lips in the sketch merged flawlessly into the Kaczynski photo.

My four and a half minutes were nearly up. Although the important academic points were coming across succinctly and clearly, instinct was telling me that things were going a little too well.

"You've walked through airports this past week," Williams said as he began to wind it down. "You've seen your work all over the nation. You've seen it for years. Now, I have to ask you"—he smiled knowingly—"what do you think? Do you think the FBI has their man?" I inhaled slowly as I comprehended what he'd done.

"You know what? Drawing that conclusion is not my job." I smiled back at him. "What *is* my job is to produce an accurate rendition of the suspect, and I can say I think that I've done that in this case." Our eyes locked in an elongated second of nonverbal tussle.

"Jeanne Boylan, we thank you for being with us this morning. And I think it's fair to say, 'Great work.' "

As the camera lights went out, he rose out of his chair and broke into a broad, toothy smile. He'd enjoyed the moment, and he'd made his point. Brian Williams wasn't going to be told how to do his job and had just let me know it. Our joust may have been imperceptible on camera, but he'd relished hitting me with the whatever-you-do-don't-ask-me question as much as I'd enjoyed squeezing out from having to answer it.

"Nice job," he said, laughing as he shook my hand a little too firmly. I stood up smiling and clenched his hand right back.

I held still while the stagehand removed the mike. Katie Couric laughed and winked at me adding, "Touché!" from her seat at the anchor desk.

———

I returned upstairs to the greenroom to wait out the rare April snowstorm. Dr. Barry Sears, author of *The Zone,* a diet book, sat down on the long sofa with his publicist and struck up a conversation. As he spoke with me, a small, frail, dark-haired woman entered the room, groping for a seat. Obviously distraught, she sat down timidly. Tears began to wash over the rims of her large, brown eyes. Another woman sat down protectively near her. I rushed over to her side to ask if there was something I could do to help.

"This is Sister Dianna Ortiz," the second woman whispered, and then introduced herself only as Pat. "Katie Couric just interviewed her about her ordeal. It's still so difficult for her to talk about it." I'd read of the Sister Ortiz story in papers, though I'd never dreamed our paths would cross.

Sister Ortiz was the Ursuline nun who was kidnapped and brutally tortured in Guatemala in 1989. Her four attackers remained unidentified, and there was strong implication of a high-ranking U.S. government official's involvement in the acts against her. For that reason, her plight had mushroomed into a hugely controversial case.

If U.S. government or CIA involvement were revealed, the political ramifications would be a nightmare, not only for the present administration, but also for the past administration under whose watch it had taken place. Ortiz had run into fierce resistance from every U.S. agency that should have been her ally. No one in the government wanted to dig toward the truth. In a final, desperate attempt to be heard, she was in the second week of a starvation and silent vigil in Lafayette Park across the street from the White House in Washington, D.C.

"No one's listening to her," Pat explained over Dianna's stilted sobs. "Under the Freedom of Information Act, she's entitled to the documents in her case, yet it seems as if they're being purposely withheld. In a press move, Hillary Clinton invited Dianna in to meet with her and even promised to help her, but there's been no follow-up to her promise. We're concerned for Dianna's safety out in that park, yet she's vowed to continue her fast until the documents in her case are released. *No one* is listening to her."

I was, and I knew of at least one way to help. If we could make the faces of her attackers tangible, it would not only increase the chances of their identification, but the interest we could generate might force the government to respond. Words alone weren't strong enough, but by making the faces of the four men real, tiny Sister Ortiz might finally be heard.

Katie Couric came into the greenroom, concerned over the fallout from her interview. She clasped her hands between her knees as she bent to speak. "Are you okay?" she asked gently.

I explained to Katie how there might still be hope of identifying the men responsible. "NBC could help you on this idea," she whispered back to me. "Be sure to keep me on top of your plans."

But there was no time to plan. Sister Ortiz was traveling back to Washington, D.C., immediately, and I was going back to Arizona the next morning. I wrote out my home telephone number on an NBC napkin and slipped it into Sister Dianna's tear-moistened hand.

If I'd questioned the logic in this sudden trip, I didn't any longer. As I sat alone after our encounter, I felt instinctively that the chance meeting with Sister Dianna was my real purpose in being there. I wasn't sure if we would ever meet again, nor was I even positive I could help her excavate the faces of her torturers from her memory.

All I knew for certain was that I felt somehow compelled to try.

By the time I got "home," the springtime temperatures in southern Arizona were climbing steadily upward. Even the wild pigs were retreating to higher elevations. As the weeks passed, I knew I needed to move soon, but any thought of leaving was forced to the back burner by a single phone call.

"Ms. Boylan, my name is José Pertierra," he said with a deep Hispanic accent. "I represent Sister Dianna Ortiz. I understand you two met on the set of the *Today* show in New York a few weeks ago and she's asked for you. Could you come to Washington, D.C., right away?" I tossed a suitcase on the bed and began packing with one hand while he talked.

Pertierra promised to fax the lengthy case history. With full knowledge of the details, I'd be able to wade through the interviews with sensitivity to key words, phrases, and references that might seem inconsequential in a normal context but could reinvoke terror with a trauma victim as affected as Sister Dianna.

Her life prior to the abduction had been tranquil. The harsh contrast from her cloistered world to her vicious assault created an emotional impact as profound as could be found in any trauma survivor, even that of a combat veteran.

Trauma has no standard measurement. To one victim, an event could lock into long-term memory as devastating; to another it could be all but forgotten as just another ordinary incident. That perspective was always crucial in understanding to what degree an image might be encoded into a victim's memory, as well as how susceptible to suggestion that person would later be.

For Sister Dianna Ortiz, nothing could make her forget. Trauma was both the lock and the key to the images that had created her nightmare. I'd need to remain alert to every potential emotional trigger. She would be highly susceptible to suggestion while her mind worked hard to keep the images buried. How I phrased questions, the voice tone I used, whether or not I continued eye contact over portions of conversation, where we worked, where I sat, the setting we used, every last detail would matter in retrieving the information accurately. Uncovering the faces of Sister Dianna's abductors would be like walking slowly and carefully through a loaded minefield.

I reached over for another page from the faxed sheets spilling over onto the terra-cotta floor.

Dianna Ortiz was twenty-eight when she left New Mexico to teach reading to grade-schoolers in Guatemala. On November 2, 1989, a man dressed as a Guatemalan policeman approached her in the schoolyard, pushed a gun into her back, and forced her onto a bus. He then prodded her into a car and drove her to a remote clandestine prison.

For twenty-four hours three men interrogated, brutalized, and repeatedly raped her. They burned her body more than a hundred times with lit cigarettes. At one point, as a foreshadowing of her own fate, she was dumped into a pit with decaying pieces of human corpses, then retrieved so the violations could continue.

Blindfolded, she heard her three attackers ask a fourth person to "come on in and have some fun." Instead, the late arrival began swearing in distinctly American phrases. He spoke Spanish, but Sister Dianna recognized his thick American accent.

The newcomer was furious. He yelled to the other three that they'd made a "mistake" and taken the wrong woman, whose disappearance had since become public in town. "I ordered you to take Veronica Ortiz Hernandez!" he screamed, then abruptly ended the torture session and demanded that Sister Dianna dress, though not before they'd videotaped the acts that her attackers vowed to her they would use against her if need be.

The three Guatemalans called the American man "Alejandro." When they removed her blindfold, Sister Dianna first saw all three. Then she saw the tall, large-framed American man in a cheap brunette wig that sat high on top of his head, his eyes masked with dark sunglasses. His beard, a different color of brown, appeared to be authentically his.

Alejandro escorted her to a jeep, telling her that he would take her to "his friend at the American embassy." Sister Dianna is bilingual, but spoke only English to him, which he understood, and he replied in a broken, heavily accented Spanish. She shook in terror as she reached for the door handle at a stoplight near Antigua, then bolted and fled through traffic in the outskirts of the city. Cornered in heavy traffic, Alejandro was unable to follow.

Sister Dianna made her way to the Maryknoll House and from there she was taken to the Papal Nuncio. The burns on her back, and the bruises and abrasions over her body, were examined and treated. After the Guatemalan archbishop examined her wounds, U.S. ambassador Thomas Stroock arrived to see her, though she was too distraught to see a stranger and declined the stranger's visit at that time.

There were four suspects in her case, the three Guatemalan rapists at the prison, and—most troubling of all—Alejandro, her fellow American, who, in a third-world country, by unspoken custom, she should have been able to rely on. None were "figments of her imagination," as the Ambassador Stroock and the political powers later tried to proclaim. One hundred and eleven burns on her body were the most solid proof.

But for the U.S. Justice and State Departments, one hundred and eleven scars seemed not to be proof enough.

Human Rights Watch reported that the CIA secretly provided millions of dollars in assistance to Guatemala's oppressive military intelligence. This and other reports filtering out of Central America validated what Sister Dianna already knew. What she did not know was who ordered her abduction and torture and why the U.S. government appeared to be concealing details of her case. Her quest for answers only uncovered more reports of Guatemalan human rights abuses and atrocities—which were routinely covered over and swept away. Sister Dianna's voice was a threat to anyone interested in maintaining secrecy. The harder she fought, the greater were the attempts to publicly discredit her.

I read the remainder of the faxed documents on the flight to Dulles Airport, then checked in at the Washington Capital Hilton, two blocks from Lafayette Park, a location chosen so that Sister Dianna would be able to come and go at will.

At first, she was afraid to come inside my room. Mary Fabri, Sister Dianna's psychologist, accompanied her and called me from a phone booth to ask if I could meet them across the street. No matter that Sister Dianna had conscious knowledge of why we were meeting, and that she herself had asked me to come, it could still have been terrifying for her to enter an enclosed room with anyone she didn't know. I was still a stranger to her. I understood, then hung up and rushed out the door.

"Sister Dianna, hello, it's Jeanne," I said gently as I approached her. She sat on a curb with her head down, her hair covering the sides of her face. Her arms embraced her legs, which were wrapped tightly inside her long, dark skirt. I knew not to touch her or to move too close. Trust would take time.

Dianna's beauty could only have been a detriment and source of conflict in the choices she'd made. At thirty-four, her good looks hadn't begun to diminish. Her dark, straight hair, cut bluntly at ear length in the austere manner of the Ursuline order, reflected the hazy afternoon sunlight. A fringe of bangs fell in strands over her large, clear brown eyes. She was a walking contradiction—a balance of physical frailty and a stunning strength of spirit.

She stood up, peering out from under the protective shield of her hair. Mary suggested we begin work at the home she shared with the other nuns. I agreed.

Alice Zachmann, head of the Guatemalan Human Rights Commission in Washington, D.C., drove us to an old brick row house in the rough and dangerous part of D.C. Oak-tree roots tilted the aged sidewalks, which bordered a lineup of common-walled porches.

We began working in the living room with a coffee table between us to give Dianna a physical zone of safety. At first I tried to look at her as I spoke, but her space had been so devastatingly shattered that even a gentle gaze was too invasive. She asked if I'd please look away.

I complied midsentence without faltering and kept myself in the center of the conversation to give her reason to stay focused on me visually while she became familiar with my presence.

In my eighteen full-time years of working with high-trauma victims from every imaginable circumstance, Sister Dianna was the most severe post-traumatic-stress-disorder victim I'd encountered. All my previous experiences were rehearsal for this moment.

To move away from the distractions of street noise, we shifted to her upstairs back bedroom. That Dianna invited me into her room showed a significant advance in trust, especially given the connotations of the setting and its physical features that may have held a trigger to her memories. Every move needed to be purely her choice, not for my convenience or at the coaxing of a counselor.

Conventional interview techniques stressed that the interviewer control the surroundings and advised never to let the subject find anything comfortable to hide behind. But these conventions, which had no understanding of the conditions of the heart, had shown no success in interviewing crime victims.

Large foam pillows formed a makeshift headboard for Dianna's single mattress on the floor, and she held one in front of her as she spoke, burying herself in its mass.

No matter how softly I constructed the questions, how slowly we moved, how gentle my voice, when the time came to interject a question even in the most indirect and subtle form, Dianna collapsed into tears. I wanted to ease her pain, but first, I had to reach after it, into the darkest depths of her mind. Dianna recoiled from the memories, but she never withdrew from the mission.

In her weakened state, her sobs led to hyperventilation, and she eventually passed out. Mary and I silently glanced at each other not with concern, but relief. Sister Dianna's breathing would smooth into a quiet rhythm as she finally drifted off to sleep. More than once, we sat still through long periods of silence, just grateful for a chance for her to rest.

Inevitably, on the street or in the alley outside the gaping, chipped-paint window frames of her weathered house, an ambulance would wail or dogs would bark, each time luring her back into her harsh reality. There was no adequate diversion for what she'd experienced. I knew Mary and I had to simply stay with her through it, as she redirected evil into good, in an effort she was fighting with her life to accomplish.

The day ended with progress. We had the faint beginnings of a single image on paper, the face of the man Sister Dianna wanted to begin with—the American man, Alejandro.

Ever since she'd begun her vigil on March 31, Sister Dianna had been surviving on only water and three pieces of bread a day, living under a blue, plastic camp awning through weather that had swung from snow to blistering heat and back to freezing temperatures.

"Physically, she's very weak," Alice Zachmann explained on our drive back to the hotel. "She's down from one hundred ten to eighty-seven pounds. The doctors say her weight loss is starting to affect her vital organs. This has got to come to an end, but she refuses. We could lose her. In fighting a battle simply to be heard, Dianna may be losing her will to survive."

The next day brought with it an encouraging sign. Sister Dianna agreed to meet me at the Capital Hilton to lessen her time away from the vigil. I pulled the sheers over the windows to soften the light and cleared out any sight or scent of food. She shyly entered and stayed for minutes, but in time, the visits turned into half hours, then full hours, taking place day or night as she decided. As further proof of the change in her, she advanced to the point of embracing me as we'd stand together at the elevator when she'd come and go, stunning me each time that she would reach out.

Sometimes she'd come in wet and nearly frozen. During an intense citywide severe-storm advisory, the wind and lightning felt as if it might bring the hotel walls down. She staggered in, shaking, the rain having saturated her simple cotton clothing. I convinced her to soak in a hot bath to take her chill away and filled the tub, sprinkling the water with salts, then left to sit by the window and read while I waited. When I heard the water splash against the porcelain, I whispered a quiet thanks to God, knowing she'd stepped into the warm water to thaw.

Working daily for a full week, the drawings emerged slowly, methodically, their startling images gradually rising to the surface of her memory and appearing in a form that she'd finally be able to confront.

"I want to see them all at once," she said when we completed the final drawing. Inside, I cringed. Every face was life-size and detailed, with dimension, depth, and realism. To see them at once could overwhelm her. I reluctantly laid the four down side by side, not knowing if I was about to undo all the healing we'd been able to achieve.

She inhaled, then moved her eyes along the line of faces, pausing at each one. She stood alone, calmly, strongly.

"That's them—all of them—exactly as they were," she said stoically, her arms wrapped tightly around her thin body. This time her eyes remained dry. For the first time, her posture was altered and upright.

"I am so sorry for what you had to go through to help me," she said, apologizing repeatedly for taking up a week of my time.

"Dianna, there's something I need for you to understand." I sat beside her and looked into her eyes. "You see, there is no city I'd rather be in, there is no restaurant I'd rather be at, no person I'd rather be with, no one I'd rather talk to. There is no place in this world that I'd rather be than right here, right now, doing exactly what I am doing—with you."

I heard the startling paradox in my words. This was work I wanted desperately to get away from. It had cost me everything—my family, my home, my marriage; I'd moved three states away to try to flee from it. Yet here I sat, meaning those words as sincerely as any I'd ever spoken.

As fiercely as I wanted to escape the work, at the same time I couldn't imagine *anyplace* more important to be.

———

With the faces captured and recorded, we finally had the lever-
age we needed to bring in the power of the press. Sister Dianna
planned to pen a statement to read from the podium at the same time
we released the drawings to the press.

I got out my thick, weathered Rolodex of reporters' names and phone
numbers, then sat cross-legged on my bed and began dialing. After all
the interviews, the invasive questions, the countless press conferences,
it was payback time.

I phoned Katie Couric at NBC, the Portland producer at CBS News,
Debbie Alpert and Gordon Recht in L.A., Vic Walter at ABC in New
York, Susan Friedman at the *Today* show, the *Washington Post,* The *New
York Times,* NPR, the reporters from the Justin Jones, Kenny Sommer,
and Cora Jones cases, and every media contact that had ever asked
favors of me. "And who did you say is your counterpart in Washington,
D.C.?" I asked, scribbling down each additional number.

Alice's office called in its resources as well. Through the Guatemalan
Human Rights Commission, we rented a meeting room in the
Washington Marriott. Next came another all-nighter at Kinko's making
up press packets with thousands of copies of all four drawings. I finally
walked out their front door as the morning work shift began filling the
sidewalks, then ran from the cab into the hotel to shower and change.
Our press conference was set for ten A.M.

The Associated Press would want just the right photograph to send
out across the country. A picture of Sister Dianna alone at a podium
wouldn't do us any good. I needed all four faces in the shot with her,
in the hope that someone would recognize Alejandro even through his
disguise. Employees at the U.S. embassy in Guatemala in 1989, visi-
tors or travelers there, someone in the U.S. government, knew this
man. Of that much we were certain. All that was needed was a single
tip.

To create the crucial shot, I needed something lightweight that Sister
Dianna could hoist easily in her weakened condition. I bought two yard-
sticks and overlapped the ends by one foot, then taped them together to
serve as a rod from which I could hang the four eleven-by-fourteen-inch
enlarged copies of the drawings. She'd be able to hold them up, all visible to the cameras at the same time.

With stacked boxes of press packets loaded in my arms, I stepped off the escalator at the upstairs foyer and went past the entrance to our pressroom and into the ladies' sitting room where Sister Dianna, Mary, and I had arranged to meet at nine forty-five.

"It's jammed out there, did you see the turnout?" Mary asked, obviously astonished. The camera tripods were so close their legs entwined and the rows of seats were rapidly filling with reporters. Attorney José Pertierra was inside the room fielding questions and informally prepping the contingent with case background.

In front of the mirrored counter, Dianna worked furiously on last-minute edits to her formal statement.

"May I borrow your scarf, please?" I asked her. I needed it to cover the sketches. Once the drawings were complete, it was crucial that she not see them again, so they would not then override the actual images embedded in her mind. The drawings can be very close, but there's only one original.

"You'll walk in from the back and carry this rod. When you reach the podium, lay it down behind you while you read your speech. You'll lift it when you are ready to reveal the faces to the press. When you *are* ready, listen to me carefully, okay? You need to lift these quickly and in one movement. Stay physically close to this display, do you understand? It's extremely important. Everything we've done boils down to this one moment."

"Okay." She looked up at me nervously, trusting my advice without question.

"And I've made this set of these drawings for you," I hurriedly told her. "But keep the faces turned away from you always, please. I want you to have this set of your own, not to look at again, but rather to tear up, to throw from a bridge or a building, to run over or to stomp on, to do with whatever you want. You are in control, not them."

I was unsure if she understood and had no time to explain further. The press conference began. Sister Dianna's mother and sister had just flown in from New Mexico and took seats in the second row behind me. The room turned silent when Sister Dianna took her place behind the podium, ready to speak publicly for the first time since March 31.

"Good morning," she began. "My name is Sister Dianna Ortiz. I am a torture survivor. Over five weeks ago, I stood in Lafayette Park, along with others whose lives had been torn apart by the violence in Guatemala."

As she read, I looked around the crowded room at the mass of cameras with tape rolling, reporters' eyes fixed on her as they scribbled every word in their notebooks. She continued speaking, telling of the horrors she had endured, describing in detail the betrayal she had experienced by the kidnappers and again by her own American justice system.

"In the five weeks of my silent vigil in Lafayette Park," she continued, "I have suffered the wind and the cold and the rain. But that is nothing. You see, in Guatemala, approximately thirty people have been tortured in just the time I have spent there. Ten more have been murdered for political motives." She stood tall and spoke with conviction. "I have struggled for the declassification of Guatemalan files. As of today, I am now suspending my fast, but the candle I lit on March thirty-first, which has burned day and night in the park as a reminder to President Clinton of the hundreds of thousands of us who have suffered in Guatemala, still burns. I hope now that its light also burns within you.

"I want to introduce you to my captors, my torturers."

As she lifted the thin rod and turned the four faces toward the crowd, a gasp rushed like a cold breeze through the room. Dozens of camera shutters clicked nearly in unison. Sister Dianna described each man's features and actions in vivid detail. Her mother wept from her seat as she looked for the first time into the eyes of her daughter's rapists. But Dianna stopped and turned her face to the reporters before describing the final sketch.

"This"—she inhaled deeply, then released her breath as well as her disdain for the man who had offended her most deeply—"is the one whom my torturers referred to as their boss, the man who gave the explicit orders, the man who had access to the U.S embassy, and to the clandestine prison in Guatemala." She looked straight into the cameras, then back at his bearded face, her spine rigid with determination as every reporter listened, every network's tape rolled.

"This is Alejandro. He is *not*"—she stressed every word, pausing to gather strength between each syllable—"a figment of my imagination."

Her eyes bore into the network lenses. Dianna spoke not to the reporters,

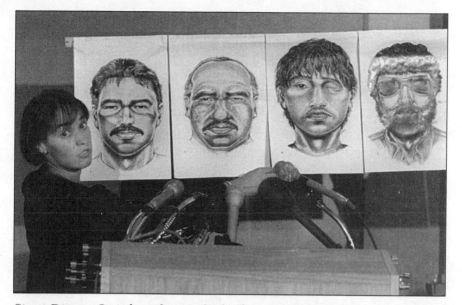

Sister Dianna Ortiz bravely reveals the faces of her four torturers at a press conference held at the conclusion of her five-week starvation and silent vigil in Washington, D.C. (Photo © AP Photo/Ron Edmonds)

but directly to Ambassador Stroock and to those in the Department of Justice who had dared to question the authenticity of her claims.

The Sister Dianna Ortiz story alongside the faces of her four torturers ran on every network and in every major newspaper across the nation and beyond by the day's end. The tiny American nun had taken back her power.

This time, the world was listening.

A procession of supporters and news cameras followed our contingent from the Washington Marriott to Lafayette Park. Sister Dianna carried the makeshift banner, her rapists' faces turned toward the crowds. When she reached the site of her vigil, she placed the sketches beside her on the ground while she knelt and began dismantling her makeshift encampment. I stood behind the crowd so the press couldn't place us in a single photograph and diffuse her story by including any mention of my involvement.

Sister Dianna stopped and looked up, searching over the rows of shoulders until she found my eyes. Oblivious to the attention of the crowd, she mouthed the words, "Jeanne, would it be all right if I burn these drawings?" Though I couldn't hear her, I understood her completely. She was ready to let her captors go.

"Yes, Dianna." I nodded slowly and mouthed the words back while tears crested over the rims of my eyes. "Yes, that would be fine."

Slowly, she peeled the tape back from the wooden rods and twisted each drawing into a cylinder, crushing each with her hands until it took the form of a long, tight wand. One at a time, she dipped the drawings into the candle's flame, holding them as they transformed into lighted torches.

Her eyes never left the fire that swallowed the emblems of the horror she'd lived through and released them into the midday air. When the last image had burned to its tip, she stood up and tucked her hair securely behind her ears and, for the first time, Sister Dianna Ortiz smiled. Her exorcism was finally complete.

As Sister Dianna Ortiz disassembles her five-week encampment, she dips each of the four drawings into the lit candles and burns the images of the faces of her abductors. (Photos: Collection of the author)

At one point during our work together, Dianna had looked over to me from the hotel couch and in her weak voice said, "You know something, it's so strange, and I can't tell you why, because I never liked them before, but all through my starvation vigil, I've been craving pork and beans."

I'd once mentioned her statement to Alice. In the park on that final day, as Dianna's five-week vigil ended, with the smoke from her captors' faces still billowing around her, a nun walked up and laid her hand gently on Dianna's shoulder. In her other hand was a gift she'd brought to help celebrate Dianna's transformation. She handed over the largest available red and white can of Campbell's pork and beans.

It took pain, protest, and amplification of the message to levels the system could no longer ignore, but at least, and at last, there was movement.

By two P.M. the same day, the Clinton administration announced that it was releasing over twenty thousand pages of official U.S. government documents regarding the Sister Dianna Ortiz kidnap-and-torture case and other human rights violations in Guatemala.

By five o'clock that afternoon I was sound asleep in an airline seat. I landed in Arizona after sunset, but even then the sweltering heat still radiated off the cement walkways of the Tucson airport. My lungs, struggling from a congestion I'd ignored throughout the stress of the last week, burned with each breath of dry desert air.

The dust was still settling in the driveway when I walked into the casita and opened all doors and windows to get the hope of an evening breeze blowing through. I switched the television on for company as I passed by it on a second trip out to the car.

Suddenly, I heard Dianna's voice and swung around to look at the TV screen. I stood motionless, stunned to hear her speaking. She was being interviewed on ABC's *Nightline*, taped, apparently, after I'd left for the

airport, their interest undoubtedly prompted by our earlier press conference. Cokie Roberts sat in for Ted Koppel.

Cokie spoke slowly, carefully, her usual political aggressiveness seemingly softened momentarily for Dianna. The interview was winding to a
close.

"So, now the administration seems to have come through. They've
released thousands and thousands of documents for you, so is that
enough?" Roberts shifted in her seat.

"It's not enough," Dianna stated quietly but emphatically. "I don't
know yet what role my government played in my abduction and my torture, and I believe I have a right to know."

Roberts pushed forward. "If, in fact, the government documents
never tell you who Alejandro is, maybe—maybe if he was a government
employee, and they didn't even put it in the documents, then what?"

"I believe that someone or maybe more than one person knows of
Alejandro," Dianna answered sternly. "I will keep knocking on doors for
as long as it takes."

"You have talked about healing"—Cokie paused briefly—"and said
that one of the reasons you are doing this is to bring it to some sort of
closure and to have some sort of healing, but it sounds like that hasn't
happened for you."

Dianna sat up so straight in her seat as to appear almost tall. She was
focused and clear, but her voice was halting, her words often parted by
seconds while she caught her breath, her frail body still weak from the
effects of her vigil.

"Healing comes in various forms. I know that I will always carry the
memory of what happened to me on November second, 1989. For more
than six and one-half years I have allowed my Guatemalan torturers and
Alejandro to haunt me. Many times, I've felt like they've danced within
me. Many times, I've felt that if I got close to anyone, I was going to
contaminate them with the evilness that they left inside me." Dianna
inhaled deeply. "But today, I can sit here and say that that evilness does
not exist inside me anymore, and that is because of the work that I was
able to accomplish with Jeanne Boylan."

I held my hands to my lips and, as my knees buckled, slowly lowered
myself to a seat on the edge of the bed.

The camera lingered on Dianna until Cokie continued, "Now let me explain for a second. Jeanne Boylan is the woman who drew the faces of the people that you saw in Guatemala. So she's now been able to put a face to those memories. Is that it?" Roberts seemed not to understand— nor would many who hadn't endured such an experience.

"That's correct," Dianna continued. "The images of my torturers and Alejandro have always stayed within me, and I have held myself responsible for the horrible things that happened on that November day, but today, because I was able, with the help of Jeanne Boylan, to put a face to these monsters, I can put them away from me. They no longer live in my soul."

"And is that why you're ending the vigil?"

"Yes. Because, you see, until I faced them, I could never be free."

18

AWAKENINGS

The summer turned a broiler on Arizona, and the months of Boeing air and artificial temperature swings finally caught up with me. Suddenly my peaceful setting burned with intolerable heat and my body temperature hovered around 103.

Still, I woke up each morning at four A.M. to fulfill more promises made for East Coast rush hour radio interviews: Miami, Atlanta, Pittsburgh, Detroit, Boston. The morning radio shows were pretty easy—in the past I'd taken calls in the bathtub, on the sundeck, wherever and however I appeared at the moment. I enjoyed the obscurity of live radio interviews, and through them I could get out solid information without worry over being reduced to an out of context sound bite on the evening news.

"Call me ten minutes before the interview to cue me, okay?" I told the scheduler for a Baltimore station. My lungs were inflamed, my temperature was stuck at the top of the thermometer, and I was beyond dizzy from flu medication. Afraid I'd sleep through the alarm clock, I knew I would never miss the sound of a ringing phone, so we made a deal that the station would provide the wake-up call. I hung up and fell back asleep.

In my dream, a talk-show host welcomed me to a cool blue set: "Thank you for joining us."

I prodded words out of my throat as if they were swimming up through deep water in slow motion. In the dream, he asked a crisp and perky deejay-style question, and I garbled a mile-long string of mumbled words, trying to make up in length for what I lacked in clarity. It was one of those dreams in which every ridiculous moment inspired another.

The host seamlessly followed each inquiry with another question, which I would answer as if talking through a snorkeling tube. "That's just as fascinating as the work you do, Ms. Boylan, so please, tell us more." Like trying to run an imaginary race with legs of concrete, I just couldn't make the effort to speak emerge from my lips in any comprehensible fashion.

I finally woke at nine-thirty, achy and still groggy from the medication. The casita was hot, the air stagnant, and the sun was blistering high in the sky when I pushed the windows open, dodging any contact with the already iron-hot metal frames.

Hey, I realized, the radio station never called. What a gift. My body was grateful for the long night's sleep.

Later I checked in with Jennifer. "You know that Baltimore station that set the interview for this morning? They never called."

"Yes they did, sweetheart," she said, pausing longer than I'd ever known her to be silent. "You, um, you talked to them for a full ten minutes."

It took all my strength to scream in my raspy voice, "I did a ten-minute radio interview? In my sleep? Are you kidding me? What did I say?"

"You were a hit. Apparently you had Baltimore's rush-hour traffic in stitches. They called back asking me to check in with you to make sure you were really all right, but I thought I'd better just let you rest. Are you okay?"

Note to self: Never, ever go to Baltimore.

A few days later my fever subsided, and I was standing at the U-Haul counter in nearby Green Valley. It was time to move on.

"Where you headed?" the woman asked as she suspended a pen over the rental contract.

"Oh, you have to have a destination?" I said, laughing but only partially kidding. What I had in mind was to drive north until the scene out the window rivaled the remote beauty I'd found in Arizona. I planned to narrow options one stop sign at a time, based purely on mood and intuition each time the road forked.

I thought of Maria Shriver's response to my "unencumbered" lifestyle: "You can just *do* that?" Yes, I can, I thought, savoring the coveted feeling of freedom. The rent-a-truck franchisee, however, wanted me to be a bit more firm in my plans.

Arizona had been good to me. I'd come to search my soul, and from my corner of the canyon, I'd managed to escape long enough to reflect and to find meaning hidden in the loss of my marriage and in the tragedies I'd witnessed firsthand. Meditations, writing, reading, listening to the teachings of my pastor on mailed cassette tapes as I'd walk the canyons at sunsets—they'd all helped. Yet it was Sister Dianna's words that had ultimately reawakened my spirit.

Sister Pat Murphy of Su Casa, the Chicago home for torture survivors where Sister Dianna had sought refuge and healing, told CNN's Brian Barger during a worldwide broadcast dedicated to her plight, "We call it a resurrection. She who was dead has come back to life."

Sister Dianna had flicked the light on in my search for why this work held such power over my life. That *was* what it was really about. Fighting an entrenched system, forging a new path, sure, but that answered only the question of what. Not why. It took working with survivors—victors—to understand why this work was important. My role was small compared to that of those who had walked every step of these anguished journeys, but such moments were enough to finally clarify what my own walk was all about.

I'd watched people step over the invisible line between victimization to victory, and their journeys had filled me with awe. Though I knew instinctively the importance of freeing a victim of the evil left from an attack, never before had I realized so clearly the emotional power that floods the soul when the residual grip of an assailant is finally loosened, and the memory is gently removed from the heart.

I drove back to the adobe to temporarily unhook the trailer, load it, and pick up Jack, a hundred-dollar investment that could be put in the passenger seat to hide the fact that I was a lone blonde in a new white car, or, better put, a car-jack waiting to happen. This would be Jack's first road trip, though he'd been with me ever since FBI agents had informed me that the beautiful strip of Arizona road between Nogales and Tucson was also the most highly drug-trafficked corridor in the USA.

Jack was my foil. Ordered from an in-flight magazine, he arrived in a square, foot-sized box branded SAFETY MAN. When the agents had suggested the idea, it seemed like a good one, but when I opened the box and pulled him out, he looked like a reject from *Revenge of the Nerds*. If anyone wanted to get to me, he appeared as if he'd jump out and flog them with a pocket protector. That wouldn't work, so I took a bit of artistic license.

After minor surgery I pushed a cubic Z stud through his left earlobe, applied a four-day stubble of rough black beard on his face, created an oversized mustache from the salt-and-pepper hair on top of his head, clipped on an artificial ponytail, put on wraparound sunglasses to conceal his wide eyes, and gave him a weathered denim shirt, faded Levi's jeans, a leather jacket, and an old pair of cowboy boots. He transformed from looking like a field geologist into a tenured member of the Mexican mafia. His appearance was so authentic and threatening that, for contrast, I wanted to give him the simplest name I could think of. I rechristened him "Jack."

While he guarded the car, I loaded up the U-Haul, saving the last few feet for trash to be dumped off at the landfill.

Once at the dump, I stood on the ledge of the pit and threw out the four Hefty bags of moving debris, but then felt an overwhelming urge to keep on tossing. I smiled inwardly and began to eye the neatly packed contents of the truck.

You know, I thought, I never liked that lamp. Out it went. I turned and began digging a little deeper. Oh, yeah, I bought that painting in Sun Valley with Robert. I reached for the frame, felt it in my hands, then suddenly I was watching it fly. Here's that jacket he loved on me.

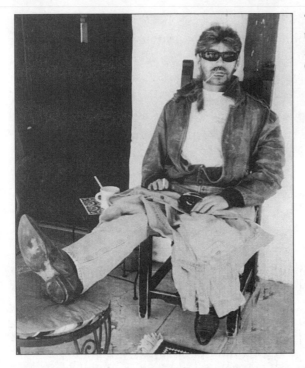

"Jack" takes a break on the front porch of the Mexican casita. (Photo: Collection of the author)

Gone. Look, it's my fishing pole. Dishes, coffee-table books, chairs, sheets, an antler candelabra, framed snapshots, old saddles—every single thing that reminded me of Robert and all his broken promises, one after another my acquisitions spiraled to the pit below. With each twist of my body the U-Haul got progressively emptier and I got progressively happier. In the end, I danced back and forth across the tailgate while Jack stared straight ahead.

Finally I turned and looked at the reopened boxes inside the nearly empty truck bed. What irony, I thought. When I was married I had so much—and felt like I had so little. Now I have so little, yet feel like I have so much.

M y first stop was Sedona. Ten months had gone by since I sat in an L.A. hotel suite watching Lisa Dahl talking with Maria Shriver about her life after Justin.

"I'm very proud of my son because his actions speak for the way he was. Justin lived his life to the fullest." Maria waited a long moment

Lisa Dahl and Andrea DiLuca celebrate Justin's life. Lisa vowed to live her life fully for her son and to continue to make him proud. They subsequently opened Dahl & DiLuca, their award-winning restaurant in Sedona, Arizona, which they created and decorated in Justin's honor. (Photo: Collection of the author)

while Lisa wiped away tears. "And I think that I have an ever-challenging job now to make him proud of me. That's what will keep us connected."

Just after our meeting, Lisa had quit her career as a shoe rep, and with Andrea, they'd sold their belongings to pursue their dreams.

I pulled the truck to a stop in front of the large white stone sign on Sedona, Arizona's Highway 89A: DAHL & DILUCA, RISTORANTE ITALIANO. In honor of Justin, angels were woven into the rich tapestry fabric over the windows and floated in frescoes along the walls and ceilings. A plaque reading VOTED BEST EUROPEAN RESTAURANT IN VERDE VALLEY was centered in the entry amid framed reviews heralding Andrea DiLuca's executive-chef capabilities and Lisa Dahl's magic touch in everything from the artistic decor to the weekend jazz bands.

The establishment's featured vocalist: Ms. Lisa Dahl. Justin Jones's last gift to his mother had been her own reawakening.

The next morning, it was open road through the Painted Desert, the Hopi and Navajo reservations, and Monument Valley. The air cooled with each degree of latitude I advanced, and Jack looked less apt to melt as we crossed into the Colorado Rockies.

Luckily, I found a hundred-year-old cabin made of hand-hewn timbers, right at the base of Mt. Sneffles in the northern shadow of the perennially snowcapped San Juan Mountains. Telluride and Ridgway were my bases for supplies, with nothing and no one around me but a few head of cattle, two horses, and a resident herd of over 250 wild elk that bellowed around the private stocked lake each evening at dusk.

I slipped into my old hometown, bypassing the road to my parents' home, my old high school, the JC Penney corner that I'd once rounded on a Greyhound bus. Little had changed. I turned in the U-Haul and, thankfully still undetected, drove the car back to my mountain cabin where I planned to spend the summer alone.

Toward the end of June, I flew to California to support Marc Klaas as he finally learned the fate of Polly's killer at the long-delayed trial of Richard Allen Davis. I spent the night at Marc's parents' home, sleeping in Polly's old bed, before meeting up with Marc and Violet at the San Jose County Courthouse. After plowing our way through the horde of cameras and the double security check, we sat together nervously holding on to each other in the front row of the packed courtroom while Davis took his seat ten feet from our chairs.

The jury had been out for three unexpected and torturously long days, allowing no one confidence in the outcome. Investigator Mike Meese grasped Marc's hand over the courtroom railing. Eddie Freyer glanced over at me as the long-awaited reading of the verdict began.

"We find the defendant guilty of murder in the first degree in the death of Polly Hannah Klaas."

Since 1993, Richard Allen Davis had avoided the cameras but, for the first time, he turned defiantly toward the networks' ready lens, then angrily jammed both middle fingers into the air.

"Did you see that?" Eddie whispered as we moved out of the courtroom along with the crowd. Marc walked ahead of us into the throng of reporters. As the decision was read, most eyes had been on the court clerk while she rapidly recited the charges count after count. The majority of those present had missed Davis's gesture.

"I heard you gasp," Eddie said.

"But, Eddie, only you and I and one juror saw it," I said.

"But the camera didn't miss it." He smiled. "That move will be all over the nation's television sets by the end of the day. The only step left for this monster is the decision for or against the death penalty. Let's be very thankful—with that gesture alone, Richard Allen Davis just sealed his own fate."

The anonymity of hiding out in a secluded cabin lasted until fall when I shattered it myself through the single, careless act of driving 55 in a 45 mph zone. The officer who wrote the ticket relayed to the local chief of police that he'd stopped "Tommy Boylan's little sister" for speeding. Three days later, Montrose had its biggest robbery in county history, and there was an eyewitness. Chief of Police Victor Bell called me in on the case.

Vic and my older brother, Tommy, had been Cub Scouts in my mother's troop when I was still too young to enter grade school. The chubby, dark-haired Vic was tall for his age, always hungry, and invariably hung around after meetings on the safe-bet chance he'd be invited for something to eat.

Now forty-seven-year-old Chief Bell walked into the police department interview room, all six feet four inches of him, his dark hair flecked with gray. He sat down on the side of the desk. "Great to see you, Jeanne. When you finish your interview, say about five o'clock, mind if I ask you one favor? Can we get a picture together?"

What I didn't know was that Vic Bell had called the Montrose version of a press conference: two reporters and a television camera with duct tape holding together its microphone wires. Harmless enough, I thought, in relation to what I was used to. But the following day, not one but both front pages of the two southwest-Colorado newspapers, featured Vic Bell, Montrose chief of police, shaking hands with me on the steps of the city hall. Calls from old friends suddenly began filling up my voice mail box, but I'd run out of time. Within a week, there would be snow covering the nine-mile dirt road to the cabin. It was time to go.

Before I left, I drove back down the main boulevard and passed my old high school, where the marquis read HOMECOMING GAME TONIGHT, seven P.M. I'd have one chance to see old friends before leaving town. I pulled in, bought a ticket, and was hopping between bleachers saying hello to everyone I knew there when I heard my name over the loud-speaker, asking me to come to the sportcasters' booth.

"Would you crown the homecoming queen for us?" the announcer asked. I looked beyond the bleachers to the dozens of red-and-white-uniformed players, the cheerleaders bounding on the sidelines, the marching band in formation on the field, their tubas and drums setting a beat that the crowd picked up with rhythmic applause. The huge banks of lights pushed a silvery fluorescence through the black night and onto the thick green turf.

At halftime, I walked out onto the track and took the hand of the six-year-old boy who was carrying the queen's tiara on a silk pillow. Together we walked under the arch of the ROTC crossed swords and onto the football field. Every detail was exactly as I'd remembered it.

"Ladies and gentlemen, MHS has a special treat for you this evening," the announcer said, blasting me away from my thoughts. "Jeanne Boylan will be crowning our homecoming queen tonight. Jeanne is one of our most celebrated alumni."

I winced at the mere thought. Then his words slowed and echoed in the cold night air. "Jeanne was our homecoming queen twenty—five—years—ago . . ."

The sting of his words echoed off the bleachers.

Twenty five years ago? *How* could that possibly be?

I stared into the hometown crowd, looking at my high school friends seated in the football stands, many who'd never left town, many who'd married each other, many occupying the same seats their parents had sat in when I was standing on that field twenty-five years earlier. Their own children were now the band members, queen candidates, and foot-ball stars.

I watched them all clapping and cheering, the noise muffled by the rapid speed of my colliding thoughts. I felt flushed, even embarrassed.

Look at them, I thought. They had children, families, homes they'd worked hard for, good businesses they'd created. Measured against their successes, what had I really achieved? And they were cheering me?

As I stood in the floodlights, feeling the crisp fall air and listening to the applause, every aspect of my high school memory came racing to the surface. As a seventeen-year-old, I'd ambitiously stood in that identical spot and vowed to myself that I would make my life unusual, unpredictable; that I'd venture out to find excitement, mystery, glamour, intrigue; that I'd work in the news, travel the world, get an education, even go live in Europe.

Sure, I couldn't join them in the stands to watch my own child play ball, but I suddenly realized that I *did* have children—children I'd loved and fought for, families I'd become a part of. My family might not be traditional, but we'd entered into each other's lives in a way that created a bond as strong as any family tie could be.

The sound of the brass band began to amplify around me again as I realized for the first time that as inadvertent as it had all seemed, as hard as I'd consciously and willfully fought to alter its path, my life had unfolded precisely—as I stood on that same field, in that same spot, twenty-five years earlier—as I had wished for it to be.

19

AMERICA'S MOST WANTED

At last, no more cases were pending and I'd disappeared permanently, I hoped, from the FBI's radar screen. I had only one more obligation, then the future was all mine to create. For financial reasons, my accountant advised me to finish out the year as an Oregon resident. It wasn't going to be an easy move. Still, finances dictated—I had to go back to Bend. I drove the hundreds of miles of interstate freeway at thirty-five miles an hour.

Somewhere between Boise and Baker City, CBS radio news broke into programming with a bulletin. "In a California courtroom, the convicted killer of Polly Klaas was given the death penalty today. Richard Allen Davis stood emotionless as—"

I reached over and snapped the radio dial off and made the remainder of the trip in silence. It wasn't satisfaction I was feeling. Nothing could lessen the sense of sadness over losing Polly, but at least for all who loved her, it would be the beginning of closure.

Though I was back in Bend against my wishes, all I had to do was lie low and stay out of sight for two short months. After New Year's Day, I'd be free to move on. But there was one place from my past I'd actually been longing to visit.

Years earlier, when I'd lost my son, my pastor suggested that I plant a tree on the grounds of the new Foursquare Church, then just a bare foundation. It would give me one sacred place, he told me, where I could go in private to stay connected to his spirit.

I tiptoed back into the courtyard. Heavy equipment had demolished every piece of foliage at the construction sight years earlier, but miraculously, in the midst of it all, they'd never touched the tiny vulnerable tree. The now tall strong boughs of my Colorado blue spruce reached skyward, shielding my eyes from the fall sun.

It seemed as though it were yesterday that I'd unwrapped the burlap blanket around its tender roots before lowering it into the bed on that cold December day, when I'd prayed for the tree to thrive in the protective shadow of the church, in my son's memory.

The opening music sounded from inside the church. I'd been lost in my thoughts and the service was already under way. The usher led me to one of the few open seats inside a row near the back of the crowded room. I mindlessly scanned the congregation but stopped suddenly when I came across a figure I knew well.

Robert was sitting just two rows in front of me.

This church was the one sanctuary where I felt certain our paths would never cross. The tree signified a memory he'd never been able to face. Yet there he was, at church and seated alone. The ambivalence of my reaction left my mind spinning. Could he possibly have changed?

As the choir began the closing song, I begged my way past the rest of the row so I could slip out without being discovered. The light from the opened door formed a beacon that I strove for with every silent, labored step. I was merely feet away when a woman on the aisle of the last row grabbed me by the arm.

"You're Jeanne Boylan, aren't you?" she whispered, taking my hand in hers. "I just wanted to tell you I've followed your work, and I think what you do is so important." She continued talking, physically restraining me, pumping my hand with both of hers, then transferring it to her husband's when I felt a gentle tug on my hair. "Jeanne?" Robert asked as I turned around. "My God, it *is* you!"

"Rob!" I feigned surprise. "How have you been?"

"It's great to see you. Have you got time for a cup of coffee?"

"Um . . . okay, sure. Where should we meet?" I made sure we went to a public meeting place and that I had my own car waiting for the get-away.

"So how's your love life?" he asked once we sat down.

"Probably a lot quieter than yours," I said, realizing that even the concept of dating was barely on my agenda.

He told me about his string of disappointing encounters and shrugged. "Nothing notable or worth a revisit," as he put it. "Just passing time."

He told good stories, made me laugh, and I relaxed into the safety of what began to feel like an old lost friendship.

When the coffee cups were empty, I said I had to run. "You know, new apartment, empty refrigerator . . . I need groceries." I searched for any excuse to get away.

"Hey, so do I," he said, and offered to walk me to the gourmet market across the street. Before long, we were laughing again. In the aisle he came up behind me and, in our old routine, reached his massive arms around me and placed his hands outside mine on the grocery cart, our legs moving in unison while we both tossed items onto the pile. In the parking lot, he swung me around, pinned me to the car, and kissed me.

I pushed him away. "You know, the last time I tried to see you, Rob, I was blinded by a prom light. It was Christmas time. Pretty tough night to forget."

"I know," he sighed. "I still hate the thought of that night. When you didn't come back from L.A., remember, when you said you wanted to give us both time to think? I thought it was just an excuse. I knew inside that you weren't coming back to me. I went into a self-destruct mode. You have no idea what I went through that night when I heard the screen door shut, then looked out to see your car pulling out of the driveway."

He turned his face away. "That woman there that night, Jeanne, she was just an anesthetic. You've got to believe me. I thought I'd lost you for good."

"Interesting way of grieving," I said, my stomach knotted while I pushed back a sudden glimpse of what could have been.

"I watched you growing," he said, "doing work that really mattered, getting all the attention, the press, the respect—pretty tough on a guy's ego, you know? You were traveling the country saving lives, and what was I doing? I was making money, but that was it. I couldn't buy your respect"—he shook his head—"or even my own."

He looked away for a long moment, then turned back. "But you, you always live your life with integrity."

"Maybe so, but look at me, Rob—it cost me everything, you, our home, all of our plans . . ."

"No, it didn't, Jeanne. It *gave* you everything. Everything that really mattered—and every single time you pulled in that driveway, I resented you a little more for it."

His words were a long-awaited salve on a barely healed wound, though I wondered if his changes were authentic, or merely the well-crafted words of a highly skilled salesman. My eyes were wide open this time. Guardedly, I agreed to see him again.

Rob was living well in an elegant, airy home on a golf course, framed by sunny fairways, stands of pine trees, and mountain views. We built fires, cooked dinners, laughed like we used to and reminisced. He asked me to come home, but I couldn't answer him—not yet.

For Christmas, I gave him an elaborately wrapped box. Inside was only a simple white dry-marker board and a note: "My gift to you—A clean slate."

When Lance Heflin, executive producer for *America's Most Wanted* in Washington, D.C., called, I thought I could hear the last pieces of my puzzle falling into place. "Television correspondent"— it was the single item on the seventeen-year-old's wish list not yet fulfilled.

Heflin invited me to sign on as one of the show's correspondents, covering crimes and investigations on the show's unsolved-case log. He explained that they wanted to get me on board for the new season, then wait for just the right case to use as a backdrop for introducing me to their national audience. While we were waiting, another call came through.

"This is Julie from the *Leeza Gibbons* show. I've taken Debbie Alpert's place. Debbie's now a producer at *Inside Edition*. Leeza would like you to come to Los Angeles for another show we're taping. We'd like you to join as the expert on eyewitness identification. Can you do it?"

The timing was ideal. I needed some room to think about what the future held for Rob and me and they needed me there early the next week. I called *America's Most Wanted* and left a message with my whereabouts, then fled Oregon's winter for a few warm days in L.A.

Paramount's lot on Melrose felt more familiar to me than a lot of neighborhoods I'd once called home. I said hello to the gate man, the makeup artists, the producers, the stage crew—and made my way through the back door of the studio to take my place on the set.

Onstage, I was seated next to a man who'd just spent half of a twenty-year sentence imprisoned on a conviction of rape. All along he'd maintained his innocence, but that wasn't enough to spare him from losing his career, his wife, and the children who hadn't spoken to him since he'd been put behind bars a decade earlier. The sole basis of his conviction? Eyewitness identification.

Then came a miracle. A discovery called DNA, which proved conclusively that he was not guilty. Yet the victim had been "positive" that his face was the right one in a lineup. But, after exposure to how much contamination? And after how many suggestive or leading interviews? He was living proof of how badly things could go wrong.

And his wasn't the only story. Defense attorneys routinely cite research indicating that up to 30 percent of people convicted and serving time are, in fact, innocent and are sitting behind bars based on the little understood topic of eyewitness identification. Is memory truly malleable? It definitely is, and I was looking at the proof as well as the consequence.

"You know what?" he whispered to me as we waited during a commercial break. "I forgave that woman who put me in jail. But I'm an honest man, you know—always have been—and when I fill out a job application now, they always ask me if I've ever been convicted of a felony. I have to tell them, yes, or I'd be lying. Once I mark that box, they won't have anything more to do with me. It's been a year since I got out of prison, but I still can't get a job."

Ten years of an innocent man's life, maybe more—it was impossible to try to calculate the price he'd paid, and his was one of a thousand stories. As a result of contaminated eyewitness recall and subsequent misidentifications, innocent men were sometimes losing their freedom, and murderers and rapists were often winning their immunity, while the number of crime victims continued to climb.

I kept thinking things were changing. And they were—at least in the academic world. But the tradition-bound criminal-justice system was still reluctant to follow.

Even the breakthroughs only perpetuated the entrenched methods. Most so-called "state-of-the-art" computer software programs allow facial composites to be created using banks of thousands of out-of-context features simply by the purchase of a disk that comes with absolutely no operator training. Agencies scramble to be the first ones to buy, moved by marketing pitches that include books of samples showing how close a laptop program can re-create the face of Michael Jackson or Pamela Anderson, as if that bears any relevance at all to the complex process of retrieving detail from a traumatized mind. Software graphics are reaching excellence, but without the comprehension of the psychological dynamics behind a memory, it's just a high tech version of a disaster-in-the-making.

Thanks to the hard work of Elizabeth Loftus, and her determined colleagues, there now exists empirical proof about how malleable the memory of an eyewitness is. DNA tests reinforce the argument with overturned convictions and indisputable facts.

If the prosecution won't recognize it, their opponents happily will. Defense teams, well paid to turn over every rock and willing to aggressively embrace any new strategy that might net results, are learning how to seize upon the pitfalls of memory contamination and using the information with increasing regularity to unravel plaintiffs' arguments.

In so doing, they use the blunders of the investigations as "technicalities" that lead—sometimes rightly, sometimes wrongly—to not-guilty verdicts. Granted, their interest in how the memory works comes after the mistakes are made, but ironically, by setting legal precedents, they may be the ones to succeed in inspiring change.

My hope is to reach the system *before* the mistakes occur.

———

Leeza sat down near the stage as the show resumed. Garrett Morris spoke next. Morris, a comedian and former cast member of *Saturday Night Live,* had once been the victim of a brutal robbery. As he voiced his frustration, he threw his hands into the air and shouted, "And now look what we have this morning right here in Los Angeles! Bill Cosby's son was shot and killed!" His outburst left everyone present stunned by the news.

Ennis William Cosby, twenty-seven years old, was murdered at one forty-five Thursday morning, January 16, 1997, near the on-ramp of the 405 freeway in Bel Air.

Bill Cosby was America's television dad, which—in this world where all lines between reality and entertainment blur—made Ennis everyone's brother. The whole country reeled from the news.

After the taping, I rushed back to the hotel room for an appointment with Debbie Alpert's camera crew from *Inside Edition,* but as they walked through the door, a call came through from *America's Most*

The crew of *America's Most Wanted* prepares to report from in front of Parker Center, Los Angeles. (Photo: Collection of the author)

Wanted, asking me to cover the Cosby case. I rushed through the interview, then left that crew and raced to meet the other for a press conference at Parker Center in downtown L.A.

With my first set of media credentials in hand and the *America's Most Wanted* producer, cameraman, and soundman alongside me, I joined the fraternity of national network correspondents, a dream I'd held for years, yet it was eclipsed by the gravity of the truth we were there to tell.

Chief of Police Willie Williams stepped behind the podium to provide the latest details. Less than twelve hours earlier, Ennis Cosby had discovered that the left rear tire of his Mercedes convertible had gone flat. He stopped near a freeway off-ramp to make the repair and used his cell phone to call the friend whose home he'd been en route to. She came to the scene to help him by lighting the back of his car with the bright headlamps of her Jaguar while he replaced the tire. It was a cold night, and she was sitting inside her car waiting when an unidentified man walked up and tapped on her partially opened driver's-side window.

She looked directly at him, frightened by the stranger's face just inches away from her own. She reacted by hitting the accelerator and racing off a short distance, then returning minutes later to see if Ennis was okay. Nothing in her imagination could have prepared her for the horror she faced when she discovered Ennis lying dead in the roadway.

"Police are withholding her identity," Chief Williams explained to the packed roomful of reporters. "The eyewitness is too traumatized to be interviewed."

"But at least they had an eyewitness!" I told Carl, the show's expert producer. *America's Most Wanted* quickly offered the LAPD my compositry services as a courtesy of the program.

First, though, the eyewitness would have to agree to be interviewed.

The camera crew drove me late that night to the crime scene where Ennis was murdered. So that I'd know precisely what to expect in terms of the witness's ability to describe, we set up the identical scenario. Fresh bloodstains on the concrete still clearly marked the exact spot that Ennis had fallen. The night sky was cloudless, identical to the conditions of twenty-four hours before, and a faint sliver of moon hung shyly over the coastal range.

We pulled a car into the space occupied the night before by the eyewitness's Jaguar. I sat in the driver's seat and watched while the producer walked toward me, emulating the movements of the stranger as he bent and tapped on my semi-opened window.

The vague glow of the partial moon, the road lights emanating up from the freeway, and the eye-level bright beams shining against the opened and light-colored trunk interior of the vehicle ahead provided ample illumination. The witness's vision hadn't been hindered by drugs or alcohol, according to the reports. Reason to encode the image was at its highest degree.

Every needed factor was in order to produce the precise image of the man down to the very texture of his skin.

Any undertone of guilt the witness might feel over having left the scene could complicate her emotions, exaggerate her willingness to comply, and put her at the highest level of susceptibility to suggestion and contamination. We'd need to work with her *very* cautiously not only to record but also to preserve her recall. If it was damaged or altered in any way, it could destroy her ability to identify the suspect. If that happened, and if the case lacked physical evidence such as the murder weapon, the unthinkable could conceivably take place: Ennis's killer could walk free.

Two and one half days after the shooting, on Saturday afternoon, January 18, at three P.M., the LAPD held another press conference. The *America's Most Wanted* crew rushed by the hotel to pick me up. Every media organization in the nation sped across town to cover the expected breaking news. Hopes ran high among reporters that the news was of the arrest of Ennis's killer.

Instead, Police Chief Williams ceremoniously entered the Parker Center Auditorium and took his place behind the podium to explain that the three-day investigation was intensively under way. Disappointingly, it was not yet focused on any suspect because the eyewitness, he maintained, "was still too traumatized to be interviewed."

There was little other news beyond the description of a vehicle, seen nearby by a different witness, that had since been located and deemed unrelated to the case. We packed up the cameras and disbanded so the crew could spend the evening with their families.

That night I went to my favorite McCormick and Schmick's restaurant at the top of the cobblestone segment of Rodeo Drive and took a table under the heater in the outdoor veranda. The owner, Bill McCormick, walked up with his hand extended. "You're Jeanne Boylan, right? I met you at a chiefs of police conference in Toronto years ago. So did you do that drawing they just released tonight of that kid who killed Ennis Cosby?"

The Cosby case eyewitness had been interviewed days earlier, and the drawing had been done shortly after Ennis was murdered, as indicated by the date scribbled on the drawing. But it wasn't released by LAPD until Saturday night, just hours after the three P.M. press conference in which Police Chief Williams had told the press about the eyewitness's continued unavailability.

The traditional procedure had been used to prepare the sketch. The result was a tube-shaped and generic depiction of a male with little dimension and none of the distinguishing details that should have been easily accessible from the vantage point of the eyewitness.

This drawing of a white male suspect in the Ennis Cosby murder was produced and released by the LAPD.

Though it was only a general suspect rendition, that the eyewitness had already been interviewed and that the drawing existed were details that had not been released at any press conference regarding the case. Only LAPD was privy to the reasons why they had withheld the information from the public for so long. Perhaps they thought the eyewitness was involved, maybe they doubted her story, or in the interest of bettering their public image after two tough, post-O.J. Simpson years, it could have been that they just hoped to solve the case without any outside assistance.

We'd never fully know their reasons, but what was known with certainty was that for those few days, while the city was jarred by fear and steeped in concern for the Cosby family, Ennis's killer had been free to roam unimpeded and his trail left to grow a little colder.

Immediately following the belated release of the suspect sketch, the Cosby case eyewitness followed what seems to be an emerging trend in criminal cases. Though an eyewitness, not a suspect, she defensively secured her own high-powered Santa Monica attorney and, according to the LAPD spokesperson, was no longer available for interview. One eyewitness, one now diluted memory, and still no suspect. There was one remaining hope, crucial to the outcome of the case: that the eyewitness hadn't lost the image from her memory completely and, along with it, her ability to identify the suspect—if and when one was finally apprehended.

I landed in Bend to a third straight day of snowfall. Everything was buried under a foot-thick blanket of fresh snow. Robert had a roaring fire waiting for me by the time I walked in his front door.

Though not anticipating calls, I'd routinely forwarded my own phone to his house after my arrival. Instinctively, I picked up the receiver when it rang.

"This is Mary Gallagher of the FBI's Psychological Profiling Unit," the caller said. I looked over at Rob kneeling near the river rock, stoking the coals in his attempt to ward off my chill.

"I'm calling you from New York City. We've got an urgent situation." She spoke rapidly. "We need you on a major serial-rapist case. Let me tell you what we've got so far: at least twenty-three cases, thirteen that we've now positively linked through DNA, and we're working on more. We've got composite drawings from nearly every case, but they are all over the damn map. No two even look alike, yet we know positively that it's the same man in at least thirteen of the rape cases."

"Who is it?" Robert asked.

"It's for me," I assured him, and walked into his office down the hall, then quietly swung the door shut.

"The New York Police Department has a task force working the case," Gallagher continued. "They've got street cops, undercover people—all of them out working this guy every weekend. It's crazy. Right now, any male on the Upper East Side between eighteen and sixty-nine is suspect. Our task force guys have no idea beyond gender of what they're even looking for. God, they aren't even sure what race he is. Some people have now been stopped multiple times by different officers. It's just a circus, and we're looking at an immense potential of lawsuits from people who've been harassed. Racial issues are popping into the picture the press is picking it up—it's a real mess.

"We know you have a different way of doing these things. We're hoping you can clean up the confusion as to why every sketch is of a totally different man. How can this happen? What do you think is wrong with these witnesses?"

Nothing, I thought.

"This animal has a defined pattern and we're expecting another hit soon," Gallagher said. "No question that he's *going* to rape again. Can you tell me what we need to do to get you here?"

All during dinner I studied Robert in the firelight, across the dining room table. I watched him laugh, watched him breathe, watched him move, wondering all the while what change my next words might bring. Just after dinner, I told him about the FBI's call.

"Damn it, Jeanne," he yelled, slamming his glass down as his fury exploded in force. "I mean this—you walk out that goddamned door, and you don't even think about coming back. Do you hear me?"

For a moment, I was reliving a past I'd fought so hard to move away from, but then I realized, nothing at all was the same. Everything had changed. This time, I didn't feel I *had* to go, this time I *wanted* to go.

I looked around at Robert's new home filled with new furniture, his beautiful new paintings, all his "things"—every luxury and physical comfort one could need and of which I now had none. I knew I was leaving all of it forever.

Then my eyes settled on the flickering candle flames between us, and I thought of the spirits of those children whose photos I still held, the life endings that had transformed me, the tragedies that had in fact left me richer in spirit than I could ever have dreamed.

"I'm going," I finally said quietly. "I don't expect you to understand."

We sat in his dining room in silence, the snow falling on the wide stretch of fairway, piling in delicate heaps on the pine boughs outside the window. The moonlight sparkled off the gemlike flakes and cast soft shadows into the room. I only wished it could illuminate for him the part of my heart that he just couldn't see.

20

LOOK THEM IN THE EYE

With John Walsh on the
set of *America's Most
Wanted* at the Fox
Television studios in
Washington, D.C.
(Photo: Collection of the
author)

By the end of January I was at Fox Television in Washington,
D.C., taping voice-over segments in the *America's Most Wanted* studios for a piece to air in an upcoming show. Jennifer called the hotel
almost hourly to remind me of the January 30 Magnificent Seven
Awards Ceremony, hosted by an organization called Business and
Professional Women/USA. She had handled all the arrangements, even
trading frequent-flier miles for a first-class ticket so my mother could
join me from Colorado.

307

At the *AMW* set, my mother waited, presumably watching the taping while I spent the afternoon upstairs in a studio sound booth. By the time I'd finished working, she'd shared most of my childhood secrets in an off-set bonding session with the program's host, John Walsh. I frantically extricated her out of there while I had any secrets left and took her back to the hotel so we could get ready for the evening's event.

"Mom, you're going to have to go ahead downstairs without me," I whispered just a few minutes before we were due at the dinner. "Just save me a seat, okay?" I was in the midst of a live telephone interview with Radio Free Europe and would be late for the ceremony being held in the grand ballroom of the Capital Hilton Hotel.

All I knew about the evening was that we'd be seated in the highest sponsorship area. For fees ranging up to $5,000, event sponsors had purchased tables, and the highest-level contributors were assigned a VIP to sit among their guests. My mother was dying to find out who the dignitary at our table would be.

By fate or coincidence, our room was in the same hotel and on the same floor on which I'd worked with Sister Dianna. As I stood waiting impatiently for the elevator, I remembered the many times she and I had stood in the identical spot embracing each other good-bye.

The door opened and I pressed my back into the crowd. Embarrassed, I rushed into the ballroom and took the seat next to my mother. Only one chair remained empty at our table.

Under the low-lit chandeliers, the room was filled to capacity with richly dressed people sitting around linen-covered round tables, each decorated with an overflowing vase of white starlilies. A program was placed above each setting. I glanced at name tags but saw no one I recognized.

In response to my mom's curiosity, I leaned toward the woman at my left and excitedly asked, "So who do you think will be the our VIP?"

She reached over my plate, opened up my program, looked over the reading glasses that dangled on the end of her long, chiseled nose, opened it up to page one for me and pointed. "Honey, it's *you.*"

Frantic, I flipped through the program. Oblivious to the honor until now, I discovered that I was one of just seven recipients chosen from a national field.

The Business and Professional Women's Magnificent Seven Award recipients, left to right: Maine Senator Olympia Snowe; Sheila Burke, executive dean of the John F. Kennedy School of Government, Harvard University; Jeanne Boylan; Angela Gittens, general manager of Hartsfield International Airport, Atlanta, Georgia; Anastasia Kelly, representing the Fannie Mae Corporation; Judy Woodruff, CNN anchor. Not pictured: Linda Miller, manager of Ford Motor Corporation, European Division. (Photo by F. Leslie Barron)

A red-suited Judy Woodruff, the impeccable CNN commentator, was finishing up her flawlessly prepared acceptance speech.

I grabbed my mother's arm and shook it in a state of panic. "I have to give a speech? Mom! What am I going to do?"

She just rolled her eyes and laughed. "Do what you always do, honey. Just stand up and tell the truth."

I watched Senator Max Cleland take his seat as former senator Warren Rudman went to the podium to present the next award to the honorable Olympia Snowe, U.S. senator from Maine.

My heart raced as I began to fully comprehend the magnitude of the award. But the ultimate panic set in as Bonnie Campbell, Director of the Violence Against Women Office of the U.S. Department of Justice, stood up to introduce me. The organization's president motioned me forward while she spoke.

"Well, Mom, this is it," I whispered in her ear. "You are about to witness your daughter's ability to wing it." I hugged her shoulders as I stood up.

"She's turned a field once considered to be simply 'artistic' into a professional and academic discipline," Ms. Campbell proclaimed. "The theme of this evening is that 'the future belongs to those who believe in the beauty of their dreams.' Our next honoree has dared to dream of changing a very outdated police system in this country, for the better. She is an inspiration to all of us, and I am honored to introduce and present this Magnificent Seven Award to Jeanne Boylan."

Bonnie handed me the elaborately engraved leaded-crystal sculpture as I stepped behind the microphone.

"Thank you very much," I said, looking out over the opulent room.

To gain a moment, I ran my fingers over the wooden podium and inhaled the fragrance of the starlilies, then took a deep breath and began.

"Have you ever been thrown into a world in which you never chose to go? Can you imagine living your life, as you would on any ordinary day, with all your plans and all your hopes in order, and suddenly having your universe turned upside down by the mere whim of a passing criminal?"

I allowed time for the audience to contemplate their response.

"The people I meet know that feeling from firsthand experience. They've been traumatized, victimized, and often second-guessed. Few feel they've been listened to. Yet held precariously inside their memories are the very keys to an assailant's capture: the images of the criminals who created their terror.

"I've spent most of my adult life probing the minds of crime victims and eyewitnesses to capture their memories, to help exorcise their fears, and to draw out the details of their violators' faces so they can be apprehended before striking again.

"But there are still two faces that have yet to be found. You see, as a twenty-one-year-old on my way to my car after a nighttime college class in rural Missouri, I was abducted from a country road. Two strangers on a dark night stole two long and unforgettable hours of my life.

"I survived. And that night, I sat on the other side of an interview table in the frightening unfamiliarity of a police precinct. The experience of that night changed me forever. It gave me the knowledge of what it feels like to need desperately to be listened to, really listened to, not judged, not second-guessed, and not forced to deliver stock answers that fit neatly into a preformatted generic report form. Answers don't come in such a shape.

"That night taught me the importance of compassion when I couldn't find any, the value of patience when I wasn't given any, and later helped me to understand the power of the heart and the mind to deeply bury a memory in order to make it just a little easier to carry on.

"My case was never resolved, but I've never stopped searching. In airports, in crowds—in fact, everywhere I go. Faces haunt me—every nuance, every angle, every shadow, every line. I've lived without the luxury of conclusion. Instead, my healing has come through this unexpected kind of work that I could have never imagined I'd be doing.

"Investigators call me a rebel, or call my methods unorthodox; the press is always asking me what makes my work so dramatically different. And the answer is so simple: I listen. Because on that night, when I had a story to tell, there was no one willing to listen to me."

The stillness of the Washington D.C. ballroom was broken by sudden applause. As I picked up the heavy crystal award, I silently committed to do what for over two decades I'd accomplished for others but had never done for myself.

I walked away from the podium understanding, for the first time, that I needed to record the faces of my attackers, to release their images from my mind so that I could finally free my own heart from the anguish of a perpetual search.

(Drawings by Jeanne Boylan, November 1999)

AFTERWORD

Unabomber

Theodore Kaczynski received four consecutive life sentences in May 1998, the result of a plea bargain that avoided the death penalty and a trial in which his lawyers planned to portray him, against his will, as deranged.

Kaczynski's plea bargain covered three deaths and the maiming of two additional victims. It included acknowledgment by Kaczynski of responsibility for all the Unabom attacks.

The judge ordered payment of more than fifteen million dollars in restitution, instructing that any funds Kaczynski receives from writings or movie rights must go to his victims. Kaczynski is serving his sentence at the Supermax federal maximum security prison in Florence, Colorado.

Polly Klaas Kidnapping/Murder

Richard Allen Davis was convicted in June 1996 by a Santa Rosa County jury of first-degree murder with four special circumstances—robbery, burglary, kidnapping, and a lewd act on a child.

In September 1996, Davis was sentenced to death. Under the auto-matic appeal allowed by California courts, the case will be contested.

Following the murder of his daughter, Marc Klaas has become in-strumental in the passage of anti-crime legislation, meeting repeatedly with President Clinton and Attorney General Janet Reno on issues of child safety. At the Federal Crime Bill signing ceremony, President Clinton dedicated the Crime Bill to Polly Klaas and two other crime victims. Marc Klaas provided the following synopsis for inclusion in this book:

> In 1990 only one state required community notification of con-victed sexual offenders. Forty-nine states now have community notification.
>
> Since Polly's death in 1993, the FBI has created an at-risk abduction protocol. They make it available for free to any law enforcement agency in the country on request.
>
> At least two special agents in every FBI field office are now trained specifically in crimes against children.
>
> Nonprofit organizations and professions that give unsupervised access of children to employees or volunteers now have the ability to conduct comprehensive FBI background checks on these indi-viduals. . . .
>
> You, nor I, nor any individual has the power to change the world. However, by holding hands and working toward common goals with a single-minded determination, we *can* change the world.
>
>   Marc Klaas

Within a year of his daughter's murder, Marc Klaas founded the KlaasKids Foundation for Children. The KlaasKids Foundation can be contacted at P.O. Box 925, Sausalito, CA 94966, 415/331-6867; *klaas@crl.com*

Ruth Mayer Kidnapping

The Ruth Mayer kidnapping investigation ultimately targeted ten sus-pects linked to the case, three of whom were charged in January 1994. One of the three suspects was subsequently released due to a lack of substantial evidence, although it was his garage in which Mrs. Mayer was held hostage. The two others were released from jail less than two weeks after their arrest when jailers mistakenly believed that charges against not just one but all three suspects had been dismissed.

In April 1996, two and a half years after the kidnapping, a Contra Costa jury awarded three million dollars to Mrs. Mayer and one and a half million dollars to her husband, Gene, assigning responsibility for the damages among four men. Three were sentenced to prison: Eural Wills, Brian Tomasello, and Francisco Sarinana. The fourth, Mark Rantissi, was to be tried in a criminal court case scheduled for a later date. A fifth suspect, Jose Luis Contreras, was determined to have no liability; however, he was sentenced on other charges and was scheduled to stand trial on kidnapping charges at a later date.

A December 1995 banner headline in the *Contra Costa Times* announced that the Mayers' "Legendary Jewelry Business Closed" and attributed the event to the personal toll from the aftermath of the kidnapping ordeal.

Martin Ganz Murder

More than nine months after the December 1993 murder of Martin Ganz, authorities charged Roger Brady, a convicted bank robber, with responsibility for the slaying. The Asian male, known to the FBI as the Clark Kent Bandit, emerged as a prime suspect in the Ganz murder when he was arrested in August 1994 on charges of murdering a woman in Oregon.

Brady is now serving a life sentence without possibility of parole in San Quentin Prison, California.

Justin Jones Murder

Jose Avina was charged in April 1994 for the March 27, 1994, strong-arm robbery and murder of Justin Wesley Jones. In November 1995, he was found guilty of second-degree murder and grand theft, and received a sentence of sixteen years to life.

In honor her son's memory, Lisa Dahl established the Justin Wesley Jones Memorial Scholarship Fund to help support programs aimed at stopping violence against youth. Contributions can be made through:

University of California, Berkeley, 2440 Bancroft Way, #4200, Berkeley, CA 94720-4200, 510-642-1212.

Kenny Sommer Murder

Kenny Sommer was murdered in Huntington Beach in April 1994. The *Rolanda Show* funded a resumption of the investigation in September 1994. More than seven months after the shooting, a sketch based on the distant memory of an eyewitness who had seen the tragedy from a distance was released.

No justice has been served, but Alice Sommer marks the moment her healing began as the day when she was able to eulogize her son using the same media outlets through which his image had been misrepresented during the early phases of his murder investigation.

The search continues. If you have any information regarding the suspect in this case, please contact: 909-730-2601. All information will be kept confidential.

Cora Jones Murder

David Spanbauer, a twice-paroled sex offender, confessed to the murder of Cora Jones, Trudy Jeschke and Ronelle Eichstedt on December 8, 1994, the day Cora Jones would have turned thirteen.

Spanbauer was sentenced to life without parole, the result of fast-track legislation proposed by Governor Tommy Thompson, advocated by Marc Klaas, and inspired by the Cora Jones murder case. Spanbauer is being held in a Minnesota state prison as part of an inmate-swap agreement.

Wisconsin's "truth in sentencing" act now eliminates the possibility of parole and requires offenders to serve one hundred percent of the prison term to which they are sentenced. The bill was advocated by Carol Grady, a 1960 victim of Spanbauer, who believed the rapist was serving a seventy-year sentence for his crime when she learned that he had been paroled after only eight years, and that since being released prematurely from prison he had murdered three young girls. The father of one of Spanbauer's victims, Tom Jeschke, joined Grady to present Wisconsin lawmakers with 6,000 signatures in support of truth in sentencing.

The Wisconsin Assembly approved the bill on an 86–8 vote, and today Wisconsin's "two-strike" law mandates life without parole for individuals convicted a second time for felony child sexual abuse.

Susan Smith Child Drownings

On November 3, 1995, Susan Smith confessed to drowning her two sons on October 25, 1995. By a vote of 12–0, a Union, South Carolina, jury rejected the death penalty and sentenced Susan Vaughan Smith, who wanted to die, to live, "tormented in her own lake of fire." She received two life terms in prison—one for the murder of three-year-old Michael, and one for that of fourteen-month-old Alex. She will be eligible for parole in thirty years.

Oklahoma City Bombing

Timothy McVeigh and Terry Nichols were both indicted on eleven criminal counts on August 10, 1995. Both pleaded not guilty.

In 1997, federal trials for both men were held in Denver, Colorado. Terry Nichols was sentenced to life in prison. Timothy McVeigh was sentenced to die.

State charges filed against Nichols are pending, with a trial expected to take place in Oklahoma.

The victim count from the Oklahoma City bombing continues to increase. A total of 168 died when the bomb exploded, one nurse rescue worker was killed by falling debris at the bomb site, and more than 500 were injured in the blast. Over the four years following the tragedy, a half dozen people committed suicide—including two rescue workers, a federal prosecutor, a bomb blast survivor and the husband of a victim— and at least twice as many attempted suicide. The related psychological wreckage is impossible to estimate.

Sister Dianna Ortiz

The Department of Justice completed its investigation and formulated a two hundred–page report on the case of Sister Dianna Ortiz. The document was "classified"—even to Sister Ortiz, who has since learned that others, including the former ambassador to Guatemala, have been granted access to the report regarding her violation.

Ten years after the abduction, the identities of Alejandro and the three other torturers remain unknown. No justice has been served.

Sister Ortiz has redirected her energy to advance human rights issues on behalf of others. She works with the Guatemalan Human Rights Commission/USA, the Torture Abolition and Survivors Support Committee (TASSC), and the National Institute of Mental Health (NIMH). She provided the following synopsis for inclusion in this book:

In 1998, the United Nations dedicated June 26 as the International Day in Support of Torture Victims/Survivors.

Several survivors and representatives of human rights organizations and treatment centers came together to form the Torture Abolition and Survivors Support Committee, which seeks to raise public awareness about the practice of torture in our world today and to offer support to survivors of political violence.

As of today, there are more than 117 governments engaged in the practice of torture. Seventy of those governments receive some form of aid from the United States.

The National Institute of Mental Health gathered a group of experts to formulate a report on the Consequences of Torture and Trauma. Sister Dianna Ortiz contributed a chapter from the survivor's perspective, incorporating the views of survivors from Asia, Europe, Latin America and Central America. The report was disseminated to the Truth and Reconciliation Commission in South Africa. It will be published in book form by Plenum Press.

Contact: Torture Abolition and Survivors Support Committee (TASSC), 3321 12th Street NE, Washington, DC 20017, 202-529-6599. Home Page: http://www.kurdistan.org/you-can-end-it

Ennis Cosby Murder

Seven weeks after the January 16, 1997, fatal shooting of Ennis William Cosby, eighteen-year-old Mikail Markhasev of San Fernando, California, was arrested on murder charges.

Markhasev's arrest followed a tip from Christopher So, who overheard

Markhasev boasting of his actions and called the *National Enquirer* in response to a $100,000 award offered by the tabloid.

Markhasev had moved through the Los Angeles area for months, unimpeded by the extensive distribution of the sketch contained in the media reports. The informant, Christopher So, led police to the murder weapon, providing the physical evidence the case needed for a conviction.

In July 1998, a Santa Monica jury convicted Markhasev of murder, attempting to rob, and using a firearm in the commission of attempted robbery. The district attorney did not seek the death penalty. Markhasev received a mandatory sentence of life in prison without parole. An appeal was announced.

The sole eyewitness in the Ennis Cosby murder was unable to identify the suspect and had "categorically eliminated" Markhasev from the police lineup after his March 12 arrest, according to the *L.A. Times*. LAPD and the district attorney's office refused comment.

In memory of their son, Drs. William H. and Camille O. Cosby established the Hello Friend/Ennis William Cosby Foundation to fulfill the goals and dreams of Ennis Cosby by supporting people with dyslexia and language-based learning differences.

Hello Friend/Ennis William Cosby Foundation, P.O. Box 4061, Santa Monica, CA 97411.

AUTHOR'S NOTE

The information in this book is based on my memories and observations, verified wherever possible against secondary news sources.

Passages that appear in first person have been edited to provide continuity, but not to alter their intent. While remembered dialogue, especially years later, is rarely an exact reproduction of the conversation, to the extent possible I have maintained the content of conversations as I recall them. When practical, I have verified quotes either through comparison with printed or broadcast sources, or through conversations with those to whom the quotes are attributed.

In some cases, the names and identifying details of certain individuals, particularly those not widely divulged through news reports, have been changed to protect their anonymity.

I used or divulged no classified material in presenting my story.

The cases are as I remember them, although, knowing memory as I do, I beg understanding if details have become blurred or overridden. The facts as I present them are true to my recollection and written with the hope that sharing them will inspire positive change.

ACKNOWLEDGMENTS

How do you thank an angel? My collaborator, Barbara Findlay Schenck, of Bend, Oregon, stayed with me through each day of this project as if we were running a marathon while holding hands. What began as a business arrangement has blossomed into the dearest friendship imaginable. I "authored" these stories in that I lived them, but she wrote this book in that she helped me craft my words and emotions into a seamless format that will let these many lessons finally be shared. For your wisdom, discernment, encouragement and unfailing faith in the true purpose of this book, thank you. You are a gift.

Linda Goldston of the San Jose *Mercury News*, thank you for reaching through that sea of reporters in the midst of a Petaluma press conference and handing me the spiral binder with your note—"Start your book NOW"—scribbled on page one. You didn't know me then, but you witnessed the ultimate price of the needless errors in the Polly Klaas case and knew I had to deliver a message even before I was aware of it. Thank you for pointing me toward a format.

Lois Mamer of Tubac, Arizona, my mentor, adopted grandmother and beloved friend, thank you for the encouragement, help in editing and also for the gift of the title. You were the other half of my Tubac team, spiritually, emotionally and grammatically.

Ann and Peter Groves, thank you for giving me a place to hide out. Your hundred-year-old adobe near the Mexican border gave me the uninterrupted solitude and privacy that was crucial to the completion of this project. I'll not forget your kindness.

Lorraine Howell of Seattle, Washington, thank you for your nurturance and support, David Howell for your bureaucratic insights and harsh but well chosen edits, and both of you for your friendship.

Paul Nagle of the William Morris Agency in Los Angeles, you took me into your care and hand-carried me to all the right places to make this book a reality. Thank you so much for believing, and thank you Dan Strone at William Morris in New York.

Mitchell Ivers and Amanda Ayers at Simon and Schuster, thank you for your patience and guidance as well as your editorial wisdom.

Jennifer Moe, my right hand, sounding board, office manager, friend, words aren't enough.

There were many cases and many people I met long before and in between those mentioned in this book. I could choose only a few, and selected these stories to provide real case illustrations of different elements of this work, each an important segment of a broad foundation for understanding this complex process of eyewitness memory. No one story is more important than any other. Each case, each person I've worked with, included in this book or not, holds an equal part of my heart.

Thank you to all those who generously allowed me to share your personal stories and photographs in the hope that the hard-earned lessons learned by these experiences will be absorbed and utilized for the better by the investigative community. We share that hope.

INDEX

Italic page numbers indicate sketches and photographs.

325